First Edition
November 2025
Third Printing

Guide to The Constitution and The Bill of Rights

for Secondary School Students

By
Michael Patrick Leahy
and Claudia Henneberry

Cover design, layout, and graphics by Christina Botteri

Star News Digital Media
Nashville, Tennessee

ISBN 978-1-7337872-0-8

Star News Digital Media

Copyright ©2025
All rights reserved

Published in the United States

This guide is dedicated to the children and grandchildren
of the students who read it today.

Contents

Chapter	Page
Chapter One: The Golden Triangle of Freedom	01
Chapter Two: A Republic, If You Can Keep It	07
Chapter Three: The Preamble	15
Chapter Four: Three Things That Make the United States Constitution Unique in World History - A Single Written Agreement Now the Highest Authority for 'The Rule of Law'	25
Chapter Five: Federalism	33
Chapter Six: The Separation of Powers	39
Chapter Seven: The Electoral College and the Selection of the President	47
Chapter Eight: How and Why Thirteen States Ratified the Constitution: 1787 - 1790	57
Chapter Nine: How and Why the First Ten Amendments - The Bill of Rights - Were Proposed and Ratified in Less Than Three Years	73
Chapter Ten: The First Amendment	85
Chapter Eleven: The Second Amendment	97
Chapter Twelve: The Third Amendment	107
Chapter Thirteen: Civil Asset Forfeiture and the Fourth Amendment	113
Chapter Fourteen: The Fifth Amendment	121
Chapter Fifteen: The Sixth Amendment	131
Chapter Sixteen: The Seventh Amendment	137
Chapter Seventeen: The Eighth Amendment	143
Chapter Eighteen: The Ninth Amendment	151
Chapter Nineteen: Revisiting the Tenth Amendment	157
Chapter Twenty: Judicial Review	163
Chapter Twenty-One: December 15, 1791: The Date Our American Republic Was Fully Formed	171
Acknowledgments	175

Appendix	
The United States Constitution	177
Amendmens 1 - 10 (The Bill of Rights)	187
Amendments 11 - 27	189
Glossary	197
Endnotes	205
About the Authors	227

 Visit nationalconstitutionbee.org

Sign up to compete in the next **National Constitution Bee.**

Listen along with co-author Michael Patrick Leahy at the podcast of *Guide to the Constitution and the Bill of Rights for Secondary School Students* at guidetotheconstitution.org.

"To live under the American Constitution is the greatest political privilege that was ever accorded the human race."

-*Calvin Coolidge*

Chapter 1

The Golden Triangle of Freedom

A remarkable aspect of the Constitution of the United States is that since its ratification in 1788 the American people have, for the most part, viewed it as a covenant agreement between themselves and the national government.

It is a powerful document not simply because of the words it contains, but because the people have freely chosen to be governed by those words.

Words written on parchment or typed into an I-phone have no impact unless they are accepted within a common belief system.

This is why "the rule of law," particularly as it has developed here in the United States, is so central to the development and growth of a vibrant and dynamic society where individual freedom flourishes. Liberty exists within a society where individual freedom is enjoyed by all members of that society.

In the United States of America, we call this freedom "constitutional liberty," because it has been acknowledged in our Constitution as the cornerstone of our system of governance.

But, as Ronald Reagan famously said, "freedom is never more than one generation away from extinction."

The Founders knew this, and recently a Chinese-born English scholar who resides in America expressed in very simple terms how freedom is gained, why it relies on the virtue of the population, how that virtue is a natural extension of faith, and how faith requires freedom, or "constitutional liberty," to thrive and prosper.

His name is Os Guinness, and he is the great-great-great grandson of the famous Irish brewer, Arthur Guinness.

Guinness introduced the simple term "The Golden Triangle of Freedom," which captures this fundamental concept, in his 2012 book, *A Free People's Suicide: Sustainable Freedom and the American Future*.

"We think of the Framers as revolutionary, and they were. But they were also rooted, in the sense they tried to use history to defy history. Because they knew if you looked at the classics you have umpteen reasons of why freedom never lasts," Guinness says.

"So, they wanted to create a political equivalent of a perpetual motion machine. A free republic that could stay free forever," he explains.

"That's incredible!" the famous brewer's descendant exclaims.

"Their answer is not what many people think. Some people think the Constitution alone. No. Law alone would never do it," Guinness asserts, a claim substantiated by the lack of freedom in a number of countries that have a document that purports to be a national Constitution.

"Others think virtue alone. No, the Framers were much more realistic than that," he adds, a notable historical reference to the failed Cromwellian theocracy in 17th century England.

"Now, they didn't give a name to their answer. Tocqueville's term is 'the habits of the heart.' My name for it is the Golden Triangle of Freedom," he adds, with a tip of the hat to the Frenchman who wrote the renowned, *Democracy in America* based on his tour of Jacksonian America in the 1830s.

"If you think of a recycling triangle of three sides that just goes round and round and round."

"The Framers' Golden Triangle is this: Freedom requires virtue. Virtue requires faith of some sort. Faith of any sort requires freedom," he explains.

"But of course that freedom requires virtue, and so on. Now you can fill out each of those legs almost ad nauseum."

"John Adams says famously 'only a virtuous people are capable of freedom,'" he adds.

"And it's not merely a moralistic saying, it's really hard prudential politics, and I call this the Golden Triangle of Freedom. If that's preserved, freedom has a chance of surviving," Guinness concludes.

One way to look at "The Golden Triangle of Freedom" is as a unique set of circumstances whose continued interactions within a society are self-perpetuating.

One side of the triangle - virtue - describes behavior, both individually and within a society as a whole. Another side of the triangle - faith - describes beliefs, also both individually and within a society as a whole. And the final side of the triangle - freedom - describes a state of being or existence which can only be fully experienced if it exists for all individuals within that society, not a select few.

Lexico.com offers these definitions for the three components of "The Golden Triangle of Freedom."

Virtue is "behavior showing high moral standards."

Faith is "strong belief in God or the doctrines of a religion."

Freedom is "the power or right to act, speak, or think as one wants without hindrance."

Author Eric Metaxas drew heavily on Guinness' "Golden Triangle of Freedom" in his 2016 book, *If You Can Keep It: The Promise of American Liberty*:

> *When I first heard my friend Os Guinness talk about the Golden Triangle of Freedom, I was taken aback. In fact, I was deeply embarrassed, because what he was describing was so central to the idea of American freedom and the American experiment that it seemed inconceivable that somehow I hadn't heard it before. I was shocked that although I'd attended decent American schools and a top American university, the concept somehow had eluded me entirely.*

"The idea that freedom requires virtue, which requires faith – which in turn requires freedom – is at once simple and elegant, but to our modern and often secularly inclined minds it can be a bit disturbing," Metaxas wrote:

> *For many the idea of faith and freedom working together to bolster each other brings about cognitive dissonance. That's because in America today we have stepped backward to a cultural situation less like the earlier times in our own country than like the France of Tocqueville's day, in which religion and freedom were thought to be bitterest enemies.*

The challenge for Americans today who wish to defend and preserve the constitutional liberty established by the Founders in 1788 extends beyond protecting the Constitution and the rule of law.

Political activism alone is insufficient.

Education of the next generation about what the Constitution means, as well as promotion of the religious liberty that creates the culture in which virtue is widespread are critical as well.

Chapter Discussion Questions

(1) Which of the three components of "The Golden Triangle of Freedom" - faith, virtue, or freedom - is most important?

(2) Do you think it is possible to have liberty, defined by Lexico.com as "the state of being free within society from oppressive restrictions imposed by authority on one's way of life, behavior, or political views" without the presence of all three components of "The Golden Triangle of Freedom" - faith, virtue, and freedom - in that society?

(3) What difficulties might the prevalence of faith alone in a society present when creating a constitutional government?

Chapter 2

A Republic, If You Can Keep It
By Claudia Henneberry

Minutes after the Constitutional Convention adjourned in Philadelphia on September 17, 1787, Elizabeth Powel, wife of the first mayor of Philadelphia and a friend of George Washington who hosted many social events for the political class of the time, asked Benjamin Franklin if the convention had given us a republic or a monarchy.

"A republic, madam, if you can keep it," the venerable 81-year-old delegate, diplomat, and inventor responded.

At one time or another, fifty-five delegates, from all the states except Rhode Island, attended that convention, which began four months earlier in May of that year under the premise of forming a more perfect union by revising the Articles of Confederation.

You see, the United States of America was not officially formed as the republic of which we are currently citizens in 1783 when the Treaty of Paris, in which Great Britain acknowledged the independence and sovereignty of its former colonies, was signed.

The Continental Congress of the 13 rebellious colonies, convening in York Town, Pennsylvania (now simply called York), proposed the Articles of Confederation in November 1777 as the contract among the 13 states they used to unite in their efforts to win their freedom from Great Britain.

The Revolutionary War had already been in progress for two-and-a-half years, and a year earlier, the colonies had signed a Declaration of Independence from Great Britain.

It was not until 1781, however, that all 13 rebellious states actually ratified the Articles of Confederation.

The U.S. Post Office issued this commemorative stamp in 1977 on the 200th anniversary of the drafting of the Articles of Confederation in York, Pennsylvania in 1777.

It took almost four long years from November 1777 until March 1781 before this mutually binding governing agreement was ratified by all 13 former colonies. But the document was so fundamentally flawed, the new government floundered until a new agreement - our Constitution - was proposed and ratified. The Articles of Confederation remain largely forgotten today, except as a precursor to the Constitution.

It became quickly apparent, however, that the Articles of Confederation was not the kind of contract - or covenant - that would keep the fledgling country in business.

The flaws in the document, in retrospect, were numerous, though it had been sufficient to bind the states together for them to win the American Revolution.

The most dramatic flaw in the Articles of Confederation was the weakness of the central government. The central government was so weak it was virtually incapable of acting on any matter of significance.

By 1787, it was clear to a number of the leading political figures - Alexander Hamilton and James Madison in particular - that a new contract between the 13 former colonies - who now called themselves states - was crucial to the survival of the young country.

So Hamilton, Madison, and a few others who wanted a new contract that gave more power to the central government persuaded state legislatures to appoint delegates to a convention for the purpose of revising and amending the Articles of Confederation. A small group of nationalists, however, wanted to do far more than revise and amend the Articles. They wanted to create a powerful new government.

Virtually everyone in the country acknowledged one main point: The Articles of Confederation as originally agreed to simply were not working.

So the legislatures of 12 of the 13 states arranged to send delegates to a convention in Philadelphia in May of 1787.

Ultimately, the convention proposed a brand new document that 42 delegates in attendance signed on September 17. This new Constitution would become the Supreme Law of the Land; a document which would set forth a government of laws, not of men, whereas the power of the government is derived from the consent of the governed, or, rather, from the people.

The Articles of Confederation loosely bound the states together with no executive, no judiciary, no taxing power and no enforcement power.

One consequence of the Confederation's lack of taxing power was that some American soldiers who served during the Revolutionary War suffered.

One of those soldiers was Daniel Shays, a 28-year old farmer with a wife and several young children from western Massachusetts who joined up in 1775. He fought the British for five years, and was promoted to captain until he was injured in 1780 and had to retire.

Shays served in the American Army for five years. After he retired from the Army and returned home he learned that he was being sued for debts he couldn't pay.

This didn't seem very fair to him, and he tried, unsuccessfully for six years to get paid for his years in his Army, but he never got a dime.

By the summer of 1786, he and a number of his neighbors, fellow veterans of the Revolutionary War who had never been paid, decided to get what they were owed.

Four thousand of them gathered together and attacked the Armory in Springfield, Massachusetts but were repelled by a larger army financed by private merchants.

When the uprising - known as Shays' Rebellion - ended in May, 1787, four "Shaysites" had been killed in battle. Two were later hanged. Shays himself was pardoned, moved to upstate New York, was granted a small pension for his service, and lived in poverty until his death in 1825.

The rebellion shocked many of the political leaders of the new country, and it gave Federalists and Anti-Federalists alike further reason to meet in Philadelphia to try and fix the Articles of Confederation.

The diminutive James Madison from Virginia - short in physical stature at 5 foot 4, but an intellectual giant - had the general outline of a plan to fix things. It was a very audacious thing for Madison, only 36 years old at the time, to even contemplate.

"The purpose of the Constitution is to restrict the majority's ability to harm a minority," he said after the document had been completed.

While the towering George Washington had led the troops for eight years, and his aide Alexander Hamilton had finally won glory on the battlefield by storming a British outpost at Yorktown, Madison's fellow Virginian James Monroe - just 19 years old - took a bullet to the chest on the day after Christmas 1777 at the Battle of Trenton. He lay bleeding to death on the ground until Washington's own surgeon intervened to save him. In contrast, Madison, a Princeton graduate, studied Greek and Roman history and did not join the Continental Army or engage in any of the fighting.

Revolutionary War veteran Daniel Shays led an ill fated but consequential rebellion.

Madison knew one thing about human nature: Every person sought to advance his or her own interests, and every person could be corrupted.

Studying the various forms of confederations deployed throughout history, Madison came to the conclusion - one that he thought should be obvious - that the only way to counteract the natural tendencies of human nature was to develop a system of checks and balances.

In a pure democracy, every citizen has one vote, and decisions are made by the vote of a majority.

That form of government, Madison and the other Founders knew, almost always led to a tyranny of the majority, where the rights of the minority were abused and trampled upon.

In a monarchy, subjects are ruled by a single ruler - a king or a queen - who inherits that role and, in some countries, exercises absolute power.

The country belongs to the monarch, rather than the citizens of that country. The "sovereignty" of the people - that is their right to choose their own form of government - is something completely missing from a monarchy.

"Power tends to corrupt, and absolute power corrupts absolutely," a famous British politician and professor by the name of Lord Acton would say almost a century later in an oft quoted phrase.

What most people forget about that phrase is the next sentence.

"Great men are almost always bad men," Acton added.

So long as a country was ruled by a good king, the people were safe. But what happens when there is a bad king? One who arbitrarily steals the property of the people, or executes his subjects on a whim?

Madison's intellectual courage matched the physical courage of Washington, Monroe, and Hamilton. Madison was 42 years old when Charles Willson Peale painted this portrait of him in 1793, six years after the Constitutional Convention and four years after its ratification. He was only 36 years old when he helped guide the development of our Constitution at the 1787 convention in Philadelphia.

For these reasons, Madison and the other delegates to the Constitutional Convention, rejected both a democracy and a monarchy.

In 1787, there were about 500 countries in the world, which had a population about 500 million.

About 499 of these countries were some form of monarchy. Only one tiny country - Switzerland - had a form of government that was an early form of a republic at the time.

A republic is a form of government in which leaders are elected by those citizens who have the right to vote. Once elected, those leaders make the key decisions of government.

Disputes in a republic are settled by "the rule of law," a system that involves courts, judges, advocacy, and precedent of earlier court rulings.

Early on in the convention, it became obvious to almost everyone that the Articles of Confederation were beyond repair. So a fresh new start was required.

Even great men - and great women, Madison and the other delegates knew, needed checks and balances in any form of government they might lead.

A republic offered those checks and balances.

"The Constitution is not an instrument for the government to restrain the people; it is an instrument for the people to restrain the government," Patrick Henry, a preeminent Anti-Federalist, said.

The idea of the Constitution was, for the first time in history, to record in a single document the contractual terms to which all the citizens agreed, and to formalize a process by which they agreed to that system of government.

In the American republic, at its inception, the central government's powers were few and defined; while the powers of the 13 states were numerous and indefinite, thereby protecting the peoples' lives, liberties and properties.

Key elements of the checks and balances contained in the final document that emerged from the Constitutional Convention were:

Federalism: Defined two distinct forms of government - the centralized national government, which had certain specified and limited powers which could be applied to every citizen of the country, and the 13 separate state governments, which had numerous and indefinite powers by which residents of those states agreed to be governed.

Separation of powers: The power of the federal government was to be distributed among three separate branches: The legislative branch, the executive branch, and the judicial branch, whereby each had specific powers that allowed it to "check" the other branches to ensure those branches were not usurping their given powers.

The legislative branch consisted of two houses - The House of Representatives, whose members were elected directly by citizens with the right to vote, and the Senate, whose members were elected by the Legislatures of each separate state. The role of the legislative branch was to make laws.

The executive branch consisted of the President, and the departments subsequently organized to implement his policies, within the laws established by Congress, the legislative branch.

The Constitution did not create the cabinet departments we currently have. It left that task to Congress, which acted during its first session in 1789 to create the first four departments - State, Treasury, War, and Justice.

The judicial branch heard disputes between the federal government and the state governments, as well as between citizens or companies of different states, and also cases involving foreigners.

In Article IV, section 4, the Constitution even guarantees each state a "Republican Form of Government."

At the Constitutional Convention, for example, large state delegates and small state delegates compromised on representation of the legislative branch by adopting a proposal suggested by Roger Sherman of Connecticut. According to the proposal, the legislative branch - which was already established as two houses - was to be apportioned differently, with proportional representation according to population (House of Representatives) and the other having equal state representation (Senate).

The framers of the Constitution knew that in order to preserve our republic, there were caveats. They knew that education and virtue were necessary. The people were expected to be educated, informed, and engaged in order to elect proper government officials.

James Madison, considered by some to be the father of the Constitution, understood that "A well-instructed people alone can be permanently a free people."

"The Constitution was made only for a moral and religious people. It is wholly inadequate to the government of any other," John Adams, who would become the second president, said.

Thomas Jefferson summed it up this way – "It is in the manners and spirit of a people which preserve a republic in vigour ... degeneracy in these is a canker which soon eats into the heart of its laws and constitution."

Ben Franklin and the other delegates to the Constitutional Convention understood the challenge that future generations would face in preserving, protecting and defending this republic.

More than two centuries ago, Franklin told Mrs. Powel we had a republic, if we can keep it.

Franklin, Mrs. Powel, and every one of their grandchildren are now long gone.

But we are their descendants, and 232 years after Franklin offered that cautionary phrase "if you can keep it," the question seems more relevant now than ever.

Franklin was concerned about the natural tendency of any government towards centralization and control.

That was why, he thought, monarchies tended to move towards "absolutism," as Louis XIV and his descendants had done in France.

That move towards centralization and control could occur in a republic as well. As a result, a republic could only survive with citizen participation and a healthy system of checks and balances.

Franklin knew all too well that such a participatory form of government was delicate and fragile, constantly in need of renewal.

What do you think?

Can we keep the American republic?

Chapter Discussion Questions

(1) In your opinion, what were the most challenging issues facing Americans in the 1780s? Were they political, economic or moral?

(2) How did the Constitution created at the Philadelphia Convention address the problems facing Americans in the 1780s?

Chapter 3

The Preamble and Its Author, Gouverneur Morris

The first 52 words of the Constitution – the Preamble – lay out The Who, the Why, the What, and the How of the 4,000 plus words that followed in the document it introduced:

WHO: We the People of the United States,

WHY: In order to form a more perfect union,

WHAT:

- establish Justice,

- insure domestic Tranquility,

- provide for the common defence,

- promote the general welfare,

- and secure the Blessings of Liberty for ourselves and our Posterity,

HOW: do ordain and establish this Constitution for the United States of America.

Black's Law Dictionary defines a preamble as "An introductory statement in a constitution, statute, or other document explaining the document's basis and objective; especially, a statutory recital of the inconveniences for which the statute is designed to provide a remedy."

The United States Constitution that was drafted by 55 delegates to the Constitutional Convention in Philadelphia in 1787 represented the first time in the history of the world that the governing laws of a country were encapsulated in a single document.

Given the historical uniqueness of such a single document, it is not surprising to see why those delegates thought that it was important to include an introductory Preamble at the very beginning of the document.

Even though the Constitutional Convention began in May of that year, it was not until September 8, 1787 – a mere nine days before the final document was signed by 39 of the delegates in attendance and

Benjamin Franklin famously told Mrs. Powel the convention had delivered "A Republic if you can keep it"- that the delegates got around to the task of writing a Preamble.

On that day, the delegates selected a Committee of Style and Arrangement, whose task was to write the final version of the Constitution and add a new Preamble for signature by the delegates followed by submission to the Confederation Congress, and then the states for ratification.

On September 8, 1787, with the convention quickly drawing to a close, a "Committee was then appointed by Ballot to revise the stile of and arrange the articles which had been agreed to by the House." The members of the committee were William Samuel Johnson, Alexander Hamilton, Gouverneur Morris, James Madison and Rufus King. These five men were known as the Committee of Style and Arrangement and it was their job to organize the layout of the numerous resolutions that had already taken shape and formed the new Constitution. (See 'Madison's Notes on the Debates in the Federal Convention' for September 8, 1787), according to Constitutionland.com:

> *Although it was a five man committee, the chairman, William Samuel Johnson, asked Gouverneur Morris to write the final draft. Remember, the committee meetings were not documented as the convention was, but both Morris and Madison confirmed Morris' authorship. (From David O. Stewart, The Summer of 1787: The Men Who Invented the Constitution p.232)...*
>
> *The phrase "We the People" has taken on a mystical quality in political history. The very concept of "the People" as the authors of this new Constitution created, in history, an element of revolution, especially considering the era in which these words were written, when most other governments in the world were ruled by, at best, constitutional monarchies, and at worst tyrannies. The birth of this phrase is not quite as miraculous as one would expect, however.*
>
> *When Morris sat at his desk in Mrs. Baily's rooming house on Market Street, where he resided during the Constitutional Convention, to polish up the Constitution, he was unsure whether all of the states would ratify it. With Rhode Island never in attendance at the Convention and the delegates from New York (besides Hamilton) having gone home, the original preamble cataloging all of the states as the authors of the Constitution, would be inaccurate and presumptuous. So, "We the People" was born of very practical parents.*
>
> *Although the extraordinary words "We the People" had a very ordinary and utilitarian birth, their power cannot be discounted. To quote Catherine Drinker Bowen: "Nor did members of the committee foresee that in Europe the phrase would serve as an inspiration, a flag of defiance against absolutist kings." (From Catherine Drinker Bowen, Miracle at Philadelphia, p. 240.)*
>
> *As for the rest of the Preamble, it did not take long for Morris to complete the entire first draft of the Constitution, so he could not dwell too much on the balance of the words. Bowen concludes, the "seven verbs...form, establish, insure, provide, promote, secure, ordain...set down a working instrument of government which must be plain, brief and strategically vague in places to give play for future circumstances." (From Bowen, Miracle at Philadelphia, p. 241.) In sum, Morris's preamble "distills the purposes of government." (From Stewart, The Summer of 1787: The Men Who Invented the Constitution, p.234).*
>
> *"Born into a New York family distinguished for its wealth, lineage, and political influence, [Gouverneur] Morris... graduated from King's College (now Columbia University) and in 1771 was admitted to the bar," according to History.com:*

In 1775, he was elected to New York's provincial congress and in 1776 served on committees that drafted the state's new constitution and that instructed New York's delegates to the Second Continental Congress to support the Declaration of Independence. In 1778, as a New York delegate to the Continental Congress, he signed the Articles of Confederation. Two years later Morris became the Confederation's assistant superintendent of finance under his political mentor, Robert Morris of Pennsylvania. In that post, he sought to expand the powers of the federal government and drafted a report to Congress recommending the first national currency-a decimal coinage based on the Spanish dollar.

In 1787, Robert Morris engineered an appointment for his protege as a Pennsylvania delegate to the Federal Convention. Brilliant and irreverent, Gouverneur Morris spoke more often and at greater length than any other delegate.

His unusual first name – Gouverneur – was the maiden name of his mother, Sarah Gouverneur. Her father, Isaac Gouverneur, was born in Amsterdam, Holland, and came to New York at an early age. Isaac's grandfather, Nicholas Pierre Gouverneur, was said to have been born in France around 1580 and served as a Captain of Arms to French King Henry IV, who was a Protestant Huguenot prior to becoming king known for his support of religious liberty and the signing of the Edict of Nantes. When Henry IV was assassinated by a Catholic fanatic in 1610, Gouverneur fled to Holland, where he was "granted arms" by William of Orange.

Morris' family lineage from his father, Lewis Morris, was equally impressive. Lewis' grandfather (Gouverneur's great-grandfather), Richard Morris, fought for Oliver Cromwell during the English Civil War in the 1640s, emigrated to Barbados, and in 1671 purchased a major 2,000 acre estate in what is now the Bronx, but was then known as Westchester County, which came to be known as Morrissania. For the next two centuries, the Morris family owned much of what is now the borough of the Bronx, as well as large tracts of land in New Jersey.

"Gouverneur Morris may not have been the most interesting man in the world, but he was the most interesting Founding Father that you probably never have heard of. Unconventional right from his odd-sounding first name, Gouverneur was never a governor, but he served in the Continental Congress, Constitutional Convention and U.S. Senate," History.com noted:

Gouverneur Morris, around the time of the Constitutional Convention in 1787

[I]n 1780 . . . a carriage accident left him with a mangled left ankle and several broken leg bones. With his regular doctor out of town, the attending physicians recommended amputation of the left leg below his knee. Morris consented. Showing a stunning lack of bedside manner, his regular doctor told Morris upon his return that the leg likely could have been saved. Rumors forever swirled that Morris, a known ladies' man, had actually injured himself jumping from a paramour's balcony to escape the wrath of an irate husband. The Founding Father didn't let the loss of a limb slow him down. According to Richard Brookhiser, author of "Gentleman Revolutionary: Gouverneur Morris - The Rake Who Wrote the Constitution," he continued to ride horses, climb church steeples, shoot river rapids and shake his (wooden) leg dancing. Nor did it diminish his trysts with married women, so much so that friend John Jay wrote that he wished Morris "had lost something else."

Although initially fearing "the domination of a riotous mob," Morris backed the patriot cause after the Battles of Lexington and Concord in April 1775. That aligned him with his half-brother Lewis Morris, who signed the Declaration of Independence. However, it set him apart from another half-brother who served as a general in the British army, two of his sisters who married Loyalists and even his Loyalist mother, whom he would not see for the duration of the war. The decision also left him homeless as his mother allowed the British to camp at Morrisania.

After living nearly a decade in Philadelphia, the New York native was a Pennsylvania delegate to the Constitutional Convention, although he wrote that he felt "in some degree as a representative of the whole human race." In spite of missing an entire month of the proceedings, Morris proved the most loquacious of the delegates. According to Brookhiser, he delivered 173 speeches, topping the 168 by James Wilson and 161 by James Madison. Morris was among the few delegates who stood up and delivered passionate orations denouncing slavery.

Theodore Roosevelt wrote a biography of Morris. It should probably be no surprise that Roosevelt, another one of the most colorful figures in American history, had an affinity for the charismatic Founding Father. "There has never been an American statesman of keener intellect or more brilliant genius," Roosevelt wrote of Morris in his 1888 biography. "Had he possessed but a little more steadiness and self-control he would have stood among the two or three very foremost."

Morris traveled to Paris on a business venture in 1789, and three years later President George Washington appointed him minister to France. Morris saw the worst violence of the French Revolution during his five years in Paris, but he was the only diplomat to remain in the city throughout the Reign of Terror. His French liaisons included a three-year love affair with the novelist Comtesse Adélaïde de Flahaut, who was married to a count 35 years her senior and lived in an apartment inside the Louvre before its conversion to an art museum. Morris shared his mistress with French diplomat Charles Maurice de Talleyrand, who would later sell the Louisiana Territory to the United States as Napoleon's foreign minister.

In August 1787, before Morris was given the editorial responsibilities, the preamble, as circulated in a draft of the entire Constitution as it existed one month before the final signing given to the delegates, read as follows:

> "We the People of the States of New-Hampshire, Massachusetts, Rhode Island and Providence Plantations, Connecticut, New-York, New-Jersey, Pennsylvania, Delaware, Maryland, Virginia, North-Carolina, South-Carolina, and Georgia, do ordain, declare and establish the following Constitution for the Government of Ourselves and Posterity."

"When he was still a young one, age thirty-five, Mr. Morris drafted the Constitution of the United States," biographer Richard Brookhiser wrote:

> *The proceedings of the Constitutional Convention were secret, to allow the delegates maximum freedom to speak their minds, so Mr. Morris's role on the Committee of Style was not generally known. But in later years he admitted to a correspondent that "that instrument was written by the fingers which write this letter." Years after Morris's death, an elderly James Madison told an inquiring historian that "the finish given to the style and arrangement of the Constitution fairly belongs to the pen of Mr. Morris."*

> *James Madison, the careful and learned theorist, is commonly called the Father of the Constitution, because he kept the most complete set of notes of the debates and made cogent arguments for ratification*

after the debates were done (he wrote one third of the Federalist Papers). But Gouverneur Morris, who put the document into its final form and who wrote the Preamble from scratch, also deserves a share of the paternity.

The founders were voluminous writers, and much of their writing is very good, but few of them had the combination of lightness and force that generates a great style. Jefferson had it; Franklin had it; Thomas Paine, the passionate and ungainly English immigrant, had it. The only other one of their number who hit that note consistently was Morris. "A better choice" for a draftsman "could not have been made," Madison concluded.

The purpose of the preamble was not to establish law - that was the purpose of the body of the Constitution that followed.

Instead, it was to provide a simple, easy to understand description of the purpose of the document.

In fact, as Constitution Law notes, only one time in the history of all Supreme Court decisions – *Jacobson v. Mass*, 197 U.S. 11 (1904) – did the Supreme Court cite the Preamble:

The only case in which the Supreme Court has directly addressed a claim based on the Preamble. In this case the court examined the Constitutional rights of Jacobson, and rejected his claim to a personal right, derived from the Preamble, to the "blessings of liberty". In rejecting Jacobson's claim, the Court wrote that "the Preamble indicates the general purpose for which the people ordained and established the Constitution" and went on to point out that "[the Preamble] has never been regarded as the source of any substantive power conferred on the Government…".

Chief Justice John Marshall, in **McCulloch v. Maryland** 17 US 316 (1819) quoted from the preamble. The issue in the case was whether the State of Maryland could tax the Bank of the Unites States, which was a federal entity. Maryland argued the Constitution was not "emanating from the people, but as the act of sovereign and independent States." To dismiss this argument, Marshall pointed to the ratification process itself. The numerous state conventions that were called, in Marshall's mind, are the original source of the federal government's power under the U.S. Constitution," Constitutionland.com notes:

"From these conventions, the Constitution derives its whole authority. The government proceeds directly from the people; is "ordained and established" in the name of the people, and is declared to be ordained 'in order to form a more perfect union, establish justice, insure domestic tranquility, and secure the blessings of liberty to themselves and to their posterity'" (McCulloch v. Maryland, 17 US 403-404).

Just like Marshall, Justice Joseph Story, in Martin v. Hunter's Lessese 14 US 304 (1816) looked to the preamble to establish the source of power in the Constitution:

"The constitution of the United States was ordained and established, not by the states in their sovereign capacities but emphatically, as the preamble of the constitution declares, by "the people of the United States. There can be no doubt that it was competent to the people to invest the general government with all the powers which they might deem proper and necessary." (Martin v. Hunter's Lessee, 14 US 324-325).

Two leading legal scholars, experts on the Constitution, offer somewhat different interpretations of meaning and interpretations of the Preamble.

"[T]he Preamble has important implications for who has the ultimate power of constitutional interpretation," Professor Michael Stokes of St. Thomas Law School writes at The Constitution Center:

> *In modern times, it has become fashionable to identify the power of constitutional interpretation almost exclusively with the decisions of courts, and particularly the U.S. Supreme Court. And yet, while it is true that the courts legitimately possess the province of constitutional interpretation in cases that come before them, it is equally true that the other branches of the national government - and of state government, too - possess a like responsibility of faithful constitutional interpretation. None of these institutions of government, created or recognized by the Constitution, is superior to the Constitution itself. None is superior to the ultimate power of the people to adopt, amend, and interpret what is, after all, the Constitution ordained and established by "We the People of the United States."*

"The Preamble to the Constitution has been largely ignored by lawyers and courts through American history," Professor Erwin Chemerinksy, Dean of the University of California at Irvine Law School responds at The Constitution Center:

> *Rarely has a Supreme Court decision relied on it, even as a guide in interpreting the Constitution. But long ago, in Marbury v. Madison (1803), the Court declared "it cannot be presumed that any clause in the constitution is intended to be without effect; and therefore such construction is inadmissible, unless the words require it." If the Preamble is read carefully and taken seriously, basic constitutional values can be found within it that should guide the interpretation of the Constitution. . .*
>
> *Equality is not mentioned in the Preamble. This is not surprising for a Constitution that explicitly protected the institution of slavery and gave women no rights. But as the Supreme Court has explained for over a half century, equality is an implicit and inherent part of liberty.*
>
> *The Preamble thus does much more than tell us that the document is to be called the "Constitution" and establish a government. The Preamble describes the core values that the Constitution exists to achieve: democratic government, effective governance, justice, freedom, and equality.*

One clause of the Preamble - the general welfare clause - is at the center of different interpretations of the Constitution.

"When challenged on the federal government's constitutional authority to create welfare programs, meddle in education or run a national healthcare system, progressives will almost always appeal to the 'general welfare clause' [of the Preamble and Article I Section 8]," Michael Maharrey, the communications director for The Tenth Amendment Center, writes:

> *The term "general welfare" actually appears twice in the Constitution. We find it first in the preamble and then in the opening line of Article I Sec. 8.*
>
> *The Congress shall have Power To lay and collect Taxes, Duties, Imposts and Excises, to pay the Debts and provide for the common Defence and general Welfare of the United States; . . .*

These words create something of a dilemma. Either the founders didn't really intend to create a general government of limited powers, or the general welfare clause doesn't really mean unlimited federal authority to fund things beneficial to the nation as a whole...

"Clearly, the words general welfare must mean something other than a grant of power for Congress to do whatever it pleased. What exactly did the framers mean?" Maharrey asks rhetorically:

Two words in the clause hold the key. General and common. The phrase simply means that any tax collected must be collected to the benefit of the United States as a whole, not for partial or sectional (i.e. special) interests.

"The federal government may promote the general welfare, or common good, but it must do so within the scope of the powers delegated and without favoritism," he concludes.

Based upon your reading of the Preamble and the Constitution, what do you think?

Chapter Discussion Questions

(1) In your opinion, should the Preamble be considered a part of the Constitution or simply an introduction?

(2) What are the advantages and disadvantages of viewing the Preamble as a part of the Constitution?

(3) What are the advantages and disadvantages of viewing the Preamble as merely an introduction to the Constitution?

Chapter 4

Three Things That Make the United States Constitution Unique in World History

Today's high school students may yawn when they hear teachers describe what a world-changing document the United States Constitution was when it was ratified in 1788 and a new government was formed a year later in 1789.

But a deeper look behind the scenes reveals the three dramatic innovations the Founding Fathers introduced in just 4,400 words that changed the course of history for the better over the next 230 years, not just in the United States of America, but around the word:

1. A Single Written Agreement Was Now the Highest Authority for "The Rule of Law" in America
2. Federalism
3. The Separation of Powers

In this chapter, we address the first of these innovations.

A Single Written Agreement Was Now the Highest Authority for "The Rule of Law" in America.

Two-thirds of the four million residents of the United States in 1789 (67 percent) were of British ancestry. Another 14 percent were from other parts of Europe. Nineteen percent (750,000) were from Africa, the vast majority of whom (700,000) were slaves, although a small number (50,000) were free.

All of the 13 original states that ratified the United States Constitution were former British colonies.

As a consequence, the government of the new United States was based on what the British called "the rule of law" - the idea that the country was governed by laws that applied to everyone, not by the arbitrary decision of one or a select

A map of the thirteen colonies that comprised British North America in 1767 (Maine was part of Massachusetts and Quebec, was a province, not a colony, acquired by Great Britain from France just a few years earlier).

group of leaders. "The rule of law" is one element that distinguishes both a republic and a constitutional monarchy from a dictatorship, an absolute monarchy, or a pure democracy.

Great Britain during the era of the Founding Fathers had a population of 14 million, and consisted of three kingdoms on the island of Britain - England, Wales, and Scotland - united under a single government whose head of state was the king and whose laws were established by the partially-elected Parliament, and a fourth kingdom - Ireland - on the island of Ireland that was a "client state" of the kingdom of England. By 1801, all four kingdoms would be united under one country, known as The United Kingdom of Great Britain and Ireland.

The kingdoms of England, Wales, and Scotland on the island of Britain and the kingdom of Ireland on the island of Ireland, circa 1789.

Great Britain had a long tradition of respect for "the rule of law," dating back more than 900 years before the American Constitution - 30 generations - to the time of the Anglo-Saxon King Alfred the Great, who created not only the country of England by uniting the ancient lands of Wessex, Anglia, Mercia, and Northumberland, but also put together the first codification of English law in the "Doom Book." (The final unification of England was accomplished by Alfred's grandson, King Aethelstan, around 927 A.D.)

The first eight decades of the settlement Colonial British North America took place as the mother country, Great Britain, underwent its own dramatic transformation from a nation that was on the verge of becoming an absolute monarchy to one that was firmly established as a constitutional monarchy.

In 1607, when the first British settlement in North America was established in Jamestown, Virginia, Great Britain was ruled by King James I, who conducted himself as an absolute monarch and considered Parliament - the country's legislative body whose tradition stretched back to the 13th century and beyond - as an annoyance to largely be ignored.

Newly installed monarchs William & Mary receive a copy of the Bill of Rights of 1689 from a representative of Parliament.

By 1689, when residents of the colony of Massachusetts successfully revolted against a tyrannical governor put in place earlier by King James II, William and Mary had assumed the throne of Great Britain as constitutional monarchs who agreed to Parliamentary supremacy.

British subjects living in the mother country celebrated this Glorious Revolution - the political uprising that began in 1688 and placed William & Mary on the throne in 1689 - as a restoration and advancement of the traditional British concept of "the rule of law."

The new Parliament after the Glorious Revolution passed a new law - the Bill of Rights of 1689 (often called the English Bill of Rights, not to be confused with our own Bill of Rights, the first ten amendments to the Constitution, all of which were ratified by 1791) - that defined the terms of this new constitutional monarchy, and protected the individual liberties of British subjects wherever they lived in the world. The agreement was hailed on both sides of the Atlantic.

British subjects living in Colonial British North America - which by this time had a population of 250,000 - celebrated the ascendancy of a constitutional monarchy as well.

John Locke, an influential English political philosopher whose ideas were central to the rise of a constitutional monarchy and whose writings profoundly influenced the thinking of many of the Founding Fathers, summed up the concept of "the rule of law" that held sway in the minds of British subjects on both sides of the Atlantic Ocean at the time.

"Freedom is constrained by laws in both the state of nature and political society," Locke wrote in a book called *Two Treatises of Government*, first published in 1689.

"Freedom of nature is to be under no other restraint but the law of nature. Freedom of people under government is to be under no restraint apart from standing rules to live by that are common to everyone in the society and made by the lawmaking power established in it," he said.

"Persons have a right or liberty to (1) follow their own will in all things that the law has not prohibited and (2) not be subject to the inconstant, uncertain, unknown, and arbitrary wills of others," Locke concluded.

John Locke's arguments, as articulated in Two Treatises of Government, made sense to the Founding Fathers.

Locke's ideas made a lot of sense to the Founding Fathers, all of whom were born well after those words were written (the oldest Founding Father, Benjamin Franklin, was born in 1706, more than 17 years after the Glorious Revolution) but began their intellectual journeys fully on board with the British concept of a constitutional monarchy.

Had the mother country adhered to those principles, there would have been no need for an American Revolution.

But, as it turned out, Parliament and King George III began to treat British subjects in British North America differently than it treated British subjects living in Great Britain.

Great Britain (now the United Kingdom of Great Britain and Northern Ireland) has never had a single document that defines its Constitution. In fact, until the ratification of the American Constitution in 1788, no country in the history of the world ever had a single document that served as its highest authority for "the rule of law."

A famous English legal scholar by the name of A.V. Dicey wrote a book in the late 19th century in which he argued that England (and by extension Great Britain and now the United Kingdom) has, in fact had a Constitution for centuries, but it is not found in a single document. Instead, it is comprised of the combination of laws passed by Parliament, the common law (the collective judicial decisions of the courts over hundreds of years), "parliamentary conventions," such as the one that enacted the reforms of the Glorious Revolution, and "works of authority," such as the document signed in 1215 by King John and the barons of England known as The Magna Carta.

Dicey is probably correct in that assertion, but the fluid nature of the "English Constitution," and the ability of Parliament to pass laws that changed what it said without giving proper consideration to the views of British subjects living in British North America was the ticking time bomb just waiting to explode during the second half of the 18th century.

This 1768 print by Paul Revere depicts the landing of British troops in Boston Harbor

And explode it did.

In 1765 Parliament passed the Quartering Act, which forced colonists to provide lodging to British soldiers living among them, and the Stamp Act, which placed an unwelcome tax on all newspapers, legal documents, and other printed documents in the colonies.

The colonists, with good reason, believed that these laws completely disregarded their rights as British subjects.

Then in 1767, Parliament passed even more onerous laws, known collectively as the Townshend Acts, which imposed more unwelcome taxes on the colonists, including the now infamous tax on tea.

In late 1767, a series of articles entitled "Letters from a Farmer in Pennsylvania" began to appear in newspapers throughout the 13 colonies. Penned by John Dickinson, who two decades later would serve as a delegate to the Constitutional Convention, these essays presented a compelling case that the imposition of taxes on the colonies by Parliament without their consent was unconstitutional - defining the English Constitution as the new agreements about governance in Great Britain arising from the Glorious Revolution almost eight decades earlier. That sentiment was widely shared in the colonies.

The usurpations of the liberties of the colonists by Parliament kept piling up.

"With a good deal of surprise I have observed that little notice has been taken of an act of Parliament, as injurious in its principle to the liberties of these colonies as the Stamp Act was: I mean the act for suspending the legislation of New York," Dickinson wrote in one of his letters.

"The assembly of that government complied with a former act of Parliament, requiring certain provisions to be made for the troops in America, in every particular, I think, except the articles of salt, pepper, and vinegar," he noted.

The suspension of New York's legislature, Dickinson wrote, "is a

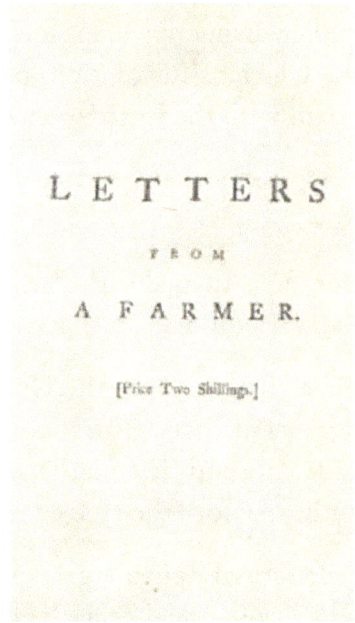
"Letters from a Farmer in Pennsylvania" were significant because they first advanced the constitutional argument for independence from Great Britain.

parliamentary assertion of the supreme authority of the British legislature over these colonies in the point of taxation; and it is intended to compel New York into a submission to that authority."

"It seems therefore to me as much a violation of the liberty of the people of that province, and consequently of all these colonies, as if the Parliament had sent a number of regiments to be quartered upon them, till they should comply," the future delegate to the Constitutional Convention concluded.

When Parliament passed The Tea Act of 1773, which removed the British East India Company's export tax for shipping tea to British America, but left the tax on tea imported to British North America intact, the call to arms, "No Taxation Without Representation" reverberated throughout the colonies.

Fourteen years later, after the American Revolution had been fought and won, and the Articles of Confederation had clearly failed, the delegates who gathered at the Constitutional Convention in Philadelphia in May of 1787 knew they had to create a single, lasting, definitive document that every colony could agree to that would be the highest authority for what "the rule of law" meant in America.

And that is exactly what they produced in the Constitution that was ratified and created the United States of America in 1789.

That highest authority could be changed, but those changes - called amendments - required a much more elaborate and participative process than the mere enacting of a single statute by the new country's legislative body.

By Charles Willson Peale -

Dickinson College in Pennsylvania is named after John Dickinson. Charles Wilson Peale painted this portrait of him around the time of the Constitutional Convention.

As for the document that emerged, it set the standard for two key concepts of governance that, while present in a few other smaller countries at the time, had never been fully developed in the creation of a major nation: federalism and the separation of powers.

Once the rest of the world saw it, they took notice. Soon, other countries began to follow the example of the United States.

Not all of the governments established by those single document constitutions have fared as well as our own.

The French Constitution of 1791, ratified just two years after the formation of the new government of the United States, established a constitutional monarchy to replace the absolute monarchy of the ill-fated King Louis XVI. That agreement barely lasted a year, and was replaced by the French Constitution of 1793, which established the first of five French republics, each with its own constitution. The current French Constitution of 1958 established the Fifth French Republic.

The Polish Constitution of 1791, which established a constitutional monarchy, also lasted less than two years.

In 1814, Norway had better luck with the Constitution of the Kingdom of Norway, which established a constitutional monarchy that continues to this day.

In 2019, more than 100 countries had a single written document that serves as their constitution. However, in many of those countries the document has little impact, since they lack the same tradition of and respect for "the rule of law" found in the United States and Great Britain.

Chapter Discussion Questions

(1) In your opinion, is a written constitution superior to an unwritten constitution?

(2) What are the advantages and disadvantages of a short and vague constitution?

(3) What are the advantages and disadvantages of a long and detailed constitution?

(4) What are the advantages and disadvantages of there being a higher law superior to a constitution?

Chapter 5

Federalism

Federalism is a foundational concept framed in the Constitution of the United States which defines the relationship between the national government and each of the state governments that comprise our republic (12 such state governments in 1789, 50 now in 2019).

A map of the fifty United States, 2019

Both entities - the national government and each state government - remain sovereign, while the powers of governance and responsibilities to the citizenry are balanced between the two. Federalism, along with The Separation of Powers within the national government (which we will discuss in Chapter Six) are the two foundational concepts of the Constitution that protect the freedoms and liberties guaranteed to individual citizens.

"In the compound republic of America, the power surrendered by the people is first divided between two distinct governments, and then the portion allotted to each subdivided among distinct and separate departments," James Madison, probably, or Alexander Hamilton, possibly, wrote of "the federal system of America" in Federalist #51, one of the famous series of essays written to persuade New York to ratify the Constitution.

"Hence a double security arises to the rights of the people. The different governments will control each other, at the same time that each will be controlled by itself," they concluded.

While revising the Articles of Confederation, delegates to the Constitutional Convention finally confronted the proper role of the states, the constitutional branch of government closest to the people.

Though the document that emerged from the convention increased the powers of the national government, which were virtually non-existent under the

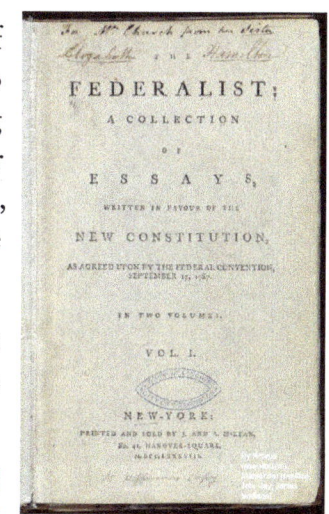

The Federalist Papers were written by Alexander Hamilton, James Madison, and John Jay between 1787 and 1788 to persuade New Yorkers to elect Federalists to their state convention.

Articles of Confederation, the complete agreement which defined that relationship was not finalized until the Tenth Amendment, the last amendment in the Bill of Rights, was ratified on December 15, 1791, just three years after the Constitution was ratified and two years after the national government was formed.

And it is the 28 simple words of the Tenth Amendment which define Federalism for us:

The powers not delegated to the United States by the Constitution, nor prohibited by it to the States, are reserved to the States respectively, or to the people.

When considering the "original agreement" of the Constitution, those first ten amendments must be considered part of the deal, because several states - Massachusetts, Virginia, and New York being the most prominent - agreed to ratify the Constitution only after instructing their representatives in the first federal Congress to consider amendments.

The motivation behind the Tenth Amendment, as expressed vehemently during the debates in ratification conventions in the 13 states, was to ensure that power didn't become centralized in the national government. It was the same notion of "checks and balances" that had been the driving force behind James Madison's original outline for the Constitution that was so influential at the Constitutional Convention in Philadelphia.

"The Constitution that was actually enacted and formally amended creates islands of government powers in a sea of liberty," Georgetown Law Professor Randy Barnett wrote in his book *Restoring The Lost Constitution: The Presumption of Liberty*, originally published in 2004.

Those government powers were balanced between the national government and the state governments.

Georgetown Law School Professor Randy Barnett.

"To better secure the natural rights of the sovereign people, the power of the national government was limited to those 'herein granted' in the written Constitution," Barnett wrote in *Our Republican Constitution: Securing the Liberty and Sovereignty of We the People*.

Under the Federalism defined in the Constitution, the national government has 33 specific limited and enumerated powers "herein granted" to its three separate branches.

Article I, Section 8 of the Constitution enumerates 19 specific powers granted to the legislative branch of the national government, one of the most important of which is the "Power to lay and collect Taxes, Duties, Imposts, and Excises."

Article II, Sections 2 and 3 of the Constitution enumerates 13 specific powers granted to the executive branch of the national government, the most significant of which states that "The President shall be Commander in Chief of the Army and Navy of the United States, and of the Militia of the several States, when called into actual Service of the United States."

Article III, Sections 1 and 2 of the Constitution enumerates the jurisdiction of the judicial branch of the national government in a single enumerated power: "The judicial Power shall extend to all Cases, in Law and Equity, arising under this Constitution, the Laws of the United States, and Treaties made, or which shall be made, under their Authority."

It also defines eight specific types of cases to which the judicial power of the judicial branch of the national government shall apply.

In the next chapter, The Separation of Powers, we'll explain how the Founding Fathers designed these three separate branches of the national government to provide "checks and balances" so that no one of the three branches would obtain powers so great as to make it capable of abusing those powers.

Here is the big, important news about the foundational concept of Federalism within the United States Constitution:

Any powers other than these 33 enumerated powers specifically given to the national government's three branches as identified above "are reserved to the States respectively, or to the people," as the Tenth Amendment makes so clear.

You may note that we have been careful in this chapter to use the term "national government" rather than "federal government."

This is intentional.

While it has been common practice for many years to refer to the "national government" as the "federal government," this terminology leads to a great deal of confusion when it comes to understanding what the foundational concept of Federalism defined in the Constitution really means.

James Monroe (left) of Virginia was a leading "Anti-Federalist" in 1788 and 1789. It was his insistence on adding a Bill of Rights during his 1789 Congressional race against James Madison (right) that persuaded Madison to champion the passage of those ten amendments in the First Congress after he defeated Monroe in the race. Monroe later served as James Madison's Secretary of State and Secretary of War, and served as the fifth President of the United States from 1817 to 1825.

As the national government has extended its powers, particularly in the last century, far beyond the very limited scope defined in the Constitution, some people are under the misimpression that Federalism means the supremacy of the national or federal government over the state governments.

Similarly, the labeling of the different groups who debated the Constitution during the ratification process has added to the confusion surrounding the true meaning of Federalism.

Those who were most insistent on the inclusion of the Bill of Rights and the Tenth Amendment into the Constitution - like James Monroe and Patrick Henry in Virginia, and Samuel Adams in Massachusetts - were called "Anti-Federalists" while those who were initially resistant to the need for a Bill of Rights - and in this category we include both Alexander Hamilton and James Madison (the latter of whom subsequently experienced such a transformation during his successful 1789 campaign to win a seat in the House of Representatives that he ultimately became the legislative champion of the Bill of Rights) - were called "Federalists."

So, it was really the "Anti-Federalists" who were ultimately responsible for the final form of Federalism incorporated in the Constitution and the Bill of Rights.

Finally, there is the Federalist Party, the first political party in America. It was in existence from about 1792 until 1816, and it advanced policies that were often at odds with the foundational constitutional concept of Federalism.

It consisted of business and banking interests who supported the economic policies of Alexander Hamilton, the first Secretary of the Treasury. Hamilton supported a national bank and the notion that the Constitution provided "implied powers" to the national government, a notion that the quickly formed second national party, the Democratic-Republicans, led by Thomas Jefferson and James Madison, vigorously disputed.

A great deal has happened in the 228 years since the Tenth Amendment was ratified, and most of it has advanced the power of the national government at the expense of state governments and individual citizens.

"Since the adoption of the Constitution, courts have eliminated clause after clause that interfered with the exercise of government power," Georgetown Law Professor Barnett wrote in his 2004 book.

The result is just the opposite of what the Founding Fathers intended when they made Federalism one of the foundational principles of the Constitution.

"The judicially redacted constitution creates islands of liberty rights in a sea of governmental powers," Barnett concluded.

What do you think?

Is it time to restore the foundational concept of Federalism the Founding Fathers installed within our Constitution to the operation of our national and state governments in 2019 and beyond?

And if it is, what specifically can be done to accomplish that?

Chapter Discussion Questions

(1) What historical events might have influenced the Founders to create a system with states retaining a degree of sovereignty?

(2) Would you alter the phrasing of the Tenth Amendment in any way? Why or why not?

(3) What are the advantages and disadvantages of returning more power to the states?

Chapter 6

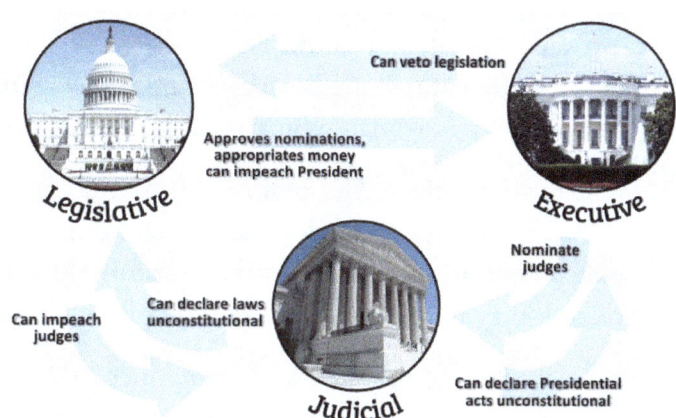

The Separation of Powers

The Separation of Powers among three branches of the national government - legislative, executive, and judicial – along with Federalism are the two foundational concepts of the Constitution of the United States that protect the freedoms and liberties guaranteed to individual citizens.

Both foundational concepts are the practical implementation of the Founding Fathers' belief in the need for checks and balances to prevent the rise of uncontrolled abuses of power within one branch of government.

"It is safe to say that a respect for the principle of separation of powers is deeply ingrained in every American," the National Archives website says:

> *The nation subscribes to the original premise of the framers of the Constitution that the way to safeguard against tyranny is to separate the powers of government among three branches so that each branch checks the other two. Even when this system thwarts the public will and paralyzes the processes of government, Americans have rallied to its defense.*

One Founding Father, more than any other, was the driving force behind the inclusion of The Separation of Powers as a foundational concept in the Constitution: James Madison, an intellectual giant who was only 36 years old when he arrived in Philadelphia in May 1787 to sit as one of 55 delegates to the Constitutional Convention. Madison, a graduate of Princeton University, came prepared. He had spent months reviewing other confederations throughout history and arrived with voluminous notes and a detailed outline of how he thought the Constitution should be written. To a large extent, the final document followed much of that outline.

James Madison lived well into his eighties. He was a young man, barely 36, when he helped guide the Constitutional Convention to create the Constitution based on his well conceived outline.

"Madison argues, it is not sufficient to list rights on parchment only. Because men are not angels - because they are so often actuated by private interest and ambition - these very motives themselves must be employed to keep the departments of government within their limited, constitutional boundaries," the Heritage Foundation writes of the bookish young man who arrived in Philadelphia wise beyond his years.

"Ambition must be made to counteract ambition. The interest of the man must be connected with the constitutional rights of the place," the author of Federalist No. 51 wrote in early 1788 as the states were selecting delegates to attend the state conventions and debate the ratification of the Constitution. Madison probably authored that essay, though it may have been Alexander Hamilton.

"Madison thus proposed a system of checks and balances that would incorporate the less than sterling side of human nature into the very workings of government," the Heritage Foundation notes:

To accomplish this, the powers of the three branches of government are partially blended, enabling each branch to guard against usurpations of power by the others and safeguard its own constitutional province. Examples of constitutional checks and balances include the executive veto of legislative bills, the legislative override of the executive veto, the required Senate confirmation of presidential appointments to the Supreme Court, and judicial review.

In essence, Madison wanted the different branches of government, as well as the two houses of Congress and the national and the state governments, to check each other in the exercise of power, thereby guaranteeing the diffusion of governmental power and the protection of the people's rights and liberties.

"The accumulation of all powers, legislative, executive, and judiciary, in the same hands, whether of one, a few, or many, and whether hereditary, self appointed, or elective, may justly be pronounced the very definition of tyranny," James Madison wrote in Federalist #47, first published in the New York Packet on February 1, 1788.

"The preservation of liberty requires that the three great departments of power should be separate and distinct," he noted in that essay.

"Where the WHOLE power of one department is exercised by the same hands which possess the WHOLE power of another department, the fundamental principles of a free constitution are subverted," he added.

The end result that emerged on parchment of this scheme of "checks and balances" known as The Separation of Powers designated specific powers to each of the three branches of the national government.

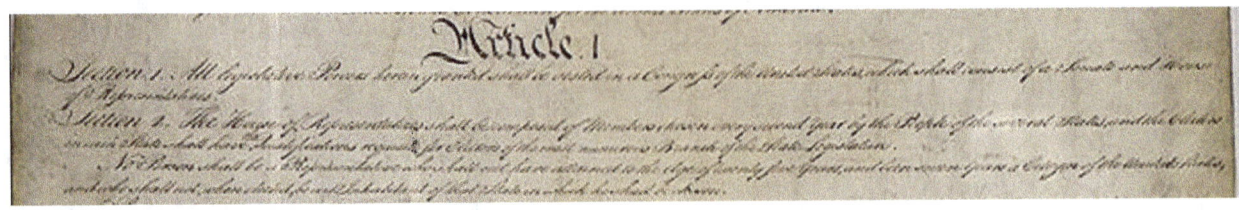

Article I, Section 8 of the Constitution enumerates 19 specific powers granted to the legislative branch of the national government:

(1) The Congress shall have Power To lay and collect Taxes, Duties, Imposts and Excises,

(2) to pay the Debts and provide for the common Defence and general Welfare of the United States; but all Duties, Imposts and Excises shall be uniform throughout the United States;

(3) To borrow Money on the credit of the United States;

(4) To regulate Commerce with foreign Nations, and among the several States, and with the Indian Tribes;

(5) To establish an uniform Rule of Naturalization, and uniform Laws on the subject of Bankruptcies throughout the United States;

(6) To coin Money, regulate the Value thereof, and of foreign Coin, and fix the Standard of Weights and Measures;

(7) To provide for the Punishment of counterfeiting the Securities and current Coin of the United States;

(8) To establish Post Offices and post Roads;

(9) To promote the Progress of Science and useful Arts, by securing for limited Times to Authors and Inventors the exclusive Right to their respective Writings and Discoveries;

(10) To constitute Tribunals inferior to the supreme Court;

(11) To define and punish Piracies and Felonies committed on the high Seas, and Offences against the Law of Nations;

(12) To declare War, grant Letters of Marque and Reprisal, and make Rules concerning Captures on Land and Water;

(13) To raise and support Armies, but no Appropriation of Money to that Use shall be for a longer Term than two Years;

(14) To provide and maintain a Navy;

(15) To make Rules for the Government and Regulation of the land and naval Forces;

(16) To provide for calling forth the Militia to execute the Laws of the Union, suppress Insurrections and repel Invasions;

(17) To provide for organizing, arming, and disciplining, the Militia, and for governing such Part of them as may be employed in the Service of the United States, reserving to the States respectively, the Appointment of the Officers, and the Authority of training the Militia according to the discipline prescribed by Congress;

(18) To exercise exclusive Legislation in all Cases whatsoever, over such District (not exceeding ten Miles square) as may, by Cession of particular States, and the Acceptance of Congress, become the Seat of the Government of the United States, and to exercise like Authority over all Places purchased by the Consent of the Legislature of the State in which the Same shall be, for the Erection of Forts, Magazines, Arsenals, dock-Yards, and other needful Buildings; - And

(19) To make all Laws which shall be necessary and proper for carrying into Execution the foregoing Powers, and all other Powers vested by this Constitution in the Government of the United States, or in any Department or Officer thereof.

The last of these 19 enumerated powers, that the legislative branch of the national government has the power "to make all Laws which shall be necessary and proper for carrying into Execution the foregoing Powers," has been at the center of debates concerning the limits or extent of the powers of the national government since the Constitution was ratified in 1789.

Debates over the "necessary and proper" clause continue to this day.

Article II, Sections 2 and 3 of the Constitution enumerates 13 specific powers granted to the executive branch of the national government:

Section. 2.

(1) The President shall be Commander in Chief of the Army and Navy of the United States, and of the Militia of the several States,

(2) he may require the Opinion, in writing, of the principal Officer in each of the executive Departments, upon any Subject relating to the Duties of their respective Offices,

(3) and he shall have Power to grant Reprieves and Pardons for Offences against the United States, except in Cases of Impeachment.

(4) He shall have Power, by and with the Advice and Consent of the Senate, to make Treaties, provided two thirds of the Senators present concur;

(5) and he shall nominate, and by and with the Advice and Consent of the Senate, shall appoint Ambassadors, other public Ministers and Consuls, Judges of the supreme Court, and all other Officers of the United States, whose Appointments are not herein otherwise provided for, and which shall be established by Law:

(6) the Congress may by Law vest the Appointment of such inferior Officers, as they think proper, in the President alone, in the Courts of Law, or in the Heads of Departments.

(7) The President shall have Power to fill up all Vacancies that may happen during the Recess of the Senate, by granting Commissions which shall expire at the End of their next Session.

Section. 3.

(8) He shall from time to time give to the Congress Information of the State of the Union, and recommend to their Consideration such Measures as he shall judge necessary and expedient;

(9) he may, on extraordinary Occasions, convene both Houses, or either of them,

(10) and in Case of Disagreement between them, with Respect to the Time of Adjournment, he may adjourn them to such Time as he shall think proper;

(11) he shall receive Ambassadors and other public Ministers;

(12) he shall take Care that the Laws be faithfully executed, and

(13) shall Commission all the Officers of the United States.

Article III, Sections 1 and 2 of the Constitution enumerates the jurisdiction of the judicial branch of the national government in a single power:

(1) The judicial Power shall extend to all Cases, in Law and Equity, arising under this Constitution, the Laws of the United States, and Treaties made, or which shall be made, under their Authority;

It also defines 8 specific types of cases to which the judicial power of the judicial branch of the national government shall apply:

(1) to all Cases affecting Ambassadors, other public Ministers and Consuls;

(2) to all Cases of admiralty and maritime Jurisdiction;

(3) to Controversies to which the United States shall be a Party;

(4) to Controversies between two or more States;

(5) between a State and Citizens of another State,

(6) between Citizens of different States,

(7) between Citizens of the same State claiming Lands under Grants of different States,

(8) and between a State, or the Citizens thereof, and foreign States, Citizens or Subjects.

Over the subsequent 230 years, as Madison predicted "Because men are not angels - because they are so often actuated by private interest and ambition," the checks and balances designated in the parchment of the Constitution has been transformed by the practices of non-angelic men and women to create a system of government that deviates substantially from the one envisioned by the Founding Fathers in two very specific ways:

First, the national government has continually usurped the power of the state governments, as envisioned in the foundational concept of Federalism.

*John Marshall, the fourth Chief Justice of the Supreme Court, established the principle of judicial review - that the Supreme Court could declare laws passed by Congress or acts of the President to be unconstitutional, in a famous 1803 case known as **Marbury v. Madison**. This judicial power was not explicitly authorized in the Constitution, but the principal of judicial review has been respected ever since.*

Second, The Separation of Powers within the national government has evolved dramatically, as both the executive branch and the judicial branch have assumed greater and greater powers, while the legislative branch has abrogated - informally in many instances - some of its most important constitutional powers.

"Abrograte" is a strong word, not often used.

Dictionary.com defines its meaning as "to abolish by formal or official means; annul by an authoritative act; repeal," or "to put aside; put an end to."

It is in the 19th enumerated power in which the legislative branch has failed so dramatically:

> *To make all Laws which shall be necessary and proper for carrying into Execution the foregoing Powers, and all other Powers vested by this Constitution in the Government of the United States, or in any Department or Officer thereof.*

The legislative branch has given away huge powers to the executive branch in the form of specific regulatory rule making based upon laws passed in Congress. This sacrifice of authority has given rise, over the past century, to the runaway regulatory bureaucratic state.

Chapter Discussion Questions

(1) How would you describe the difference between checks and balances and separation of powers?

(2) In your opinion, does the "necessary and proper" clause grant more powers to Congress? Why or why not?

(3) In your opinion, does the "necessary and proper" clause infer there are implied powers in the Constitution? Why or why not?

(4) What are the advantages and disadvantages of viewing the "necessary and proper" clause of inferring there are implied powers in the Constitution?

Chapter 7

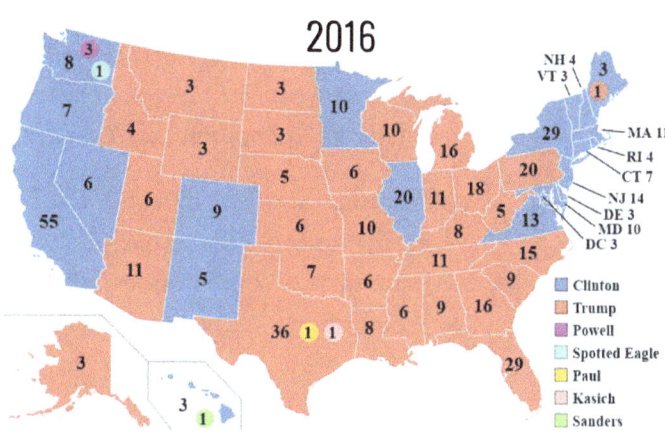

The Electoral College and the Selection of the President

The method of selection of a President to head the executive branch for a term of four years is the most notable illustration of the foundational concept of Federalism seen in the body of the text of the Constitution of the United States that emerged from the Constitutional Convention.

Federalism, as we explained earlier, "defines the relationship between the national government and each of the state governments that comprise our republic. Both entities - the national government and each state government - remain sovereign, while the powers of governance and responsibilities to the citizenry are balanced between the two." And it was the Tenth Amendment, ratified in 1791 and part of the original constitutional "compact" or "covenant" between the states and the national government upon which our republic was organized:

> *The powers not delegated to the United States by the Constitution, nor prohibited by it to the States, are reserved to the States respectively, or to the people.*

"The executive Power shall be vested in a President of the United States of America. He shall hold his Office during the Term of four Years, and, together with the Vice President, chosen for the same Term, be elected, as follows," Article II, Section 1 of the Constitution reads.

It then explains the method to be used in the new American republic to select that President.

"Each State shall appoint, **in such Manner as the Legislature thereof may direct, a Number of Electors, equal to the whole Number of Senators and Representatives to which the State may be entitled in the Congress:** but no Senator or Representative, or Person holding an Office of Trust or Profit under the United States, shall be appointed an Elector," (emphasis added) it begins.

"This language in fact paralleled the provisions for state legislative appointment of congressional delegates in the Articles of Confederation, and of U.S. Senators under Article I of the Constitution," the Heritage Guide to the Constitution notes.

Article II, Section 1 then describes the method of Presidential selection by these Electors:

> *The Electors shall meet in their respective States, and vote by Ballot for two Persons, of whom one at least shall not be an Inhabitant of the same State with themselves.*

One month after the general election for a President is held, the Electors selected in each state convene in their State capital to cast their ballots for President. They then sign a Certificate of Vote, which is sent to the Capitol in Washington, D.C. for review and acceptance by the Congress of the United States.

And they shall make a List of all the Persons voted for, and of the Number of Votes for each; which List they shall sign and certify, and transmit sealed to the Seat of the Government of the United States, directed to the President of the Senate.

After the Electors meet in their State capitals to sign their Certificate of Vote, that document is transmitted to the Senate of the United States, where the Electoral College votes are counted:

The President of the Senate shall, in the Presence of the Senate and House of Representatives, open all the Certificates, and the Votes shall then be counted.

The Person having the greatest Number of Votes shall be the President, if such Number be a Majority of the whole Number of Electors appointed; and if there be more than one who have such Majority, and have an equal Number of Votes, then the House of Representatives shall immediately chuse by Ballot one of them for President; and if no Person have a Majority, then from the five highest on the List the said House shall in like Manner chuse the President.

So, the House of Representatives then, will select the President if no candidate has a majority of the Electoral College votes, as Article II, Section 1 continues:

But in chusing the President, the Votes shall be taken by States, the Representation from each State having one Vote; A quorum for this Purpose shall consist of a Member or Members from two thirds of the States, and a Majority of all the States shall be necessary to a Choice. In every Case, after the Choice of the President, the Person having the greatest Number of Votes of the Electors shall be the Vice President. But if there should remain two or more who have equal Votes, the Senate shall chuse from them by Ballot the Vice President.

The Congress may determine the Time of chusing the Electors, and the Day on which they shall give their Votes; which Day shall be the same throughout the United States.

Critics of the Electoral College system argue it is "unfair," and that a simple majority of all the votes cast should determine the election outcome. But to do so would be a direct violation of the foundational constitutional concept of Federalism, which specifically recognizes the sovereignty of each state.

Direct election of the President by nationwide popular vote is a concept suitable with a pure democracy, but is entirely unfit for a constitutional federal republic like the United States of America.

The President of the Senate counts the Electoral College votes submitted by the state legislatures in the presence of all the members of the House of Representatives and the Senate. C-SPAN cameras show members of the Senate and House emerging from the joint session of Congress held on January 6, 2017 that declared Donald Trump the winner of the 2016 Presidential election.

Article II Section 1 recognizes the sovereignty of each state in the Presidential selection process.

Note first that it says "Each State shall appoint, in such Manner as the Legislature thereof may direct, a Number of Electors, equal to the whole Number of Senators and Representatives to which the State may be entitled in the Congress,"

Under the Constitution, then, the State Legislature of any state could choose a manner of selecting presidential Electors that differs from the popular vote within the state which has so long been the tradition among most states.

In fact, during the first ten Presidential elections between 1788-89 and 1824, Electors in most states were appointed by their state legislatures. In the very first presidential election, which was conducted between December 1788 and January 1789, George Washington was unanimously elected by the ten states that selected Electors.

George Washington was unanimously elected President in the election of 1788-1789 by the Electoral College. He was the only candidate on the ballot in those six states that selected Electors by some form of popular vote, and he won the popular vote virtually unanimously as well.

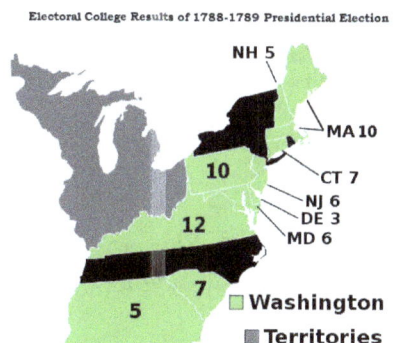

George Washington was unanimously elected President in the election of 1788-1789 by the Electoral College. He was the only candidate on the ballot in those six states that selected Electors by some form of popular vote, and he won the popular vote by virtually unanimously as well.

The legislatures of six states - Delaware, Massachusetts, Maryland, New Hampshire, Pennsylvania, and Virginia - decided to select Electors based on some form of popular vote. But the legislatures of four states - Georgia, South Carolina, New Jersey, and Connecticut - chose to select Electors themselves. New York did not select any Electors that year because the State Legislature there was deadlocked over the procedure of choosing electors. Neither North Carolina nor Rhode Island participated because they had not yet ratified the Constitution.

By 1828, when Andrew Jackson was elected President, 20 of the country's 22 states selected Electors by some form of popular vote. Only Delaware and South Carolina selected Electors in the state legislature. By 1840, South Carolina was the only state in which the state legislature still selected Electors. It was not until the election of 1868 that every state in the union selected Electors by some form of popular vote.

The Constitution itself offers no insight into the qualifications and duties of an Elector, it leaves that entirely to the States, who can set the rules as to both the selection of the Electors and their specific duties, responsibilities, and authorities: "Each State shall appoint, in such Manner as the Legislature thereof may direct, a Number of Electors . . ."

Alexander Hamilton, however, did offer significant insight into those qualities in The Federalist essays.

He commented extensively on this in Federalist #68, published in the *New York Packet* on March 14, 1788:

It was equally desirable, that the immediate election should be made by men most capable of analyzing the qualities adapted to the station, and acting under circumstances favorable to deliberation, and to a judicious combination of all the reasons and inducements which were proper to govern their choice. A small number of persons, selected by their fellow-citizens from the general mass, will be most likely to possess the information and discernment requisite to such complicated investigations.

It was also peculiarly desirable to afford as little opportunity as possible to tumult and disorder. This evil was not least to be dreaded in the election of a magistrate, who was to have so important an agency in the administration of the government as the President of the United States. But the precautions which have been so happily concerted in the system under consideration, promise an effectual security against this mischief. The choice of SEVERAL, to form an intermediate body of electors, will be much less apt to convulse the community with any extraordinary or violent movements, than the choice of ONE who was himself to be the final object of the public wishes. And as the electors, chosen in each State, are to assemble and vote in the State in which they are chosen, this detached and divided situation will expose them much less to heats and ferments, which might be communicated from them to the people, than if they were all to be convened at one time, in one place.

Alexander Hamilton, who later became our first Secretary of the Treasury under President George Washington, offered his views on the qualities needed in a Presidential Elector in The Federalist #68.

Under the concept of sovereignty, the states can provide detailed instructions to Electors. In other words, they can say - you are instructed to vote for the candidate for President who receives the most votes in our state.

The Founding Fathers failed to anticipate one particular piece of skullduggery by a Vice-Presidential candidate that surfaced in the election of 1800, when Aaron Burr was running as Thomas Jefferson's Vice-President.

When the Electoral College votes were cast in the United States Senates in that election, both men had an equal number of votes, 73, out of a total of 276 cast. (Remember, under the Constitution each Elector cast two votes for President, and the top vote-getter was elected President if they obtained a majority, and the second vote-getter was Vice-President).

Guess what?

Burr decided that he wanted to be President, not Vice-President, and a heated political battle ensued.

With Burr and Jefferson tied, the election was thrown into the lame-duck House of Representatives still controlled by the

Aaron Burr decided he wanted to be President, not Vice-President, in 1801.

Federalists, where it wasn't until the 36th ballot that Jefferson was elected.

Ultimately, Burr lost out, but the Congress realized this flaw in the Constitution had to be remedied.

"By the election of 1800, the nation's first two parties were beginning to take shape. The Presidential race was hotly contested between the Federalist President, John Adams, and the Democratic-Republican candidate, Thomas Jefferson. Because the Constitution did not distinguish between President and Vice-President in the votes cast by each state's electors in the Electoral College, both Jefferson and his running mate Aaron Burr received 73 votes," the National Archives notes.

According to Article II, Section 1 of the Constitution, if two candidates each received a majority of the electoral votes but are tied, the House of Representatives would determine which one would be President. Therefore, the decision rested with the lame duck, Federalist-controlled House of Representatives. Thirty-five ballots were cast over five days but neither candidate received a majority. Many Federalists saw Jefferson as their principal foe, whose election was to be avoided at all costs. But Alexander Hamilton, a well-respected Federalist party leader, hated Burr and advised Federalists in Congress that Jefferson was the safer choice. Finally, on February 17, 1801, on the thirty-sixth ballot, the House elected Thomas Jefferson to be President.

If no Presidential candidates receives a majority of the Electoral College votes, the House of Representatives selects the President.

The tie vote between Jefferson and Burr in the 1801 Electoral College pointed out problems with the electoral system. The framers of the Constitution had not anticipated such a tie, nor had they considered the possibility of the election of a President or Vice President from opposing factions – which had been the case in the 1796 election when Federalist John Adams was elected President and Democratic-Republican Thomas Jefferson was elected Vice-President. In 1804, the passage of the 12th Amendment corrected these problems by providing for separate Electoral College votes for President and Vice President.

"Passed by Congress December 9, 1803, and ratified June 15, 1804, the 12th Amendment provided for separate Electoral College votes for President and Vice President, correcting weaknesses in the earlier electoral system which were responsible for the controversial Presidential Election of 1800," the National Archives says.

The text of the 12th Amendment reads as follows:

The Electors shall meet in their respective states, and vote by ballot for President and Vice-President, one of whom, at least, shall not be an inhabitant of the same state with themselves; they shall name in their ballots the person voted for as President, and in distinct ballots the person voted for as Vice-President, and they shall make distinct lists of all persons voted for as President, and all persons voted for as Vice-President and of the number of votes for each, which lists they shall sign and certify, and transmit sealed to the seat of the government of the United States, directed to the President of the Senate.

The President of the Senate shall, in the presence of the Senate and House of Representatives, open all the certificates and the votes shall then be counted.

The person having the greatest number of votes for President, shall be the President, if such number be a majority of the whole number of Electors appointed; and if no person have such majority, then from the persons having the highest numbers not exceeding three on the list of those voted for as President, the House of Representatives shall choose immediately, by ballot, the President. But in choosing the President, the votes shall be taken by states, the representation from each state having one vote; a quorum for this purpose shall consist of a member or members from two-thirds of the states, and a majority of all the states shall be necessary to a choice. And if the House of Representatives shall not choose a President whenever the right of choice shall devolve upon them, before the fourth day of March next following, then the Vice-President shall act as President, as in the case of the death or other constitutional disability of the President.

The person having the greatest number of votes as Vice-President, shall be the Vice-President, if such number be a majority of the whole number of Electors appointed, and if no person have a majority, then from the two highest numbers on the list, the Senate shall choose the Vice-President; a quorum for the purpose shall consist of two-thirds of the whole number of Senators, and a majority of the whole number shall be necessary to a choice. But no person constitutionally ineligible to the office of President shall be eligible to that of Vice-President of the United States.

In one of the bitter ironies of history, Aaron Burr killed Alexander Hamilton in a duel on July 11, 1804 (Hamilton died the following day), less than a month after the 12th Amendment was ratified.

In recent years, a number of political figures and commentators have criticized the Electoral College and want the President selected by direct popular vote.

Four times since 1868, the first year in which all states selected Electors by some form of popular vote, the candidate who received the most popular vote did not win the Electoral College, and therefore was not elected President.

In 1876, Democrat Samuel Tilden received 50.9 percent of the popular vote to Republican Rutherford B. Hayes' 47.9 percent. But Hayes was elected President because he won a majority of the Electoral College votes, 185 to 184.

In 1888, Democrat Grover Cleveland, the incumbent President, received 48.6 percent of the popular vote to Republican Benjamin Harrison's 47.8 percent. But Harrison was elected President because he won a majority of the Electoral College votes, 233 to 168.

Burr and Hamilton held their duel on a ledge above Hudson River in what is now Weehawken, New Jersey on July 11, 1804. The details of how the duel ended in an uninjured Vice President Burr and a mortally wounded Hamilton are unclear.

In 2000, Democrat Al Gore received 48.4 percent of the popular vote to Republican George W. Bush's 47.9 percent. But Bush was elected President because he won a majority of the Electoral College votes, 271 to 266.

In the presidential election of 2016, Democrat Hillary Clinton received 48 percent of the popular vote to Republican Donald Trump's 46 percent. But Trump was elected President because he won the majority of the Electoral College votes, 304 to 227 (7 Electoral College votes were split between other candidates).

Clinton's popular vote margin of 2.8 million was the highest of any Presidential candidate who won the popular vote but lost the Electoral College vote (though her 2 percent margin was less than Samuel Tilden's 3 percent margin in 1876), and therefore the Presidency.

A closer look at the state by state breakdown of the 2016 Presidential Election results reveals the wisdom of the Founding Fathers in establishing an Electoral College method for selecting a President.

Hillary Clinton won the state of California resoundingly, beating Donald Trump there by more than 4.2 million votes – a 61 percent to 31 percent thumping.

Had the Founders selected direct popular vote as the means for electing a President, the residents of California would have dictated to the other 49 states who would have served as our President.

Looking at the total combined vote in the other 49 states, Donald Trump won 1.4 million votes more than Hillary Clinton, taking 58.5 million votes to her 57.1 million votes.

But because of the Electoral College, Hillary Clinton's huge vote margin in California earned her the state's 55 Electoral College votes, and no more.

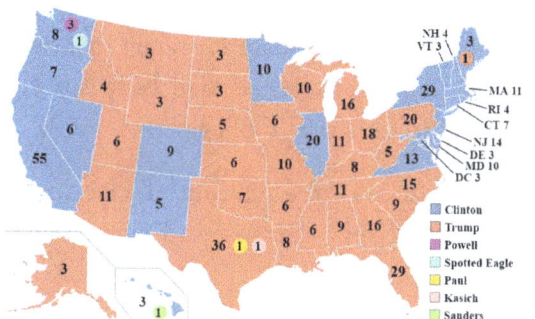

Donald Trump easily won the 2016 Electoral College vote, 304 to 227, despite losing the popular vote 48 percent to 46 percent.

The Founding Fathers had an idea that the Electors would be of a high personal character, wisdom, and that intelligence, and would exercise those qualities in their selection.

They also hoped against the development of factions and competing political powers, a hope in retrospect was inevitably bound to be disappointed, given the foibles of human nature.

By tradition, and in many instances as a consequence of state law, Electors have followed the directions of their State Legislatures, and by extension for most of the past 200 years, the expressed will of the voters in their states when it comes to casting their ballot for President.

"Developments since [the ratification of the Constitution and the Bill of Rights] have changed much of the expected practice, but cases have confirmed the original understanding regarding electoral powers absent constitutional alteration. Our democratic ethos increasingly embraced popular elections, leading all state legislatures by 1880 to provide for popular election of presidential electors, and the Sixteenth Amendment in 1913 mandated the same for Senators," the Heritage Guide to the Constitution notes:

> *This development, and the growing view that political party politics reflected rather than undermined democratic choice, made the notion of electors exercising their own independent judgment seem dubious by the early 1800s. Current case law such as Ray v. Blair (1952) allows the states to present voters with ballots that list only the presidential candidates (even though the votes for a candidate are really for his party's slate of electors), and also permits the states to pass laws requiring electors to pledge that, if chosen, they will vote for their party's candidate. Electors rarely do otherwise, though the enforceability of those pledges against a wayward elector remains unsettled.*

In some cases, "Faithless Electors" have gone against that tradition in those states that have not explicitly instructed them how to cast their ballot.

Until 2016, there had been only 20 Faithless Electors in 14 separate Presidential elections (out of the 57 Presidential elections between 1788 and 2012) who cast their ballots for a Presidential candidate other than the one who had won the votes of their state, or whom they had committed to their state legislatures they would back–who was still living at the time the electoral college convened. (Sixty-three electors who were pledged to Democratic candidate Horace Greeley in 1872 did not vote for him because he died between election day and the day the Electoral College convened).

In 43 of those 57 Presidential elections, every elector was a "Faithful" Elector and voted as he or she had pledged.

A number of "Faithless Electors" failed in 2016 because state laws did not allow them to exercise their personal discretion when casting their ballots.

2016 saw the highest number of Faithless Electors–seven–in the history of the country for any Presidential election in which both candidates were still living at the time the Electoral College convened, in part due to the increasingly polarized nature of the country.

Four Electors in the state of Washington, which Hillary Clinton won, were "Faithless" Electors. Three voted for Colin Powell and one voted for Faith Spotted Eagle.

One Elector in the state of Hawaii, which Hillary Clinton won, was a "Faithless" Elector who voted for Sen. Bernie Sanders (I-VT).

Two Electors in the state of Texas, which Donald Trump won, were "Faithless" Electors. One voted for Ohio Governor John Kasich, the other voted for former Congressman Ron Paul.

Most state legislatures look askance at such free lancing. A number of state legislatures which did not provide explicit guidance to Electors prior to 2016 (Texas and Washington in particular) appear to be in the process of tightening those directions for 2020 and beyond.

Chapter Discussion Questions

(1) In your opinion, do the states have too much power over national elections?

(2) What modifications, if any, would you make to the Electoral College?

(3) To what extent did Hamilton's view of the electors of the Electoral College reflect an elitist view?

(4) Were the Founders naïve to assume there would not be parties in the American political system?

Chapter 8

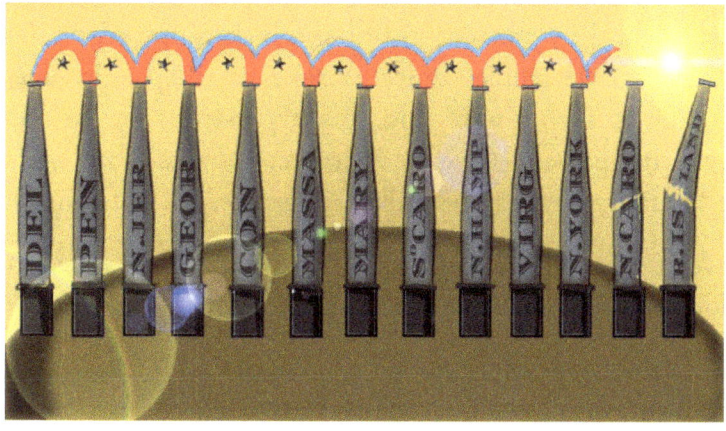

How and Why Thirteen States Ratified the Constitution: 1787 - 1790

When Benjamin Franklin emerged from the Constitutional Convention in Philadelphia on September 17, 1787 and told Mrs. Powel the delegates had given Americans "a republic, if you can keep it," he was anticipating that at least nine of the 13 states who were joined together under the Articles of Confederation would eventually ratify the Constitution.

Franklin was right, of course, but it would take two-and-a-half long years before all 13 states were in the fold of the new republic.

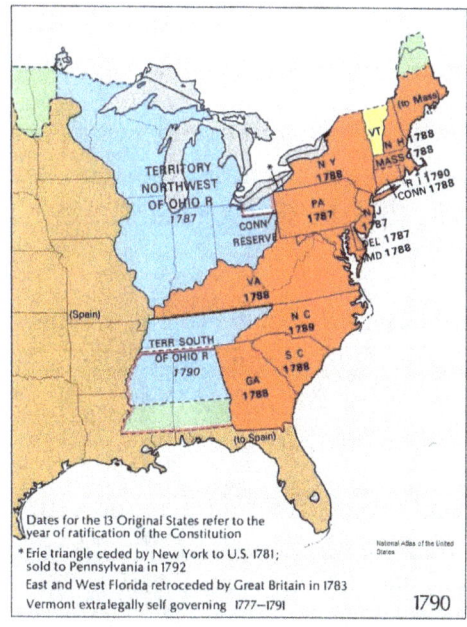

A map of the thirteen states that comprised the Confederation of the United States of America during its short existence between 1777 and 1789.

The delegates to the Constitutional Convention believed in the concept of the sovereignty of the people, so they made sure that the new republic would not be formally organized until two-thirds of the states - nine out of 13 - held conventions that ratified the Constitution.

Until then, the United States of America, as a country, existed, but under the weak terms of the Articles of Confederation.

Once nine states ratified the Constitution, that old form of government would dissolve, and the remaining four states would be left to fend for themselves as independent sovereign "country-states," a rather impractical, though possible, proposition.

This was a very intelligent way to frame the issue of ratification, and it avoided the weakness of the ratification process of the Articles of Confederation. The Continental Congress proposed that document in November 1777, and required ratification by all of the state legislatures. That process took until 1781, and was one of the reasons the document had to be drafted providing so few powers to the national government.

The first problem for the delegates to the Constitutional Convention was to determine how to deal with the Confederation Congress organized under the Articles that was convening at that time in New York

City. The Confederation Congress was "unicameral," that is, it had only one elected body, as opposed to the "bicameral" Congress provided by the Constitution, which proposed two elected bodies, the Senate, which represented the States, and the House, which represented the people. The Confederation Congress also had executive powers, limited as they were, and legislative powers, unlike the Constitution's Congress, which had primarily legislative powers. (The new Senate, however, had executive power to confirm Presidential appointments, to ratify treaties, and judicial power as well to try impeachments.)

Each session of the Confederation Congress lasted for only a year, and the 8th such session was drawing to a close when the Constitution was signed on September 17, 1787.

Remember, the new Constitution would, in effect, do away with that body, so you can see why its members might oppose the new Constitution.

On the other hand, several delegates to the Constitutional Convention, including James Madison, were also members of the Congress.

"When the Constitution was signed on the 17th of September, the question was, 'Shall we take it to Congress?'" Professor Gordon Lloyd wrote:

> *The Pennsylvania Assembly was nearing the end of its session, and what they wanted to do was to authorize the calling of a ratifying convention. But they had a problem: "Should the Congress of the United States approve this document before they issued a call for elections to a state ratifying convention?"*

In the end, the Pennsylvania Assembly "decided to go to Congress" for approval before deciding to hold a ratifying convention in the state.

So on September 19, Madison and several other Constitutional Convention delegates who were also members of the Confederation Congress, rode from Philadelphia to New York City to make their case.

William Jackson, the Secretary of the Constitutional Convention, left for New York City from Philadelphia with the four-page engrossed parchment Constitution.

Madison wanted the Confederation Congress to endorse the new Constitution, which he thought would give it the very best chance for quick ratification by the requisite nine states to form a new republic.

During the ratification debates that would follow, Madison and the other Federalists would argue that the new Constitution had to be accepted or rejected as it stood, without any changes or amendments.

But Madison and his colleagues received an icy reception from Virginia's Richard Henry Lee, (first cousin to the grandfather of the famous Confederate Civil War General Robert E. Lee) a prominent member of the Confederation Congress, when they arrived in New York City.

Though there was not a possibility that the Confederation Congress would refuse to send the Constitution to the states for ratification, there was a debate about whether it would be sent with that legislative body's approval.

After three days of debate, the Confederation Congress agreed on September 28, 1787 to send the Constitution to each state for ratification, without a recommendation either way. Madison was disappointed, but reasoned that it was an acceptable start. He was still unconvinced of the need for a Bill of Rights.

William Jackson, who brought the engrossed Constitution on parchment with him to the Confederation Congress in New York "made his way back to Pennsylvania with the Constitution on the very day [September 29] that the Pennsylvania Assembly was supposed to adjourn," Lloyd wrote:

The Pennsylvania Constitution provides for quorum requirement of two-thirds of the membership. In practice that means that 46 members must be present. Since a few of the Federalist members were indisposed, a handful of Antifederalists were needed to secure a quorum. Knowing this, they hid in churches and taverns only to be forcefully removed and seated in the Assembly to secure the quorum and the vote needed to authorize the calling of the state ratifying convention.

So the Pennsylvania Assembly called for election of delegates to a state ratifying convention, to be held seven weeks later, starting on November 20.

The Confederation Congress was meeting in Federal Hall in New York City when James Madison and several other Constitutional Convention delegates who were also members of the Confederation Congress arrived there on September 20, 1787.

By mid October 1787, every state governor had officially received the new Constitution from the Confederation Congress. Soon, each state legislature began deliberating whether - and when and how - to hold a state ratification convention.

(The state legislatures of 11 states would soon call for the election of delegates to state ratifying conventions. The North Carolina state legislature meeting in December 1787 called its convention for July 1788. Rhode Island - which had refused to send a delegation to the Constitutional Convention - called for a statewide referendum to be held in the state's thirty towns on March 24, 1788, but would not actually hold a ratifying convention until March 1790.)

The "Anti-Federalists" soon emerged as powerful opponents of the new Constitution. They opposed it because it failed to include a specific protection of individual liberties - a bill of rights - and also objected to the way it changed the federal-state relationship. They struck first in the arena of public opinion to register their opposition.

It was likely New York's Governor George Clinton - who had been in office for more than a decade - writing as "Cato" - who penned the first such letter, which was published in the *New York Journal* in late September 1787. That opposition was quickly followed by another letter published in the *New York Journal* on October 18 written by a New Yorker (Melancton Smith), under the pseudonym "Brutus."

Soon after, in early November, "Letters from a Federal Farmer," were published in both the *Poughkeepsie Country Journal* (90 miles north of New York City on the Hudson) and the *New York Journal*.

"The letters, skillfully written, moderate in tone, and thoughtful, were perhaps the most eloquent and persuasive anti-federalist writings," historian Ralph Ketcham wrote in 1986.

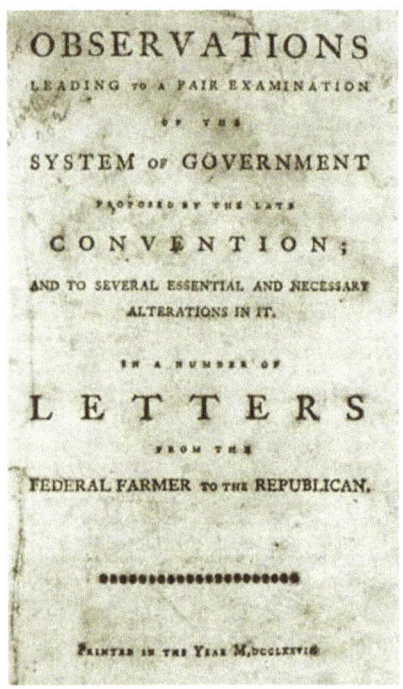

Alexander Hamilton considered "Letters from a Federal Farmer" the most effective presentation of the Anti-Federalist case. Significantly, he never responded to the arguments made by the Federal Farmer in the Federalist Papers.

"I can consent to no government, which, in my opinion, is not calculated equally to preserve the rights of all orders of men in the community," the Federal Farmer wrote.

"A federal government of some sort is necessary," he conceded. "A constitution is now presented which we may reject, or which we may accept, with or without amendments," he continued.

"We are hardly recovered from a long and distressing war ... It must however, be admitted, that our [current] federal system is defective, and that some of the states are not well administered," he conceded even further.

"But I do not pay much regard to the reasons given for not bottoming the new constitution on a better bill of rights," the Federal Farmer wrote, hitting at the core problem with the proposed new system of government:

There are certain unalienable and fundamental rights, which in forming the social compact, ought to be explicitly ascertained and fixed–a free and enlightened people, in forming this compact, will not resign all their rights to those who govern, and they will fix limits to their legislators and rulers, which will soon be plainly seen by those who are governed, as well as those who govern; and the latter will know they cannot be unperceived by the former, and without giving a general alarm —

These rights should be the basis of every constitution. (emphasis added)

At the time, the identity of Federal Farmer was unknown, but more recently historians believe it was either New York's Melancton Smith or Elbridge Gerry of Massachusetts.

Virginia and New York were both influential states, critically important because of their geographical location. Should both fail to ratify the Constitution, the new country would be composed of three geographically separated regions - New England, the Middle Atlantic, and the South.

Opposition to the Constitution in those key states for its failure to include a Bill of Rights – we would call them "swing states" today – was a huge warning sign that alarmed Alexander Hamilton, a New York City lawyer.

An organized media counter-offensive had to be mounted quickly, Hamilton realized, and he set out to do just that.

Just a few weeks after the publication of the first Anti-Federalist letter, Federalist #1, written under the pseudonym "Publius" by Hamilton, was published on October 27 in three New York City newspapers: the *New York Packet*, the *Daily Advertiser*, and the *Independent Journal*.

George Clinton was a political powerhouse in New York who sided with the Anti-Federalists. He served as Governor from 1777 to 1795, and again from 1801 to 1804, and was twice Vice-President, first under Thomas Jefferson, subsequently under James Madison.

"I propose, in a series of papers, to discuss the following interesting particulars," Hamilton wrote in this first "general introduction" article, capitalizing each of the six "particulars" for emphasis:

(1) THE UTILITY OF THE UNION TO YOUR POLITICAL PROSPERITY

(2) THE INSUFFICIENCY OF THE PRESENT CONFEDERATION TO PRESERVE THAT UNION

(3) THE NECESSITY OF A GOVERNMENT, AT LEAST EQUALLY ENERGETIC WITH THE ONE PROPOSED, TO THE ATTAINMENT OF THIS OBJECT

(4) THE CONFORMITY OF THE PROPOSED CONSTITUTION TO THE TRUE PRINCIPLES OF REPUBLICAN GOVERNMENT

(5) ITS ANALOGY TO YOUR OWN STATE CONSTITUTION and lastly,

(6) THE ADDITIONAL SECURITY WHICH ITS ADOPTION WILL AFFORD TO THE PRESERVATION OF THAT SPECIES OF GOVERNMENT, TO LIBERTY, AND TO PROPERTY.

One area in which Hamilton differed dramatically from the Anti-Federalists was on the need for a specifically articulated Bill of Rights.

To Hamilton, those rights were implicit within the Constitution, and did not require explicit articulation.

"Both James Madison and Alexander Hamilton expressed grave reservations about Thomas Jefferson's, George Mason's and others insistence that the Constitution be amended by the Bill of Rights. It wasn't because they had little concern with liberty guarantees. Quite to the contrary they were concerned about the loss of liberties," George Mason University Professor of Economics Walter Williams wrote in 2000.

The first supporter of the new Constitution to publicly advance the argument that a Bill of Rights was unnecessary was neither Madison, nor Hamilton. Instead it was James Wilson, a Philadelphia lawyer, who had been a delegate to the Constitutional Convention from Pennsylvania.

"The Pennsylvania State Legislature was in session when the new Constitution was proposed, so the ratification campaign proceeded immediately, and a large public meeting held October 6, 1787, in the State House (Independence Hall) yard to nominate delegates to the next Pennsylvania Legislature became a forum for debate on ratification," The Constitution Society notes.

"Wilson . . was asked to speak to the gathering to explain the proposed Constitution and answer some of the criticisms that had been made of it. His speech was printed in the Pennsylvania Packet on October 10, 1787, and it was soon reprinted throughout the states, receiving more coverage than the more detailed arguments made [later] in The Federalist," the Constitution Society adds.

"In delegating federal powers," Wilson began, "the congressional power is to be collected, not from tacit implication, but from the positive grant expressed in the instrument of the union. Hence, it is evident, that in the former case everything which is not reserved is given; but in the latter the reverse of the proposition prevails, and everything which is not given is reserved."

"This distinction being recognized, will furnish an answer to those who think the omission of a bill of rights a defect in the proposed constitution; for it would have been superfluous and absurd to have stipulated with a federal body of our own creation, that we should enjoy those privileges of which we are not divested, either by the intention or the act that has brought the body into existence," he continued that October day in 1787:

> *For instance, the liberty of the press, which has been a copious source of declamation and opposition — what control can proceed from the Federal government to shackle or destroy that sacred palladium of national freedom?*
>
> *If, indeed, a power similar to that which has been granted for the regulation of commerce had been granted to regulate literary publications, it would have been as necessary to stipulate that the liberty of the press should be preserved inviolate, as that the impost should be general in its operation...*
>
> *In truth, then, the proposed system possesses no influence whatever upon the press, and it would have been merely nugatory to have introduced a formal declaration upon the subject — nay, that very declaration might have been construed to imply that some degree of power was given, since we undertook to define its extent.*

Seven months later, when Federalist #84 was published on May 28, 1788 after eight states had ratified the Constitution, one shy of the requisite nine to form the new republic, Hamilton advanced the argument first made in Federalist #1:

Bills of Rights have "no application to constitutions professedly founded upon the power of the people, and executed by their immediate representatives and servants. Here, in strictness, the people surrender nothing; and as they retain every thing they have no need of particular reservations," Hamilton wrote:

> *"WE, THE PEOPLE of the United States, to secure the blessings of liberty to ourselves and our posterity, do ORDAIN and ESTABLISH this Constitution for the United States of America."*
>
> *Here is a better recognition of popular rights, than volumes of those aphorisms which make the principal figure in several of our State bills of rights, and which would sound much better in a treatise of ethics than in a constitution of government.*
>
> *But a minute detail of particular rights is certainly far less applicable to a Constitution like that under consideration, which is merely intended to regulate the general political interests of the nation, than to a constitution which has the regulation of every species of personal and private concerns. If, therefore, the loud clamors against the plan of the convention, on this score, are well founded, no epithets of reprobation will be too strong for the constitution of this State. But the truth is, that both of them contain all which, in relation to their objects, is reasonably to be desired.*

"I go further, and affirm that bills of rights, in the sense and to the extent in which they are contended for, are not only unnecessary in the proposed Constitution, but would even be dangerous. They would contain various exceptions to powers not granted; and, on this very account, would afford a colorable pretext to claim more than were granted . . . [it] would furnish, to men disposed to usurp, a plausible pretense for claiming that power, " Hamilton concluded.

It was an argument the Anti-Federalists were not buying.

Federalist #1 was quickly followed by Federalist #2 through #5, also published under the pseudonym "Publius," but authored by veteran New York lawyer John Jay. Since 1785, he was the Confederation's Secretary of Foreign Affairs, in which capacity he acted as the de facto prime minister of the United States.

When Jay fell ill, Hamilton needed another co-author. He looked around the fellow backers of the Constitution living in New York City at the time and found James Madison, in the city serving as a delegate from Virginia to the Confederation Congress. Hamilton recruited Madison, who readily agreed to join the task.

By May of 1788, a total of 85 essays signed by Publius had appeared in New York newspapers. Five were written by Jay, 29 by Madison, and a whopping 51 by Hamilton. Today, these essays are collectively known as The Federalist Papers and are considered to be a masterpiece of political philosophy.

Madison (left), Jay (center), and Hamilton (right).

Though originally published in New York City, these essays were shared far and wide across all 13 states who were in the process of electing delegates for their state ratification conventions.

While the state legislatures of the two key "swing" states of New York and Virginia did not immediately decide when and how to hold their conventions, several states where popular sentiment supported the Constitution jumped into the fray.

By the end of the first week of November, when the newspaper battle between Publius in support of the Constitution, on the one hand, and Brutus, Cato, and Federal Farmer opposing it without a Bill of Rights, on the other, was fully engaged, Pennsylvania had already elected delegates to the state's ratifying convention to be held later that month.

The Delaware state legislature followed quickly, setting the start date for its state ratifying convention at December 4.

It took Delaware's convention just three days to ratify the Constitution. On December 7, Delaware became the first state in the not-yet formed new American republic. To this day, the state issues license plates for cars that say "The First State."

Pennsylvania, which started two weeks earlier, took a full three weeks to ratify the Constitution, but on December 12, they also ratified the Constitution. New Jersey, which began on December 11, took just a week to ratify the Constitution, which they did by December 18. Georgia, which began on Christmas Day, December 25 ratified the Constitution on the very last day of 1787.

The 85 Federalist essays were originally published in two volumes, in March and May of 1788. Originally called "The Federalist," they were known as "The Federalist Papers" in the 20th century. Lacking a single individual orchestrating a specific game plan, Anti-Federalists essays were not put into a single volume until late in the 20th Century when historian Herbert Storing compiled and published "The Anti-Federalists Papers," which included some, but not nearly all, of the Anti-Federalist essays from the era.

Among the Anti-Federalist writers continuing to advance their case against the Constitution as 1787 came to a close was a woman from Massachusetts. Mercy Otis Warren wrote an influential pamphlet in early 1788, "Observations on the new Constitution, and on the Federal and State Conventions," under the pseudonym "A Columbian Patriot." Her authorship of the pamphlet would not be discovered until almost 100 years later.

Born to a prominent Massachusetts family, Mercy Otis Warren was sister to the famous pre-Revolutionary pamphleteer James Otis and was married to the Massachusetts Speaker of the House James Warren.

(Seventeen years later, in 1805, she wrote and published a landmark history of the American Revolution under her own name titled, *History of the Rise, Progress, and Termination of the American Revolution*.)

As 1787 turned to 1788, Connecticut held its ratifying convention in the first week of the new year. After six days, they ratified the Constitution on January 9, 1788.

Five down, four to go until the formation of a new country.

It had been a very fast start. In the six weeks since the first convention opened in Pennsylvania, five states had convened their conventions and ratified the Constitution.

But things were about to get bumpy, and the trouble would begin in Boston, where another large state, Massachusetts, was ready to begin its ratifying convention.

On January 9, the same day Connecticut officially said yes, 370 delegates to the Massachusetts ratifying convention convened at the Massachusetts State House in Boston.

Everyone knew that the outcome in Massachusetts, the second most populous of the 13 states, was critical, and that the issue was very much in doubt, as Federalists and Anti-Federalists jockeyed for position in the lead up to the convention.

"When Paul Revere learned that Sam Adams and John Hancock were reluctant to offer their support for the Constitution during the ratification fight, he organized the Boston mechanics into a powerful force and worked behind the scenes for the successful approval by the Massachusetts convention," Constitution Facts notes.

Proceedings began on a sour note, an indication of the contentious discussions yet to come, when the delegates began to complain about their meeting location, which was designed to house the state's much smaller legislative bodies.

"The delegates complained that the State House facilities were overcrowded. On January 17, the convention moved to the Long Lane Congregational Church," Teaching American History notes.

"The Old State House, the oldest surviving public building in Boston, was built in 1713 to house the government offices of the Massachusetts Bay Colony. It stands on the site of Boston's first Town House of 1657-8, which was destroyed by fire in 1711. As the center of civic, political, and business life, the Old State House was a natural meeting place for the exchange of economic and local news. A merchant's exchange occupied the first floor, and John Hancock and others rented warehouse space in the basement. The National Historic Sites Commission has called the Old State House one of the most important public buildings in Colonial America. . . The central area of the second floor was the meeting place of the Massachusetts Assembly, the most independent of the colonial legislatures, and the first to call for sectional unity and the formation of a Stamp Act Congress," the Bostonian Society website says.

The Long Lane Meeting House was torn down long ago, but the congregation, now part of the Unitarian Church, continues to exist under another name at a different location in Boston.

Prominent Boston merchant John Hancock, famous for his outsized signature on the Declaration of Independence, was a delegate to the ratifying convention who had originally leaned in favor of the Anti-Federalist position. He proposed "The Massachusetts Compromise" – ratify now, amend with a Bill of Rights later – and Samuel Adams, the famous firebrand who helped start the Revolution, another Anti-Federalist, supported the compromise.

On February 6, 1788, the ratifying convention voted in favor of ratifying the Constitution, bringing the number of states that had ratified it to six, just three shy of the nine needed to create the new government.

"What is clear is that the Massachusetts Compromise secured the victory for the proponents of the Constitution because roughly ten delegates changed their mind to secure ratification by a 187-168 vote," Professor Gordon Lloyd wrote.

Prominent Boston merchant John Hancock, famous for his outsized signature on the Declaration of Independence, proposed "The Massachusetts Compromise" of 'ratify now, amend later.'

The Massachusetts Centinel, a Federalist newspaper "published in Boston on Wednesdays and Saturdays by Benjamin Russell (1761–1845) . . . specialized in the brief article that, in vigorous and colorful language, extolled the Constitution or scored its critics," according to the Documentary History of the Ratification of the Constitution.

"Russell was an early advocate of increasing the powers of the central government. While the Constitutional Convention sat, the *Centinel* was filled with articles that advocated strengthening Congress," the Documentary History notes:

> *He attended the Massachusetts convention and took notes of the debates, which were published in the **Centinel**. No other printer celebrated the ratification of the Constitution more originally than Russell.* **On 16 January 1788, a week after Connecticut had ratified, Russell printed an illustration of five pillars, each representing a state that had ratified the Constitution. Each time a state ratified, he added another pillar. Russell's originality and partisanship made the Centinel one of the most often reprinted newspapers in America.** *(emphasis added)*

Up next was New Hampshire, where, as Professor Lloyd noted, "many a campaign has fallen on hard times . . . in February."

The New Hampshire convention met on February 13. To the surprise of the pro-Constitution forces, it was discovered that a majority of the delegates were actually opposed to ratification! Of the 108 delegates in attendance, fewer than 50 were in favor of adoption. According to Jackson Turner Main, "only thirty favored ratification."

Samuel Adams supported the Massachusetts Compromise.

And the going was so tough that the Madisonian forces proposed a

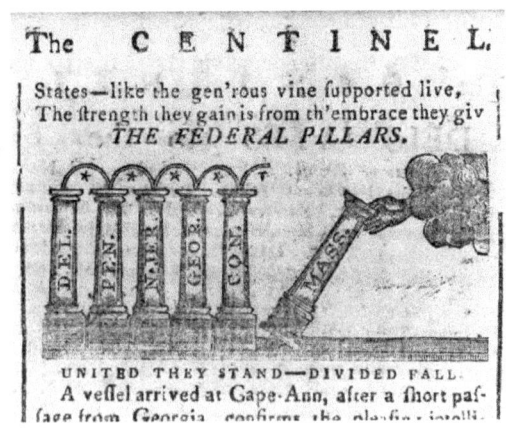

The Centinel's publisher, Benjamin Russell, showed the hand of God pushing the Massachusetts pillar to an upright position in this illustration for his paper published about the same time as the Massachusetts ratifying convention convened in Boston.

strategy that they implemented on February 22. The strategy in New Hampshire was to adjourn in order to avoid what was beginning to look like the first ratification defeat. So they postponed with the intention of coming back later. That's the low-ground explanation for the delay. The high-ground explanation was that the delay allowed the delegates who were elected, perhaps even instructed by their constituents to oppose ratification, before they knew that five states would ratify before New Hampshire's convention even met, to go back to their district and make sure that their constituency still felt the same way about rejecting the Constitution.

With New Hampshire "on hold," all eyes turned southward.

"Given the concerns expressed by the delegates from Maryland and South Carolina at the Philadelphia Convention, one might anticipate that there would be quite a confrontation in Maryland and South Carolina," Lloyd wrote:

> But the delegates from these two states adopted the Constitution very easily: 63 to 11 [in Maryland on April 26, 1788], and 149 to 73 [in South Carolina on May 23, 1788], respectively. More importantly, these "exit votes" were virtually the same as the "entrance votes" going in to the ratifying conventions. Moreover, there wasn't much of a debate despite the official declarations that the proposed Constitution had been "fully considered." The problem is that we will never know why Maryland and South Carolina didn't put up much of an opposition. The official records are very sparse. We can only speculate as to why the Antifederalists failed to mount a credible challenge at this stage of ratification. Jackson Turner Main puts it down to a biased press and the location of the state ratifying conventions.

The ratification count was now up to eight states, just one shy of the needed nine.

"The fate of the Constitution virtually hung in the balance during the summer of 1788. While it was true that Federalists only needed the affirmative vote of one of those three state ratifying conventions and the Antifederalists needed all three, if you look at the predicted vote going in, then it was clear that Federalists had some very real problems. New Hampshire was 52-52, Virginia was 84-84, and New York was 19 in favor and 46 against by what today we might call 'entrance polls.' It was going to be an extremely close call," Lloyd explained:

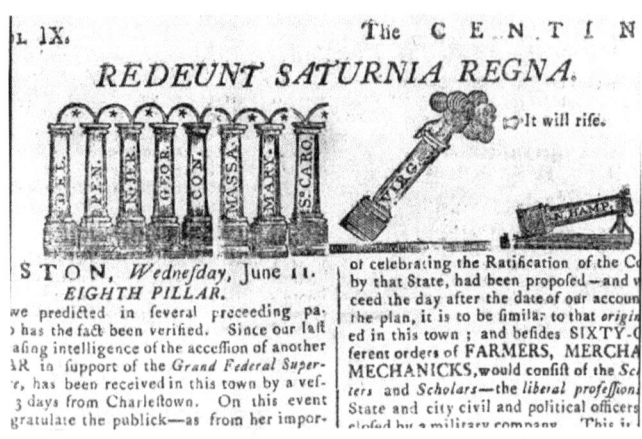

The Centinel published this version of the Federal Pillars as one state remained to reach the magic number of nine that would form a new republic under the Constitution.

> In preparation for the June New Hampshire ratifying convention, the Federalist leaders were far more active in their campaigning than in February. Even then, it turned out that the vote was virtually even going into the convention. It turns out, furthermore, that five delegates adopted the Massachusetts Compromise in New Hampshire after three days of debate. Thus the Constitution was officially ratified

on June 21, 1788 by a vote of 57-47. According to Jere Daniell, only calculated and manipulative political maneuvering by Sullivan and Langdon carried the day.

Nine states had ratified the Constitution, and the constitutional republic of the United States of America was now officially in existence.

Immediately after the news of the new nation spread throughout the state, the first of the public celebrations - which would be referred to as "Federal Processions" took place in Portsmouth, New Hampshire.

The second session of the New Hampshire ratifying convention met in the Old North Meeting House in Concord, New Hampshire.

Now, there was a new country consisting of nine states, but it was divided into three disconnected geographic regions: New England (without Rhode Island), which was separated from the Mid-Atlantic states by New York, which were in turn separated from the Southern states by Virginia and North Carolina.

For the entire enterprise to work, both Virginia and New York needed to ratify the Constitution, but that remained very much in doubt.

"Governor Edmund Randolph presented the proposed Constitution to the Virginia Assembly in mid-October 1787 and the legislative branch provided for the election of delegates to a state ratifying convention," Lloyd wrote:

"Two delegates were selected from each of the 84 counties," and the ratification convention began on June 2, 1788:

> *Among those delegates who defended the Constitution at the Virginia Ratifying Convention were James Madison, "father of the Constitution;" John Marshall, future Chief Justice of the Supreme Court; and Governor Randolph who nearly a year earlier introduced the Virginia Plan and was one of two Virginia delegates to the Constitutional Convention who refused to sign on September 17, 1787. Opposing adoption of the Constitution were such heavyweights as George Mason, author of the Virginia Bill of Rights and the other non-signer in Philadelphia; Patrick Henry, renowned for his inflammatory, dominating, and passionate speeches; William Grayson, delegate to the Confederation Congress, and James Monroe, future President of the United States and author of the Monroe Doctrine.*

Three weeks later, on June 25, "The delegates then voted 89-79 to ratify the Constitution with a recommendation that "subsequent amendments" be sent to the First Congress for their consideration," an outcome made possible only because several delegates who arrived as Anti-Federalists changed their minds during the debates.

Now the Mid-Atlantic states were connected to the South, but New England remained separated by New York, which, "in many ways, was at the center of the ratification controversy," according to Lloyd.

On June 16, 1788 the New York ratification convention convened in Poughkeepsie, 90 miles north of New York City. Alexander Hamilton was the most prominent Federalist delegate in attendance:

> *Starting June 17, the delegates proceeded to go paragraph by paragraph through the Constitution during the first week of the Convention. Early in the second week - June 24 - the delegates received news that*

New Hampshire, the critical ninth state, had ratified. But the debate continued. Then news that Virginia had ratified reached New York at the end of June. Although the delegates continued their discussion through July 7, there were various moves taking place to seek a compromise solution. Between July 7 and July 14, Antifederalist attempts to secure conditional amendments as well as secession guarantees were defeated. On July 26, New York, by a vote of 30-27 - on the promise of recommended amendments - ratified the Constitution and proposed 25 items in a bill of rights and 31 amendments.

The Massachusetts Centinel celebrated by publishing an updated version of its now famous "Federal Pillars" drawing, which showed eleven strong upright pillars, and only two - North Carolina and Rhode Island - falling towards the ground.

In New York City, the grandest of all "Federal Processions" was held on July 23, featuring a horse drawn vessel bearing the name "Hamilton."

By this time, the North Carolina ratification convention was finally under way. News of New York's ratification reached them just before they adjourned, but lacking a clear commitment to a Bill of Rights, the vote for ratification failed.

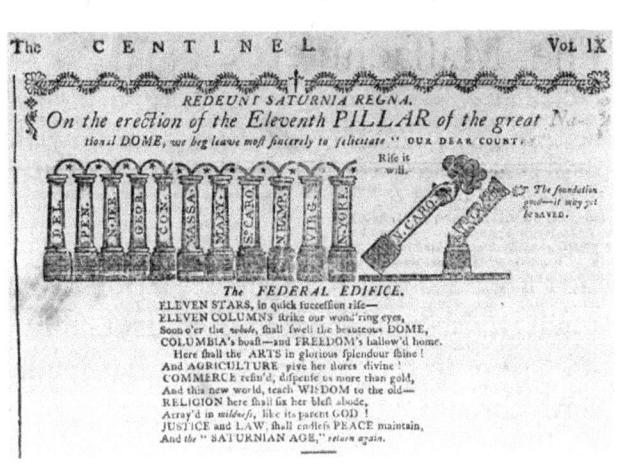

After New York and Virginia ratified the Constitution, bringing the total number of states participating in the new republic to eleven, the Centinel published this image of the Federal Pillars, indicating the danger for North Carolina and Rhode Island if they failed to become the twelfth and thirteenth states to ratify.

"Meeting in Hillsborough, North Carolina, delegates convened from July 21 to August 4, 1788 to consider ratification of the newly proposed federal Constitution. Key state Federalists were James Iredell, William R. Davie, Archibald Maclaine and William Blount. Antifederalist leaders included Willie Jones, Samuel Spencer, and Timothy Bloodworth. Governor Samuel Johnston presided over the Convention. The two-week long deliberations resulted in neither ratification nor rejection. The 1789 Fayetteville Convention continued the debate," North Carolina History.org reports.

Another key Federalist delegate in attendance was Dr. Hugh Williamson, for whom Williamson County in Tennessee was named.

Alexander Hamilton was the hero of the day during the Federal Procession in New York City celebrating the state's ratification of the new Constitution.

But with or without North Carolina and Rhode Island, the other 11 states were determined to move quickly in establishing the new government.

"Congressional and Presidential elections took place in November 1788, and the First Congress met in March 1789," Lloyd wrote.

James Madison, one of the two most well known Federalists in the country, won a hard fought campaign to represent his Virginia Congressional District against his Anti-Federalist opponent, James Monroe, largely on the basis of his promise to introduce and support a Bill of Rights when the first Congress convened.

When the first Congress convened in New York City in March, 1789, Madison was true to his word.

"Learning that Congress endorsed a version of Madison's Bill of Rights proposal, North Carolina held a second ratifying convention. This time, on November 21, 1789, the delegates ratified the Constitution," Lloyd wrote.

"And then there is Rhode Island. Between February 1788 and January 1790, the Assembly refused 11 times to call a ratifying convention. At the end of the second session of the First Congress, the Senate sent Rhode Island a message which, in effect, said: "Join or die." Rhode Island finally held a convention, having rejected earlier attempts to hold a ratifying convention, and they joined the Union. The delegates ratified the Constitution by a vote of 34 to 32 on May 29, 1790. They also had the nerve to propose that the First Congress recommend the adoption of a bill of rights as well as amendments to the Philadelphia Constitution," Lloyd noted.

"Rhode Islanders finally acted after several neighboring states threatened to tax its exports as though it were a foreign country. All in all, 11 attempts to hold constitutional ratifying conventions failed, along with several unsuccessful referenda. Residents of the former British colony rejected the first effort to approve the Constitution by a margin of 10-to-1," Andrew Glass wrote:

> *Rural areas voiced particularly strong opposition to the Constitution; from 1786 to 1790, an anti-federalist "Country Party" controlled the General Assembly. In 1788, William West, an anti-federalist politician and Revolutionary War general from Scituate, led an armed force of 1,000 men to Providence, the colonial capital, with the aim of breaking up a Fourth of July celebration marking New Hampshire's breakthrough ratification vote.*

"Rhode Island was the only state not to send delegates to Philadelphia in 1787. At that time the state legislature was controlled by the agrarian party and was fearful that a stronger central government would demand that debts be paid in specie (hard money). It was the last state to ratify the Constitution on May 29, 1790 (over a year after President George Washington's inauguration) by a vote of 34-32," Constitution Facts notes.

Three full years after the delegates gathered at the Constitutional Convention, all 13 states were now joined in the new republic.

But there was still more than a year of work ahead before the entire covenant that bound the new country together was completely sealed.

Chapter Discussion Questions

(1) What were the advantages and disadvantages of sending the Constitution to state conventions for ratification?

(2) Would you have been in favor of sending the Constitution to Congress for ratification? Why are why not?

(3) Would you have been in favor of allowing the state conventions to be able to make changes/amendments to the proposed Constitution?

(4) How does the ratification process illustrate the principle of popular sovereignty?

Chapter 9

How and Why the First Ten Amendments - The Bill of Rights - Were Proposed and Ratified in Less Than Three Years

The first ten amendments to the Constitution - the Bill of Rights - were proposed in Congress and ratified by the necessary three-fourths of the states in less than three years, a speed of action that seems improbable, given the undeveloped state of travel and communications at the time and the lengthy process more recent amendments to the Constitution have undergone.

But the urgency with which the new nation acted upon the Bill of Rights simply confirms this key point: the secular covenant by which the citizens of the United States agreed to be governed consists of both the Constitution document delivered to the country by the Constitutional Convention and ratified by the States, and the Ten Amendments that comprise the Bill of Rights proposed by the Congress and ratified by the States.

One of fourteen engrossed parchments copies of the twelve amendments proposed by the Congress in 1789 which was sent to the states for their ratification.

There were four distinct phases in the formation of this secular covenant, or "solemn agreement." Had not all four phases been completed, the agreement might not have held.

(1) The Constitutional Convention held in Philadelphia over four months between May 14, 1787 and September 17, 1787 that created the Constitution document, which would give Americans "a republic, if you can keep it," as Benjamin Franklin told Mrs. Powel.

(2) The State ratification conventions, beginning on November 20, 1788, when the first such gathering convened in Pennsylvania, until the formation of the new country with the ratification by the ninth state, New Hampshire, on June 21, 1788, but continuing on to the ratification by the 13th state, Rhode Island, in May 1790.

(3) The proposal of 19 amendments and a new preamble, by James Madison, the representative from Virginia's Fifth Congressional District to the newly formed House of Representatives on June 8, 1789, and

debates that led to the passage of 12 of those amendments by Congress on a two-thirds vote, as the new Constitution proscribed, for presentation to the states for ratification as The Bill of Rights, on September 25, 1789.

(4) The ratification of ten of those 12 amendments, which we call the Bill of Rights, by the state legislatures of the requisite 3/4 states, a process that started when the New Jersey state legislature ratified all ten amendment on November 20, 1789 and ended when the Virginia state legislature ratified the ten amendment on December 15, 1791.

It is our good fortune that the Founding Fathers were able to complete all four phases, thus cementing the bond that holds us together as a country today.

But for a while there, it was touch-and-go.

To understand why, we need to understand what the Americans who chose to be governed by this "solemn agreement" or "secular covenant" understood the terms of that agreement to be.

Actor Charlton Heston portrayed Moses in the 1956 film "The Bible," directed by Cecil B. DeMille.

We've combined two words with which you may be familiar, but whose specific definitions may not be at the forefront of your thoughts, to describe the agreement formed by the Constitution and the Bill of Rights: "secular" and "covenant."

The first use of the word "covenant" is found in the Old Testament, and it describes "the agreement between God and the ancient Israelites, in which God promised to protect them if they kept His law and were faithful to Him."

For those of you familiar with the Old Testament, that covenant usually refers to God's agreement with Abraham (circa 2,300 B.C), and his subsequent agreement with Moses (circa 1,400 B.C.), in which the Ten Commandments were delivered.

Another definition of covenant, one that would have resonated with 18th century Americans, calls it "a solemn agreement between the members of a church to act together in harmony with the precepts of the gospel."

The New England states – Massachusetts, Rhode Island, and Connecticut in particular – were founded as colonies in the 17th century built around congregations of Christian churches, each of which had its own solemn agreement among its members.

The second word, "secular," means "of or relating to worldly things or to things that are not regarded as religious, spiritual, or sacred."

Putting those two together, we can define the secular covenant of the Constitution as "a solemn agreement between the states, and

17th century New England church service in a congregation formed by a "covenant" among all its members.

the citizens of those states, to form a government guided by the foundational principles of Federalism and the Separation of Powers as defined in the Constitution and the Bill of Rights."

Another important element of an agreement – and especially a solemn agreement like this secular covenant – is this: it must be freely entered into by all parties.

And that was the issue facing the newly formed United States after the first two phases had been completed and the Constitution was ratified. Without a Bill of Rights as they believed they had been promised in the Massachusetts Compromise, the Anti-Federalists – as well as a great number of Americans who may not have specifically given themselves a label one way or the other at the time–would not freely enter into the agreement.

Patrick Henry delivers his "If this be treason, make the most of it!" speech to the Virginia House of Burgesses in 1765.

While it was true that a new government was formed when New Hampshire became the ninth state to ratify the Constitution, the short-lived government of the United States under the Articles of Confederation had begun to unravel when the Philadelphia convention was called in 1787 ostensibly to simply "improve upon" that arrangement.

Lacking a Bill of Rights – amendments to be proposed by the first Congress – Article V of the new Constitution offered the states another mechanism for introducing those amendments should the first Congress fail to act.

"The Congress, whenever two thirds of both Houses shall deem it necessary, shall propose Amendments to this Constitution, or, on the Application of the Legislatures of two thirds of the several States, shall call a Convention for proposing Amendments," Article V of the Constitution began.

If two-thirds of the states – and there were only eleven on board at the time, so that meant only eight needed to agree – called for yet another convention, who knew where that might end up?

Many Federalists wanted to define this agreement as one that was completely operational after the second of these two phases – the ratification of the Constitution by nine states – was completed in June of 1788.

You may recall that back in February 1788, the Constitution was ratified by the sixth state - Massachusetts - only after the Massachusetts Compromise proposed by John Hancock and supported by Samuel Adams - was accepted by the ratifying convention in Boston. The delegates agreed to ratify the Constitution without amendments with the recommendation that the state's future members of Congress would support the proposal of nine amendments to the Constitution recommended by the Massachusetts convention. Though there was no specific promise of a "bill of rights" in this compromise, there was clearly a spirit on both sides to accommodate the Anti-Federalists desire for a "bill of rights."

That method of ratification was also championed by delegates to ratifying conventions in South Carolina, New Hampshire, Virginia, and New York, North Carolina, and Rhode Island who ratified the Constitution.

Now, in the fall of 1788 with the new government adopted and in the process of being organized, it was time for the Federalists to deliver on that promise.

And if they failed to deliver, one of the leading Anti-Federalists in the country, Virginia's Patrick Henry, was determined to hold them to account.

Henry was famous for his oratory.

In 1765, he introduced the Virginia Stamp Act Resolutions to the colony's House of Burgesses. He reportedly said, "Caesar had his Brutus; Charles the First his Cromwell; and George the Third… may he profit by their example. If this be treason, make the most of it!"

Ten years later, in a speech to the Second Virginia Convention in St. John's Church in Richmond, Virginia on March 23, 1775, he delivered another barn-burner.

"Give me liberty, or give me death!" those who were in attendance quoted him as saying that day.

A leading Anti-Federalist, he was bitterly disappointed when the Virginia Ratifying Convention approved the new Constitution in June 1788.

But the new nation had been formed, and Henry had a role to play in where it went next.

It is interesting to note that the process of ratifying an amendment to the Constitution had a slightly higher bar than did the process of ratifying the Constitution itself.

Article VII of the Constitution simply said "The Ratification of the Conventions of nine States, shall be sufficient for the Establishment of this Constitution between the States so ratifying the Same."

Since there were only 13 states at the time, that meant that the Constitution could be ratified with the support of 69 percent - or nine - of those states.

Article V of the Constitution stated that amendments proposed by either the Congress or an Article V convention "shall be valid to all Intents and Purposes, as Part of this Constitution, when ratified by the Legislatures of three fourths of the several States, or by Conventions in three-fourths thereof, as the one or the other Mode of Ratification may be proposed by the Congress;"

Ten states out of the original thirteen (77 percent) had to ratify an amendment to exceed the three-fourth standard in Article V for it to become part of the Constitution.

A former governor of the state, Henry was by far the most powerful member of the Virginia state legislature when it convened in the fall of 1788 to elect two United States Senators and draw up the state's ten Congressional Districts to elect members of the new House of Representatives.

"His influence over the legislature was so evident that George Washington observed that 'He has only to say let this be Law - and it is Law,'" Professor Richard Labunski wrote in his 2006 book, *James Madison and the Struggle for the Bill of Rights*.

Henry used that influence in two ways to damage the ambitions of James Madison.

First, he ensured that Madison was not elected to the U.S. Senate by the Virginia legislature. Second, he gerrymandered the Fifth Congressional District, which included Orange County, where Madison's Montpelier residence was located, and recruited a strong Anti-Federalist candidate, James Monroe, to run against him in the elections scheduled for the following February.

Then, to add insult to injury, on November 14, 1788, barely five months after the new government had been ratified, Henry made sure the Virginia legislature passed an application to the soon-to-be-elected first Congress to hold an Article V convention, although the language did not specifically mention Article V:

> *We do, therefore, in behalf of our constituents, in the most earnest and solemn manner, make this application to Congress, that a convention be immediately called, of deputies from the several States, with full power to take into consideration the defects of the constitution that have been suggested by the State Conventions, and report such amendments thereto as they find best suited to promote our common interests, and secure to ourselves and our latest posterity the great and unalienable rights of mankind.*

On February 5, 1789, the state legislature of New York passed its own Article V application to Congress, and Federalists worried that more states might join them.

Anti-Federalists in several other state legislatures – particularly in Massachusetts and other states that ratified after the Massachusetts Compromise was proposed, like New Hampshire – were poised to pass their own Article V petitions.

Madison learned of Henry's gerrymandering and the challenge by Monroe a few weeks later in New York City, where he was serving as a delegate to the soon to be dissolved Confederation Congress.

He hated campaigning, and debated for some time whether he should make the arduous journey back to Virginia to electioneer for his seat. After several friends back home wrote that Monroe presented a serious challenge, he reluctantly packed his bags and headed south.

The diminutive Madison, who stood barely 5 foot 4, and the towering Monroe, who stood just more than 6 feet tall, were friends despite their differing political philosophies at the time.

The two had purchased 1,000 acres of land together in upstate New York several years earlier, a speculative real estate venture. When Monroe got into financial trouble, Madison bought his interest out at a fair price. He later sold the land at a modest profit.

Madison had arrived back in Montpelier in late December, and campaigning across the wide expanse of the new Congressional District - which included Amherst County in the south west of the state, Culpeper County in the north of the state, Goochland County in the center, and Orange, Spottsylvania, Fluvanna, Louisa, and Albemarle Counties in between - began in early January.

JAMES MADISON (left) stood 5 foot 4, and his friend and political opponent in Virginia's Fifth Congressional District election of 1789, JAMES MONROE, stood over 6 feet tall.

"Madison would have a very difficult five weeks ahead of him," Labunski wrote.

"Patrick Henry had done an extraordinary job of creating a congressional district in the Piedmont area of central Virginia that would be hostile to Madison and his supporters," he added.

In mid January, "Madison and Monroe traveled together to Culpeper to address a Lutheran congregation. On January 26 [they] spoke together to citizens in Orange, the county seat of Orange County. [At the end of January they] spoke to 'a nest of Dutchmen' at what is today the Hebron Church in present day Madison County," Labunski noted.

Along the campaign trail that wintry January, Madison "offered what amounted to a campaign pledge that if he was elected he would sponsor a bill of rights and work diligently towards its passage," Labunski added:

> Several groups in the district needed to be assured that Madison was genuinely committed to working for a bill of rights. Baptists, who would play a crucial role in the election, wanted Madison's pledge that he believed an amendment protecting religious freedom was necessary and he would work towards its approval in Congress.

In the end, Madison's diligence paid off. He defeated Monroe on election day, February 2, 1789 1,308 votes to 972 votes. Forty-four percent of eligible voters turned out.

The new Congress convened in New York City on April 1, 1789, but Madison took his time to carefully prepare his Bill of Rights proposal so he could present it at the right time.

One month into the new Congress, Virginia Rep. Theodorick Bland presented the Virginia legislature's application for an Article V Convention on May 5, 1789 and asked that a committee take it under consideration.

Madison noted that "he had no doubt but the House was inclined to treat the present application with respect, but he doubted the propriety of committing it [to a committee of the whole House] because it would seem to imply that the House had a right to deliberate upon the subject. This he believed was not the case until two-thirds of the State Legislatures concurred in such application, and then it is out of the power of Congress to decline complying," the Annals of Congress reported.

Finally, one month later, on June 8, 1789, Madison proposed his 19 amendments and new preamble to the House of Representatives.

First Session of House of Representatives in New York City

The preamble was quickly discarded, and after three months of debate and deliberation, both the House and Senate agreed to 12 amendments to be submitted to the states for their legislatures' consideration.

One noticeable thing happened during this period of debate: Federalists seemed to soften in their opposition to the Bill of Rights, and many opinions on both sides changed.

A month and a half later, meeting in the port city of Perth Amboy, the New Jersey state

The New Jersey State Legislature met in this building in Perth Amboy, now the City Hall, on November 20, 1789 when it became the first state to ratify the Bill of Rights.

legislature became the first to ratify all ten amendments of the Bill of Rights on November 20, 1789.

By June 7, 1790, nine states - New Jersey, Maryland, North Carolina, South Carolina, New Hampshire, Delaware, New York, Pennsylvania, Rhode Island - had ratified all ten amendments in the Bill of Rights.

In four states - Virginia, Connecticut, Georgia, and Massachusetts - ratification of the Bill of Rights languished.

When Vermont joined the Union as the fourteenth state on March 4, 1791, the three-fourth required to ratify the ten amendments that comprised the Bill of Rights jumped from 10 states to 11 states.

By November, Vermont ratified all ten amendments, but the deficit of one state remained.

Once again, Patrick Henry's Virginia became the focal point, this time for the final battle.

"A less formidable and determined foe than Patrick Henry would have given up by now," Professor Richard Labunski wrote.

"But Henry was not through. Having failed to obtain the radical amendments he had long demanded, he would do everything he could to prevent Virginia from approving the Bill of Rights. He told Senator Richard Henry Lee that the proposed amendments 'will tend to injure rather than serve the Cause of Liberty,' and he believed they were intended to 'lull Suspicion totally on this Subject,' to prevent changing the 'exorbitancy of Power granted away by the Constitution from the People,' Labunski added.

Henry had succeeded in delaying a vote on ratification on the Bill of Rights in the Virginia Assembly in 1789, but now, two years later, in the fall of 1791 with only one state needed to make it part of the Constitution, it was on the agenda again.

Though still influential, Henry was not a member of either the House or the Senate, now, so his spell binding oratory was limited in its effectiveness.

Finally, four and a half years after the Constitutional Convention convened in Philadelphia in May 1787, and two years, six months, and seven days after James Madison first proposed the amendments that became the Bill of Rights in Congress, the secular covenant that formed the Constitution and the Bill of Rights was finally sealed.

On December 15, 1791 the Virginia state legislature ratified all ten amendments included in the Bill of Rights, making Virginia the 11th state to ratify them. Since there were now 14 states (Vermont had been granted entry as a state earlier in the year), the three-quarters of all states ratification standard for amendments established in the Constitution had now been met, and the Bill of Rights was officially now part of the Constitution. (For those of you who want to work the math, three-quarters of 14 is 10.5, so 11 clearly surpasses the three-quarters mark.)

The Virginia Assembly ratified all ten amendments of the Bill of Rights at the State Capitol in Richmond on December 15, 1791, making them "valid as part of this Constitution."

The Ten Amendments Included in the Bill of Rights

Here are those first ten amendments, the Bill of Rights, as ratified on December 15, 1791:

First Amendment

Congress shall make no law respecting an establishment of religion, or prohibiting the free exercise thereof; or abridging the freedom of speech, or of the press; or the right of the people peaceably to assemble, and to petition the Government for a redress of grievances.

Second Amendment

A well regulated Militia, being necessary to the security of a free State, the right of the people to keep and bear Arms, shall not be infringed.

Third Amendment

No soldier shall, in time of peace, be quartered in any house without the consent of the owner, nor in time of war, but in a manner to be prescribed by law.

Fourth Amendment

The right of the People to be secure in their persons, houses, papers and effects, against unreasonable searches and seizures, shall not be violated, and no warrants shall issue, but upon probable cause supported by oath or affirmation, and particularly describing the place to be searched, and the persons or things to be seized.

Fifth Amendment

No person shall be held to answer for a capital, or otherwise infamous crime, unless on a presentment or indictment of a Grand Jury, except in cases arising in the land or naval forces, or in the Militia, when in actual service in time of War or public danger; nor shall any person be subject for the same offence to be twice put in jeopardy of life or limb; nor shall be compelled in any criminal case to be a witness against himself, nor be deprived of life, liberty, or property, without due process of law; nor shall private property be taken for public use, without just compensation.

Sixth Amendment

In all criminal prosecutions, the accused shall enjoy the right to a speedy and public trial, by an impartial jury of the State and district wherein the crime shall have been committed, which district shall have been previously ascertained by law, and to be informed of the nature and cause of the accusation; to be confronted with the witnesses against him; to have compulsory process for obtaining witnesses in his favor, and to have the Assistance of Counsel for his defence.

Seventh Amendment

In suits at common law, where the value in controversy shall exceed twenty dollars, the right of trial by Jury shall be preserved, and no fact, tried by a Jury, shall be otherwise re-examined in any court of the United States, than according to the rules of the common law.

Eighth Amendment

Excessive bail shall not be required, nor excessive fines imposed, nor cruel and unusual punishments inflicted.

Ninth Amendment

The enumeration in the Constitution, of certain rights, shall not be construed to deny or disparage others retained by the people.

Tenth Amendment

The powers not delegated to the United States by the Constitution, nor prohibited by it to the States, are reserved to the States respectively, or to the people.

What Became of the Two Other Amendments Passed by the First Congress?

The first Congress passed a total of 12 amendments, which they sent to the states for ratification.

Ten were ratified on December 15, 1791. Of the remaining two, one was ratified eventually and the other remains unratified.

It took more than 200 years for that 11th proposed amendment to be ratified as the Twenty-Seventh Amendment. That finally happened on May 5, 1992, when Missouri became the 38th of the 50 states that formed the United States by then to reach the requisite three-fourths required for ratification.

Twenty-Seventh Amendment

No law, varying the compensation for the services of the Senators and Representatives, shall take effect, until an election of Representatives shall have intervened.

How this eleventh amendment proposed by Congress in 1791 ultimately became the 27th Amendment to the Constitution is quite a story.

"In 1982, a college undergraduate student, Gregory Watson, discovered that the proposed amendment could still be ratified and started a grassroots campaign. Watson was also an aide to Texas state senator Ric Williamson," the Constitution Center reported:

Shortly after the amendment was ratified a decade later, New York Law School professor Richard B. Bernstein traced the journey from 1789 to 1992 in a Fordham Law Review article. Bernstein called Watson the "step-father" of the 27th Amendment. Watson was a sophomore at the University of Texas-Austin in 1982 and he needed a topic for a government course. Watson researched what became the 27th Amendment and found that six states had ratified it by 1792, and then there was little activity about it.

*Watson concluded that the amendment could still be ratified, because Congress had never stipulated a time limit for states to consider it for ratification. Watson's professor gave him a C for the paper, calling the whole idea a "dead letter" issue and saying it would never become part of the Constitution. "The professor gave me a C on the paper. When I protested she said I had not convinced her the amendment was still pending," Watson told **USA Today** back in 1992.*

Undeterred, Watson started a self-financed campaign to get the amendment ratified. He wrote letters to state officials, and the amendment was ratified in Maine in 1983 and Colorado in 1984. The story appeared in a magazine called State Legislatures, and an official from Wyoming, reading the magazine, confirmed his state had ratified the amendment, too, six years earlier.

In 2017, the same teacher who gave Watson a "C" on his paper in 1982, petitioned the University of Texas to change it to an "A+."

The 12th proposed amendment passed by Congress in 1789 and sent to the states for ratification has never reached the requisite three-fourths state approvals for ratification.

That unratified amendment reads as follows:

After the first enumeration required by the first article of the Constitution, there shall be one Representative for every thirty thousand, until the number shall amount to one hundred, after which the proportion shall be so regulated by Congress, that there shall be not less than one hundred Representatives, nor less than one Representative for every forty thousand persons, until the number of Representatives shall amount to two hundred; after which the proportion shall be so regulated by Congress, that there shall not be less than two hundred Representatives, nor more than one Representative for every fifty thousand persons.

In 2019, there are now 435 members of the House of Representatives, each representing approximately 700,000 residents.

Chapter Discussion Questions

(1) Why do you think the delegates at the Philadelphia Convention did not include a bill of rights to the Constitution?

(2) If you were an Anti-Federalist, would you have voted to approve the Constitution based on the promise that a bill of rights would be added later?

(3) Would you have been in favor of a second constitutional convention to add a bill of rights to the Constitution? Why or why not?

Chapter 10

The First Amendment
By Claudia Henneberry

The First Amendment was approved by Congress September 25, 1789, and ratified on December 15, 1791 along with the nine other amendments that comprise The Bill of Rights. It reads:

> *Congress shall make no law respecting an establishment of religion, or prohibiting the free exercise thereof; or abridging the freedom of speech, or of the press; or the right of the people peaceably to assemble, and to petition the Government for a redress of grievances.*

The First Amendment combines five specific rights into one fundamental law guaranteeing freedom of expression:

(1) Freedom of **Religion**

(2) Freedom of **Speech**

(3) Freedom of the **Press**

(4) Right to **Peaceably Assemble**

(5) Right to **Petition** the government

"The first amendment is the most important in the American Constitution because it protects the things that make us what we are, including talking, and writing, and worshiping," Dr. Larry Arnn, professor of politics and history and president of Hillsdale College, wrote recently.

The Founding Fathers knew that these unalienable rights already belonged to the people naturally, given to them by God, their Creator. All that was needed was for certain of these unalienable rights to be included in the Bill of Rights to be protected from government.

The First Amendment is first, not simply because it falls at the beginning of a list of amendments, but because it articulates the first freedom and the nature of that freedom. It guarantees the freedom essential to humans as rational beings: the freedom to reason and form thoughts.

Freedom of Religion

The first clause of the First Amendment protects religious liberty, which the founders considered to be of paramount importance. They knew that religion increased virtue among the people, and they contended such public virtue was necessary to maintain good government in a free republic.

"The only foundation for a useful education in a republic is to be laid in religion. Without this, there can be no virtue, and without virtue there can be no liberty, and liberty is the object and life of all republican governments," Benjamin Rush, a signer of the Declaration of Independence, said in 1806, as he reflected back on the earlier events of his life.

To which "religion" does the First Amendment refer?

The men who created the republic understood that it must refer to "all sound religions," which, from their various personal writings on the topic, contained the following fundamental beliefs, in their view: There exists a Creator who made all

Normal Rockwell's Classic 1943 illustration of Freedom of Religion, part of his "Four Freedoms" series for Life Magazine.

things and should be worshiped; The Creator has revealed a moral code which distinguishes right from wrong; The Creator holds mankind responsible for the way they treat one another; There is a life after this one where mankind will be judged.

In the founding era, these beliefs were considered basic and necessary for the well-being and happiness of the people.

The original intent of the first part of the religious liberty clause was simply to limit Congress, and thus the national government, from establishing an official national religion – "Congress shall make no law respecting the establishment of religion."

The second part of the clause was to prevent Congress from restricting people's actions upon their beliefs – "… or prohibiting the free exercise thereof." The religious liberty clause restrained the federal government but did not restrain the states. The states were free to make their own laws concerning religious beliefs and practices.

In 1775, no fewer than nine colonies had an established state religion. Massachusetts, Connecticut, and New Hampshire had systems of local church establishment in favor of the Congregationalists. In the South, from Maryland on down, the establishments were Episcopal. In New York, there was a system of locally supported Protestant clergy.

After the Constitution and the Bill of Rights were ratified by 1791, several of these former colonies continued to have some element of established state religions for a time.

Religions that were not established in those states were concerned about their rights, and, though they believed the "establishment clause" of the First Amendment - "Congress shall make no law respecting an establishment of religion" - protected those rights at a national level, they remained unsure about how well those rights were protected within their own states.

In Virginia, for instance, Baptists had been treated unfairly during the Colonial period when the Anglican Church was the officially established religion of the colony.

In 1786, the Virginia State Legislature and the governor formally disestablished the Anglican Church, but the Baptists were still concerned, a concern they expressed effectively to James Madison, who eventually became the champion of the Bill of Rights in the first Congress.

The Baptists of Danbury, Connecticut were still concerned about their own state of Connecticut infringing on their religious liberty a decade after the First Amendment was ratified. So in 1801 they wrote a famous letter to President Thomas Jefferson in which they asked for his opinion on the issue.

> *Our [state] constitution of government is not specific. Our ancient charter, together with the laws made coincident therewith, were adapted as the basis of our government at the time of our revolution. And such has been our laws and usages, and such still are, [so] that Religion is considered as the first object of Legislation, and therefore what religious privileges we enjoy (as a minor part of the State) we enjoy as favors granted, and not as inalienable rights.*

"I contemplate with sovereign reverence that act of the whole American people which declared that their legislature would 'make no law respecting an establishment of religion, or prohibiting the free exercise thereof,' thus building a wall of separation between Church and State," Jefferson responded.

Jeffersons' response asserting "a wall of separation between Church and State," though not specifically language found in the Constitution or any amendment, was cited frequently in decisions by the Supreme Court in the 20th century.

In a 1940 Supreme Court case, for instance, *Cantwell v. Connecticut*, Jesse Cantwell, a Jehovah's Witness, was distributing religious materials in a Catholic neighborhood. Connecticut required a permit to solicit religious materials which he did not possess, so he was arrested. Ultimately, the case was decided by the Supreme Court which ruled that the First Amendment guaranteed freedom of belief as well as freedom to act on that belief and that it was unconstitutional for a state to require a permit.

Some believe that current court decisions prohibiting prayer in public schools, and particularly Christian prayer in public schools, are a dramatic misinterpretation of the actual establishment clause of the First Amendment, which says only that "Congress shall make no law respecting an establishment of religion."

Freedom of Speech

The next two clauses of the First Amendment protect Freedom of Speech and Freedom of the Press. These two are similar in nature in that "speech" in the broadest sense can be vocal, written, published, broadcast or displayed.

Narrowly defined, Freedom of Speech refers only to the right to speak freely in either a private or public setting. The Federalist Party leaders in the 1790s would call this narrowly defined speech "utterances."

Speech can also refer to personal expressions that are not simply verbal "utterances," such as holding a sign or engaging in specific conduct, such as burning of an American flag, a Bible, or a Koran.

More broadly, speech also refers to "speaking" via the written word in letters or in publications, such as newspapers and magazines or books, and on broadcast media, such as radio, television, and the internet, so in this sense Freedom of the Press is a subset of Freedom of Speech.

These rights were not well-defined by the men who created the First Amendment because there were not a lot of cases concerning speech or press in the beginning of the republic, but it is thought the original intent of these rights was to primarily protect political speech, for the people to be free to criticize the government.

The Founding Fathers - and the framers of the Constitution - likewise knew such freedoms were vital in protecting advancement of truth, science, morality and arts.

If there was any doubt in the minds of Samuel Adams and the other Anti-Federalists in the wisdom the Massachusetts Compromise - the insistence that ratification of the Constitution could only come on the promise by the Federalists that a Bill of Rights, and in particular the First Amendment, would be added to the Constitution - the conduct of his own distant cousin, now the President of the United States and leader of the Federalist Party, quickly disabused them of that notion.

Less than seven years after the First Amendment was ratified, President John Adams signed into law the Sedition Act on July 14, 1798. It was one of four bills signed by President Adams at about the same time that, together, are referred to as The Alien and Sedition Acts. It was the Sedition Act, however, that undermined the First Amendment in a way that many opponents at the time - and almost every legal scholar today - considered unconstitutional.

The Alien Acts extended the number of years immigrants had to remain in the country before becoming citizens from 5 to 14; in the case of war, males of the enemy nation could be arrested and detained; also, non-citizens suspected of plotting against the U. S. could be deported.

The Sedition Act made it a crime to publish writings intended to defame the government, Congress, or the President or to incite unrest in the nation. Federalist supporters of the Sedition Act argued that freedom of the press did not extend to seditious speech against the government because it destroys confidence in government.

The second illustration of Norman Rockwell's classic 1943 illustrations of the Four Freedoms, his "Freedom of Speech" showed a member of the community speaking his mind about a particular public issue at a classic New England town hall, the annual meeting where citizens vote on the town's budget and elect representatives for the next year. Notice in particular the interest and respect shown for what the speaker has to say by his fellow towns people.

In effect, the Sedition Act utterly gutted the First Amendment.

The doctrine of Judicial Review - the idea that the Supreme Court could invalidate a law if it deemed it unconstitutional - had not yet been established, and so this unconstitutional act would stay on the books until it expired and a new President, Thomas Jefferson, elected in a thorough trouncing of Adams in 1800, would not renew it.

The language of the Sedition Act was a full throated rejection of both the Freedom of Speech and Freedom of the Press clauses of the First Amendment:

> *If any person shall write, print, utter or publish, or shall cause or procure to be written, printed, uttered or published, or shall knowingly and willingly assist or aid in writing, printing, uttering or publishing any false, scandalous and malicious writing or writings against the government of the United States, or either house of the Congress of the United States, or the President of the United States, with intent to defame the said government, or either house of the said Congress . . . then such a person, being thereof convicted before any court of the United States having jurisdiction thereof, shall be punished by a fine not exceeding two thousand dollars, and by imprisonment not exceeding two years.*

The Jeffersonian Republicans argued at the time that criticism of the government was absolutely protected because it was the main intent of the Freedom of Speech and Freedom of the Press clauses of the First Amendment.

James Madison, for instance, who had been, along with Alexander Hamilton, one of the leading Federalists arguing on behalf of ratification of the Constitution, now had become one of the leading members of the emerging Democratic-Republican Party, along with Thomas Jefferson, that opposed the Federalist Party of Adams and Hamilton. Madison said that the Sedition Act attacked the "right of freely examining public characters and measures and of free communication among the people."

The Federalist Party, which controlled the Presidency under John Adams, as well as the Senate and the House of Representatives, paid scant attention to Madison's criticism.

The Sedition Act passed the Senate on a 22-9 party line vote, and in the House on a 60-46 party line vote. Adams quickly signed it into law.

The "speech" or "utterance" prohibition in the Sedition Act was soon tested by a citizen by the name of Luther Baldwin in Newark, New Jersey. Baldwin was in the crowd as President Adams passed by with his entourage.

A cannon blast saluted the president:

> *When one in the crowd commented that "there goes the President and they are firing at his ass," Luther Baldwin replied that he didn't care "if they fired through his ass." Incredibly, Baldwin was arrested, convicted and imprisoned for this remark. He remained in prison until he paid the hefty fine specified in the law, as well as the associated court fees.*

Having been successfully used to attack the Freedom of Speech clause of the First Amendment, The Sedition Act was soon used to successfully attack the Freedom of the Press clause as well.

Freedom of the Press

Both clauses of the First Amendment were at play in the case of Matthew Lyon, a Vermont Republican congressman, who was put on trial under The Sedition Act in October 1798.

Lyon had written a letter which was published in a Republican newspaper criticizing President Adams for 'a continued grasp for power.' Lyon had also read a poem at several public meetings written by Joel Barlow who jokingly wondered why Congress had not sent Adams to a mad-house. Lyon was against a potential war with France and a land tax to raise money for war preparations.

The U. S. marshal, a Federalist appointee, indicted Lyon and assembled a jury from Vermont towns know to be Federalist strongholds.

Lyon was quickly found guilty on October 10, 1798, sent to jail for 4 months, and fined $1,000. While in jail, he was re-elected to Congress.

Benjamin Franklin's grandson, Benjamin Franklin Bache, was another critic of Adams arrested under The Sedition Act, specifically for what he published in his newspaper, *The Philadelphia Aurora*, printed ironically on printing presses he had inherited from his famous grandfather.

President Adams, Bache wrote in *The Aurora*, "has appointed Alexander Hamilton inspector general of the Army, the same Hamilton who published a book to prove he is an adulterer … Mr. Adams ought hereafter to be silent about French principles."

"Soon Bache was arrested for violating the law. He died of yellow fever in the summer of 1799, before his case was brought to trial, but during more than two years the law was in effect, twenty-five Americans were prosecuted and imprisoned based upon its provisions," Michael Patrick Leahy wrote in his 2012 book, *Covenant of Liberty*:

> *[The Sedition Act] had been so unpopular it fueled Jefferson's 1800 presidential victory and, equally important, it swept the Federalists out of their majority in both houses. . . It was also the first time in American political history that the people had risen up in an election and "thrown the bums out." . . . The Federalist Party would never again hold a majority in either house of Congress. Though the body would not be buried officially for another decade, the Federalist Party of Washington, Adams, and Hamilton was dead.*

The Sedition Act expired after John Adams left office and Thomas Jefferson was President in 1801.

At the time of the ratification of the First Amendment, "the Press" referred to individuals or businesses who printed newspapers, pamphlets, almanacs, broadsides, journals, or books on paper - in bound or unbound form - and expressed in written format ideas that could also be expressed verbally by conversations or speeches. As technology advanced, "the Press" quickly came to include for-profit or non-profit expressions of these thoughts in other media, telegraph, radio, television, and now the internet.

The Federalist Party's demise was a clear sign that the American people strongly supported the First Amendment. Over time, as individuals who felt their First Amendment rights had been violated brought their cases before the federal courts, our modern understanding of its vibrant meaning developed.

Over the years, the Supreme Court has developed its own set of categories of protected and unprotected speech and press. The guarantees in these two clauses protect individuals against the actions of government, not against the actions of private individuals. They apply to both state and national governments. They cover speakers and writers regardless of media source (books, magazines, or internet.) Radio and television receive less constitutional protection.

The Freedom of Speech clause covers expressive actions such as carrying a flag, wearing a symbol, and actions that are necessary in expressing one's opinion like buying a microphone. Political speech includes giving money contributions to candidates who run for office. Free speech extends to all viewpoints.

And, yes, there are certain limitations on freedom of speech and press. These include speech inciting individuals to break the law; obscene works; threats of violence; fighting words or personal insults directed toward a specific person that are likely to cause a fight; speech owned by others that may violate intellectual property laws; and certain types of commercial advertising such as misleading claims on products.

One of those limits results from the "clear and present danger" standard established in 1917 when the country was at war.

The Supreme Court case, *Schenck v. U. S.*, involved Charles Schenck, general secretary of the Socialist Party of America, and the Espionage Act of 1917, passed by Congress in order to prohibit interference with military operations, recruitment, insubordination and support of hostile enemies during wartime.

This case would define the limits of the First Amendment's right to free speech.

Schenck organized the distribution of 15,000 flyers advocating that draftees should resist the draft, that they would relinquish their constitutional rights as soldiers and enter into involuntary servitude, which the 13th Amendment outlawed.

He was arrested along with another member of his group, convicted and sentenced to six months in prison. They appealed to the U. S. Supreme Court, contending that the Espionage Act violated the First Amendment's protection of free speech.

In his majority opinion, Justice Oliver Wendell Holmes wrote that during wartime " …The question in every case is whether the words are used in such circumstances and are of such a nature as to create a clear and present danger that they will bring about the substantive evils that Congress has a right to prevent."

Until a court case in 1925, *Gitlow v. New York*, when Benjamin Gitlow was arrested for distributing copies of a left-wing manifesto which advocated the "forceful" overthrow of the U. S. government, the First Amendment only applied to the national government.

The Supreme Court ruled that since Gitlow's actions did not result in violence, that his speech and publication rights had been violated in New York, resulting in the beginning of a precedent that the First Amendment rights would also apply to the states based on the due process clause within the Fourteenth

Amendment. (Amendment 14, Section 1). Gitlow's speech advocating forceful overthrow, however, was not protected by the First Amendment as a result of the court's "clear and present danger" test.

The Supreme Court replaced the "clear and present danger" standard with the "imminent lawless action" test. This standard is still applied by the Court today to free speech cases involving advocacy of violence.

In recent times, the Espionage Act also remains intact with Chelsea Manning and Edward Snowden having been charged with its violation.

Right to Peaceably Assemble

The First Amendment protects "the right of the people peaceably to assemble." In 1774, the Declaration and Resolves of the First Continental Congress proclaimed that colonists "have a right peaceably to assemble, consider of their grievances, and petition the King; and that all prosecutions, prohibitory proclamations, and commitments for the same, are illegal." By 1789, four of the 13 original colonies included the right to assemble in their constitutions or charters.

During the debate in Congress in the summer of 1789 over the details of the amendments we now know as the Bill of Rights, Representative Theodore Sedgwick, a member of the Federalist Party, moved to take out the words "to assemble" from the wording of the First Amendment. He thought the words were unnecessary.

"If people freely converse together, they must assemble for that purpose; it is a self-evident, unalienable right which the people possess," he argued.

Sedgwick was here offering a very detailed version of the broader case made against the entire Bill of Rights by his fellow Federalist, Alexander Hamilton.

But Sedgwick's argument was rejected by Congress, which passed the First Amendment on September 25, 1789 that included the language "the right of the people peaceably to assemble."

So that fourth right within the First Amendment became part of the Constitution when it was ratified by the requisite number of states on December 15, 1791.

"The freedom of assembly has been at the heart of some of the most important social movements in American history: antebellum abolitionism, women's suffrage in the nineteenth and twentieth centuries, the labor movement in the Progressive Era and after the New Deal, and the Civil Rights movement," John D. Inazu wrote in the Tulane Law Review in 2010.

Contemporary political movements, such as the Tea Party Movement, have also grown through the exercise of the freedom of assembly. In fact, it was the exercise of that right in more than 900 cities by an estimated one million Americans on April 15, 2009 that launched that movement onto the national political scene, and led directly, in turn, to the Republican takeover of the House of Representatives in 2010 and indirectly to the election of President Trump in 2016.

Tennesseans exercised the right to peaceably assemble on March 4, 2017 at the Legislative Plaza in Nashville.

A key word included in this clause of the First Amendment, one that is uniquely part of the American tradition is "peaceably."

"Abraham Lincoln once called 'the right of peaceable assembly' part of 'the Constitutional substitute for revolution,'" Inazu remarked.

Americans have traditionally understood the importance of "peaceably" assembling. Unlike other countries where public assemblies often disintegrate into violent encounters between opposing groups, Americans have, for the most part, not only enjoyed their own right to peaceably assemble–they have respected the rights of their political opponents to peaceably assemble.

"Groups invoking the right of assembly have inherently been those that dissent from the majority and consensus standards endorsed by government," Inazu noted:

Second, claims of assembly have been public claims that advocate for a visible political space distinguishable from government.

Finally, manifestations of assembly have themselves been forms of expression - parades, strikes, and demonstrations, but also more creative forms of engagement like pageants, religious worship, and the sharing of meals.

"These three themes - the dissenting assembly, the public assembly, and the expressive assembly - emerge from the groups that have gathered throughout our nation's history," Inazu concluded.

Right to Petition

The final clause of the free expression amendment is "Congress shall make no law … abridging … the right of the people … to petition the Government for a redress of grievances." The right to petition a monarch, or, a government, dates all the way back to the Magna Carta of 1215. It originally was a right given only to noblemen. By 1669, every British citizen had the right to petition Parliament, then, by 1689, The Declaration of Rights made it law that citizens petitioning a monarch with a list of complaints could not be punished.

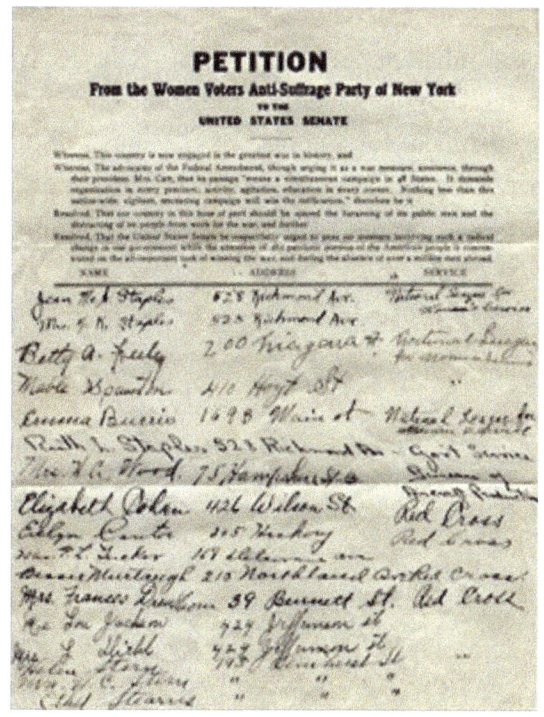

By 1642, Massachusetts, in its "Body of Liberties," became the first of the British colonies to add the right to petition any governmental body or official. North Carolina, Pennsylvania, Delaware, New Hampshire and Vermont also wrote it into their constitutions while the rest of the colonies had an implied right to petition.

In 1776, of course, Thomas Jefferson listed the grievances against King George III in the Declaration of Independence.

Historically, petitioning the government was one of the only recourses the people had to communicate with monarchs, appointed or elected officials. Petitions were taken seriously in early days and, quite frequently, the government would not only hear the grievances, but would enact laws to satisfy those grievances.

The right to petition the government did not guarantee that the government had to take action, however. After the Constitution established separation of powers within the national government, these petitions would be presented then handed down to a committee where they might be lost or ignored.

In 1836, the U. S. House of Representatives decided that it would not entertain petitions concerning slavery nor concerning the abolition of slavery. Those would simply be "tabled." "All petitions relating . . . to the subject of slavery . . . shall, without being either printed or referred, be laid upon the table and that no further action whatever be had thereon."

By 1840, thanks to Congressman John Quincy Adams, the former president, what was known as the "gag rule" on slavery was repealed. Regardless, petitions on anti-slavery were subsequently sent to committees, where they died.

Other famous petitions include those, beginning in 1871, submitted to the United States Congress which asked for women to be granted the right to vote in the form of a constitutional amendment. One such petition from 1917 petitioning the U. S. Senate is pictured on the previous page. The women's suffrage movement, their peaceful assemblies and petitions, was victorious as a result of the 19th amendment having been added to the Constitution in 1920.

Petitioning the government today means to provide information to elected leaders about unpopular policies; to expose misconduct, waste, corruption, and incompetence; and to vent popular frustrations without endangering the public order.

Lobbying, letter-writing, email or social media campaigns, testifying before a government body, filing lawsuits, collecting signatures for ballot initiatives, peaceful protests and picketing, as well as all public articulation of issues, complaints and interests requesting government action qualify under the petition clause.

Our inherent and unalienable right to freedom of expression is outlined within our First Amendment specifically as freedom of religion, speech and press and the right to peaceably assemble and to petition the government for a redress of grievances. The guarantee that government will protect these rights is necessary for the virtue and happiness of the people and the survivability of our republic. Freedom of expression is the very essence of what it means to be American.

Chapter Discussion Questions

(1) Would the First Amendment be better off by being written as "Congress shall make no law abridging the freedom of expression?"

(2) The First Amendment is stated in absolute terms: Congress shall make no law respecting an establishment of religion." Does this wording reflect a hostility toward religion? Why or why not?

(3) Why is it important to keep the church and the state separate?

(4) In your opinion, should the freedom of speech be interpreted narrowly or broadly?

(5) What limits, if any, would you place on the rights in the First Amendment?

Chapter 11

The Second Amendment

The language of the Second Amendment is clear and unambiguous.

"A well regulated Militia, being necessary to the security of a free State, the right of the people to keep and bear Arms, shall not be infringed."

On June 8, 1789 James Madison, then a Congressman from Virginia, proposed the Second Amendment to the House and Senate, along with the other nine amendments that comprise the Bill of Rights, just three months after the very first Congress convened in New York City. On September 25, 1789, Madison secured the passage of all ten of these amendments with the necessary two-thirds vote in both the House and the Senate, the first step required by Article V of the Constitution towards the inclusion of amendments to the Constitution.

From there, the Second Amendment and the other nine amendments of the Bill of Rights went to the state legislatures (now numbering fourteen with the addition of Vermont as a state) for ratification by three-fourths of the states (eleven), as required by Article V. On December 15, 1791, the state legislature of Rhode Island became the eleventh state to ratify all ten amendments of the Bill of Rights, and those amendments became part of our Constitution.

"The Death of General Mercer" by Turnbull

During this two-and-a-half year process of introduction and ratification, there was virtually no public opposition to the Second Amendment.

The fourteen states in 1791 had an estimated population of almost 4 million, 700,000 of whom were slaves, primarily in the southern states.

Gun ownership within the free population of the United States in 1791 of 3.3 million was high. Some historians estimate that between 50 percent and 80 percent of all households owned at least one firearm at the time. With an average household size of five to six individuals, this suggests that there was as many as 1 million guns owned by private citizens in the United States in 1791.

Support for the rights of private citizens to bear arms had long been almost universal in the thirteen colonies that comprised what was known as British North America until these colonies formed the United States of America and declared their independence from Great Britain in 1776.

It is easy to understand why there was such widespread public support in British North America and subsequently the newly-formed United States of America for private ownership of guns.

The early colonists lived in a hostile environment in a wild land where their survival depended on their own abilities to find food and defend themselves. Virtually every frontier household relied upon guns for food -  hunting wild game such as deer, and wild fowl such as ducks and turkeys - as well as self-defense. Until the French and Indian Wars of 1754 to 1763, there was virtually no British military presence in the colonies, and when relations with Native American tribes descended into warfare, it was the locally armed militia which provided the only reliable defense.

On the frontier in particular, every free male over the age of 18 was often compelled to participate in the armed defense of the community, when called upon. Thus, the tradition of average citizens owning guns and participating in a local militia when called upon by local, state, and colonial authorities, was long established by the time the 13 colonies declared their independence from Great Britain in 1776.

"It has always been widely understood that the Second Amendment, like the First and Fourth Amendments, codified a pre-existing right. The very text of the Second Amendment implicitly recognizes the pre-existence of the right and declares only that 'it shall not be infringed'," Supreme Court Justice Antonin Scalia wrote in the majority opinion in the landmark case *District of Columbia v. Heller* (2008).

Scalia went on to note that this pre-existing right was recognized in 17th century England, the country of origin for the majority of colonists in British North America.

> *Between the Restoration [in 1660] and the Glorious Revolution [in 1689], the Stuart Kings Charles II and James II succeeded in using select militias loyal to them to suppress political dissidents, in part by disarming their opponents. . . Under the auspices of the 1671 Game Act, for example, the Catholic Charles II had ordered general disarmaments of regions home to his Protestant enemies. . . These experiences caused Englishmen to be extremely wary of concentrated military forces run by the state and to be jealous of their arms. They accordingly obtained an assurance from William and Mary, in the Declaration of Right (which was codified as the English Bill of Rights), that Protestants would never be disarmed. . .*
>
> *It was clearly an individual right, having nothing whatever to do with service in a militia. To be sure, it was an individual right not available to the whole population, given that it was restricted to Protestants, and like all written English rights it was held only against the Crown, not Parliament. . . But it was secured to them as individuals, according to "libertarian political principles," not as members of a fighting force.*

No other country in the world recognized the right of private citizens to keep and bear arms until 1917, when Mexico did so. Today only two additional countries - Guatemala and Haiti - recognize that right, while the English origins of that right are being limited in unrecognizable ways in Canada, Australia, and the United Kingdom.

For more than a century, there was a consensus among the American public, Congress, and the Supreme Court, that "the right of the people to keep and bear Arms shall not be infringed." This virtually unanimous sentiment later came to be known as "the individual rights approach" to the Second Amendment.

That consensus, however, began to change ever so slightly in 1915 when a retired judge from Maine, Lucilius A. Emery, a champion of the Progressive movement, wrote an article for the Harvard Law Review that highlighted the first phrase of the Second Amendment regarding a militia, "**A well regulated Militia, being necessary to the security of a free state**," and made subordinate the phrase that had been primary for over a 100 years, "**the right of the people to keep and bear arms, shall not be infringed.**"

Thomas Jefferson by Rembrandt Peale, c.1800

In the article titled "*The Right to Keep and Bear Arms in the Light of Its Historical Development*," Emery wrote:

> [T]he right guaranteed is not so much to the individual for his private quarrels or feuds as to the people collectively for the common defense against the common enemy, foreign or domestic. The guaranty is to insure the safety of the people, their "laws and liberties," against assaults from any sourcor quarter, but not to give individuals singly or in groups uncontrollable means of aggression upon the rights of others.
>
> Granting that the individual may carry weapons when necessary for his personal defense or that of his family or property, it is submitted that he may be forbidden to carry dangerous weapons except in cases where he has reason to believe and does believe that it is necessary for such defense.

By the 1930s, when President Franklin Roosevelt appointed four of the nine members of the Supreme Court, this "collective rights approach" to the Second Amendment was embraced by the highest court in the land, as Cornell Law School's Legal Information Institution notes:

> [S]ome believe that the Amendment's phrase "the right of the people to keep and bear Arms" creates an individual constitutional right to possess firearms. Under this "individual right theory," the United States Constitution restricts legislative bodies from prohibiting firearm possession, or at the very least, the Amendment renders prohibitory and restrictive regulation presumptively unconstitutional. On the other hand, some scholars point to the prefatory language "a well regulated Militia" to argue that the Framers intended only to restrict Congress from legislating away a state's right to self-defense. Scholars call this theory "the collective rights theory." A collective rights theory of the Second Amendment asserts that citizens do not have an individual right to possess guns and that local, state, and federal legislative bodies therefore possess the authority to regulate firearms without implicating a constitutional right.

> In 1939 the U.S. Supreme Court considered the matter in *United States v. Miller, 307 U.S. 174*. There, the

Richard Heller was a special police officer and litigant in the landmark 2008 Supreme Court Case.

Court adopted a collective rights approach, determining that Congress could regulate a sawed-off shotgun which moved in interstate commerce under the National Firearms Act of 1934 because the evidence did not suggest that the shotgun "has some reasonable relationship to the preservation or efficiency of a well regulated militia . . . ." The Court then explained that the Framers included the Second Amendment to ensure the effectiveness of the military.

But just as the election of Franklin Delano Roosevelt as president from 1933 to 1945 allowed a Democrat president to appoint a total of eight new members to the Supreme Court over a period of a dozen years, shifting its interpretation of the Constitution away from an originalist perspective, the election of two Republican presidents - George H.W. Bush and Ronald Reagan, dramatically changed the perspective of the Court. Reagan appointed Antonin Scalia in 1986, and Bush appointed Clarence Thomas in 1991.

Writing in 2004, Professor Randy Barnett previewed what this more originalist court meant for the Second Amendment, in his article "*Was the Right to Keep and Bear Arms Conditioned on Service in An Organized Militia?*" Barnett concluded that it was not.

Arguments that "the right to keep and bear arms was expressly conditioned on its exercise as part of a militia that no longer exists . . . is belied by contemporaneous statements about the nature of the right and the meaning of the Amendment before, during, and after its ratification, by evidence of later usage, by the original meaning of the Fourteenth Amendment, by repeated affinnations by Congress, and by the current statutes of the United States."

> *Notwithstanding the . . . opinion [of collective rights approach supporters] that "it would be difficult to conceive of any institution less necessary to the security of the fifty free states at the beginning of the new millennium, than the now disorganized common militia," we may just need the militia again one day, as we did on September 11th. When we do, it may well be under circumstances where it would be better if its members have access to their own weapons to arm themselves.*
>
> *Fortunately, as the evidence shows, the Founders had the foresight to enshrine an individual right of the people to keep and bear arms in the Constitution when they added the Second Amendment. Though it has often been ignored by courts, and sometimes squelched by [collective right] scholars . . . who wish that it was not there, the Second Amendment has not been repealed and it has never fallen silent.*

Four years later, in 2008, the Supreme Court re-established the "individual rights approach" to the Second Amendment, as Cornell Law School's Legal Information Institution notes:

> *This precedent stood for nearly 70 years until 2008, when the U.S. Supreme Court revisited the issue in the case of*

Antonin Scalia was nominated to the Supreme Court by President Ronald Reagan in 1986, and served after his confirmation that same year until his death in 2016.

District of Columbia v. Heller, 478 F.3d 370. The plaintiff in Heller challenged the constitutionality of a Washington D.C. law which prohibited the possession of handguns. In a 5-4 decision, the Court struck down the D.C. handgun ban as violative of that right. The Court meticulously detailed the history and tradition of the Second Amendment at the time of the Constitutional Convention and proclaimed that the Second Amendment established an individual right for U.S. citizens to possess firearms. The Court carved out Miller as an exception to the general rule that Americans may possess firearms, claiming that law-abiding citizens cannot use sawed-off shotguns for any law-abiding purpose. Similarly, the Court in dicta stated that firearm regulations would not implicate the Second Amendment if that weaponry cannot be used for law-abiding purposes. Further, the Court suggested that the United States Constitution would not disallow regulations prohibiting criminals and the mentally ill from firearm possession.

Supreme Court Justice Antonin Scalia, c.2013

"In interpreting [the Second Amendment], we are guided by the principle that '[t]he Constitution was written to be understood by the voters; its words and phrases were used in their normal and ordinary as distinguished from technical meaning.' The two sides in this case have set out very different interpretations of the Amendment. Petitioners and today's dissenting Justices believe that it protects only the right to possess and carry a firearm in connection with militia service. . . Respondent argues that it protects an individual right to possess a firearm unconnected with service in a militia, and to use that arm for traditionally lawful purposes, such as self-defense within the home," Justice Scalia wrote in the 5-4 majority decision in *District of Columbia v. Heller*:

The Second Amendment is naturally divided into two parts: its prefatory clause and its operative clause. The former does not limit the latter grammatically, but rather announces a purpose. The Amendment could be rephrased, "Because a well regulated Militia is necessary to the security of a free State, the right of the people to keep and bear Arms shall not be infringed." . . . Although this structure of the Second Amendment is unique in our Constitution, other legal documents of the founding era, particularly individual rights provisions of state constitutions, commonly included a prefatory statement of purpose.

"By the time of the founding, the right to have arms had become fundamental for English subjects. . . Blackstone [writing in 1765], whose works, we have said [in our 1999 decision in *Alden v. Maine*], 'constituted the preeminent authority on English law for the founding generation,' cited the arms provision of the Bill of Rights as one of the fundamental rights of Englishmen. . . His description of it cannot possibly be thought to tie it to militia or military service," Scalia noted:

It was, he said, "the natural right of resistance and self-preservation," and "the right of having and using arms for selfpreservation and defence," (1768). Other contemporary authorities concurred. Thus, the right secured in 1689 as a result of the Stuarts' abuses was by the time of the founding understood to be an individual right protecting against both public and private violence.

"Three important founding-era legal scholars interpreted the Second Amendment in published writings. All three understood it to protect an individual right unconnected with militia service." Scalia continued:

> St. George Tucker's version of Blackstone's Commentaries, as we explained above, conceived of the Blackstonian arms right as necessary for self-defense. He equated that right, absent the religious and class-based restrictions, with the Second Amendment:

> In 1825, William Rawle, a prominent lawyer who had been a member of the Pennsylvania Assembly that ratified the Bill of Rights, published an influential treatise, which analyzed the Second Amendment as follows: "The first [principle] is a declaration that a well regulated militia is necessary to the security of a free state; a proposition from which few will dissent. . . . "The corollary, from the first position is, that the right of the people to keep and bear arms shall not be infringed. "The prohibition is general. No clause in the constitution could by any rule of construction be conceived to give to congress a power to disarm the people. Such a flagitious attempt could only be made under some general pretence by a state legislature. But if in any blind pursuit of inordinate power, either should attempt it, this amendment may be appealed to as a restraint on both."

> [Supreme Court Justice] Joseph Story published his famous Commentaries on the Constitution of the United States in 1833. Story explained that the English Bill of Rights had also included a "right to bear arms," a right that, as we have discussed, had nothing to do with militia service. He then equated the English right with the Second Amendment. . . As the Tennessee Supreme Court recognized 38 years after Story wrote his Commentaries, "Story shows clearly that this right was intended . . . and was guaranteed to, and to be exercised and enjoyed by the citizen, as such, and not by him as a soldier, or in defense solely of his political rights."

"Like most rights, the right secured by the Second Amendment is not unlimited. . . . [N]othing in our opinion should be taken to cast doubt on longstanding prohibitions on the possession of firearms by felons or the mentally ill, or laws forbidding the carrying of firearms in sensitive places such as schools and government buildings, or laws imposing conditions and qualifications on the commercial sale of arms," Scalia concluded.

Revolutionary militia fire on the British.

In 2010, the Supreme Court made another signifcant Second Amendment ruling in *McDonald v. City of Chicago*. Professors Calvin Massey and Brannon P. Denning, writing in *American Constitutional Law: Powers and Liberty*, noted in this decision the Court concluded "that the Second Amendment right to possession of a firearm for purposes of self-defense 'was fundamental to our scheme of ordered liberty' and 'deeply rooted in this Nation's history and tradition.' Thus, the Fourteenth Amendment made the Second Amendment right applicable to the states."

In 2022, fourteen years after *Heller*, and a dozen years after *McDonald*, the Supreme Court delivered an emphatic endorsement of the "individual rights approach" to the Second Amendment in the 6 to 3 decision in *New York State Rifle & Pistol Association, Inc. v. Bruen*.

Brandon Koch and Robert Nash - both members of the New York State Rifle and Pistol Association - applied to the proper state licensing official to obtain a permit to carry a concealed weapons, "citing self-defense as their reason." Both Koch and Nash received permits to concealed carry, but those permits only allowed them to carry for hunting and target shooting, not for self-defense. Their requests to have the restrictions on their concealed carry permits removed were denied by a state licensing official, and they filed suit.

Justice Clarence Thomas described how the New York statute was applied to Koch and Nash at the start of his majority opinion in the case:

Supreme Court Justice Clarence Thomas (cir. 2018)

> *New York State has regulated the public carry of handguns at least since the early 20th century . . . Today's licensing scheme largely tracks that of the early 1900s. It is a crime in New York to possess "any firearm" without a license, whether inside or outside the home, punishable by up to four years in prison or a $5,000 fine for a felony offense, and one year in prison or a $1,000 fine for a misdemeanor. . . Meanwhile, possessing a loaded firearm outside one's home or place of business without a license is a felony punishable by up to 15 years in prison.*

> *A license applicant who wants to possess a firearm at home (or in his place of business) must convince a "licensing officer" - usually a judge or law enforcement officer - that, among other things, he is of good moral character, has no history of crime or mental illness, and that "no good cause exists for the denial of the license." . . . If he wants to carry a firearm outside his home or place of business for self-defense, the applicant must obtain an unrestricted license to "have and carry" a concealed "pistol or revolver." . . . To secure that license, the applicant must prove that "proper cause exists" to issue it. . . If an applicant cannot make that showing, he can receive only a "restricted" license for public carry, which allows him to carry a firearm for a limited purpose, such as hunting, target shooting, or employment.*

Thomas then explained how state courts in New York interpreted "proper cause."

> *No New York statute defines "proper cause." But New York courts have held that an applicant shows proper cause only if he can "demonstrate a special need for self-protection distinguishable from that of the general community." . . . This "special need" standard is demanding. For example, living or working in an area "noted for criminal activity does not suffice" . . . Rather, New York courts generally require evidence "of particular threats, attacks or other extraordinary danger to personal safety."*

> *When a licensing officer denies an application, judicial review is limited. New York courts defer to an officer's application of the proper-cause standard unless it is "arbitrary and capricious." . . . In other words, the decision **must be upheld if the record shows a rational basis for it.** The rule leaves applicants little recourse if their local licensing officer denies a permit. (emphasis added)*

"The constitutional right to bear arms in public for self-defense is not 'a second-class right, subject to an entirely different body of rules than the other Bill of Rights guarantees.' We know of no other constitutional right that an individual may exercise only after demonstrating to government officers some special need," Justice Alito wrote in his concurring opinion:

> *That is not how the First Amendment works when it comes to unpopular speech or the free exercise of religion. It is not how the Sixth Amendment works when it comes to a defendant's right to confront the witnesses against him. And it is not how the Second Amendment works when it comes to public carry for self-defense.*
>
> *New York's proper-cause requirement violates the Fourteenth Amendment in that it prevents law-abiding citizens with ordinary self-defense needs from exercising their right to keep and bear arms. We therefore reverse the judgment of the Court of Appeals...*

Political controversy over the Second Amendment continues, as is evidenced by the dissenting opinion in *Bruen* by Justice Breyer, who wrote:

> *In 2020, 45,222 Americans were killed by firearms... Since the start of this year (2022), there have been 277 reported mass shootings - an average of more than one per day... Gun violence has now surpassed motor vehicle crashes as the leading cause of death among children and adolescents...*
>
> *Many States have tried to address some of the dangers of gun violence just described by passing laws that limit, in various ways, who may purchase, carry, or use firearms of different kinds. The Court today severely burdens States' efforts to do so. It invokes the Second Amendment to strike down a New York law regulating the public carriage of concealed handguns. In my view, that decision rests upon several serious mistakes.*

Despite that political controversy, especially as it exist in states where the governors and attorneys generals are members of the Democrat Party which has politically attached itself to the "collective rights approach," the trio of major Supreme Court Second Amendment cases over the past two decades - *Heller*, *McDonald*, and *Bruen* - have firmly re-established the "individual rights approach" to the interpretation of the Second Amendment in courts throughout the United States of America for the foreseeable future.

Chapter Discussion Questions

1. Describe the "collective rights" approach to the Second Amendment of the Constitution.

2. Describe the "individual rights" approach to the Second Amendment of the Constitution.

3. What is the significance of the 2010 *McDonald* case?

4. In light of the 2008 *Heller* and 2022 *Bruen* decisions, what limitations does the Supreme Court place on gun ownership under the Second Amendment?

Chapter 12

The Third Amendment

To modern eyes, the Third Amendment seems anachronistic. To the Founders, however, it was a critical protection of individual liberty:

> *No Soldier shall, in time of peace be quartered in any house, without the consent of the Owner, nor in time of war, but in a manner to be prescribed by law.*

The unwelcome quartering of troops was fresh in the minds of newly independent Americans, who rankled at the memory of their homes being taken over by British troops, almost always against the wishes of the owners, during the American Revolution.

"The Third Amendment seems to have no direct constitutional relevance at present; indeed, not only is it the least litigated amendment in the Bill of Rights, but the Supreme Court has never decided a case on the basis of it," Professor Gordon Wood of Brown University, a leading expert on the Federal Era of the new American Republic, wrote:

> *The federal government today is not likely to ask people to house soldiers in their homes, even in time of war. Nevertheless, the amendment has some modern implications. It suggests the individual's right of domestic privacy - that people are protected from governmental intrusion into their homes; and it is the only part of the Constitution that deals directly with the relationship between the rights of individuals and the military in both peace and war - rights that emphasize the importance of civilian control over the armed forces. Some legal scholars have even begun to argue that the amendment might be applied to the government's response to terror attacks and natural disasters, and to issues involving eminent domain and the militarization of the police.*

> *When the amendment was written in the eighteenth century, Americans and Englishmen in general believed that the issue of quartering troops in private homes was of great and palpable significance. During the course of their history the English had developed a deep dislike of standing armies; they especially objected to the government's compelling them to quarter soldiers in their homes.*

> *Yet the English attitude was contradictory. At the same time as the English protested the quartering of troops in private homes, they were reluctant to house the soldiers in barracks separated from the civilian*

population. The English remained so suspicious of standing armies that they feared that concentrations of soldiers in barracks might pose military threats to the people's liberties. Thus, the English concluded that if they had to have an army, it must be scattered among the populace and housed preferably in inns, alehouses, stables, and private homes. But as Parliament made clear in the Glorious Revolution of 1688-89, the government could not billet troops in private homes without the consent of the owners. So the English fear of standing armies was inextricably connected to their fear of having soldiers quartered in their homes without their consent.

"The idea of quartering soldiers in private homes without the owners' consent, even in wartime, had been illegal in England for many years before the American Revolution. The English Bill of Rights of 1689 listed the right of the king's subjects 'not to be burdened with the sojourning of soldiers against their will,'" the Constitutional Rights Foundation wrote:

In America during 1754, the question of quartering troops first arose, when British soldiers began arriving to fight in the French and Indian War. Lord Loudoun, the commander-in-chief of the British army in North America, realized that the quartering provisions of the Mutiny Act applied only to England and not to its colonies. Using his military authority, Lord Loudoun decreed that if barracks were not available, then the owners of both public and private houses would have to provide accommodations for his men. Loudoun left it up to local civilian officials to make the necessary arrangements and to secure reimbursement from their colonial legislatures...

In 1763, when the French and Indian War ended, the British government decided to keep a standing (permanent) army in North America. Although the mission of the peacetime army was not clearly defined, it seemed to be a combination of defending newly acquired Canada and Florida and managing Indian affairs. Some colonists welcomed British military assistance in protecting them from hostile Indian attacks. The British government, however, never stated the most important purpose. The army was to act as a police force to keep the king's subjects in line...

On October 26, 1768, the Massachusetts Council announced its "definitive refusal" to provide and pay for the quartering of British soldiers inside the town of Boston. The following day, soldiers moved into stores, warehouses, and other commercial buildings that had been rented by Lt. Col. Dalrymple at the Crown's expense. Eventually, as local toughs and soldiers repeatedly clashed, virtual warfare raged on the streets of Boston. On March 5, 1770, a crowd gathered before the Customs House, taunted the sentry and began throwing stones and snowballs. The crowd became increasingly aggressive, eventually goading British soldiers into firing their muskets into the crowd, killing five people.

Anger over the Boston Massacre led to the Boston Tea Party of 1773, which in turn fueled opposition to British rule and ultimately, the Declaration of Independence and the American Revolution.

The treaty ending that war and formalizing American independence was signed in 1783. Four years later, the Constitutional Convention met in Philadelphia.

"[W]hen the new federal Congress came to write the Third Amendment to the Constitution in 1789, it had considerable experience and precedent to rely on. There was nothing new about the Third Amendment; it simply declared what had become conventional American wisdom," Wood concluded.

That lack of controversy about the Third Amendment at the time of its introduction and ratification is universally acknowledged.

"The brief congressional debates on the text [in 1789] make clear that the amendment reflects an effort to balance private property rights and the potential wartime need for military quarters," Professor Andrew P. Morriss of the University of Alabama School of Law wrote:

> *The Anti-Federalists used the absence of a ban on quartering as an argument against ratification. Once the concept of a Bill of Rights was agreed upon, however, there was little controversy over the inclusion of a ban on quartering. Six of the original thirteen states also adopted constitutional provisions banning the quartering of soldiers.*
>
> *The British practice of quartering soldiers in America grew out of the lack of regular army bases, unclear legislative authority for British army quartering in America, and the need to move large bodies of troops about the country during conflicts with the French and Indians. Although there were numerous conflicts over quartering in both Britain and America before the 1770s, the most significant episodes concerned the British quartering of soldiers in private homes to punish the people of Boston under the Intolerable Acts of 1774.*
>
> *Because of its clear text, there have been few court opinions discussing the Third Amendment. The quartering problem has largely been solved today by paying communities to host military bases.*

"When the Supreme Court has cited the Third Amendment, it has been as part of nonoriginalist interpretations that list it as one of the sources of 'penumbras, formed by emanations' that created a zone of privacy in no specific clause of the Constitution. For example, the Court cited it in the name of marital privacy as support for constitutional restrictions on state governments' abilities to regulate the sale of contraceptives in *Griswold v. Connecticut* (1965)," Morriss concluded.

If the Third Amendment is ever seen again at the Supreme Court, it will almost certainly come in connection to a nonoriginalist interpretation surrounding "zones of privacy" rather than the clear quartering of troops issue addressed by the actual text of the amendment.

Chapter Discussion Questions

(1) In your opinion, should the Third Amendment principle of privacy be limited to and apply to privacy as it relates to property?

(2) Does the fact that the Supreme Court has never decided a case on the Third Amendment mean it is not necessary?

Chapter 13

Civil Asset Forfeiture and the Fourth Amendment

The Bill of Rights - the first ten amendments to the Constitution - were included in the "covenant" that created the United States because many Americans feared that unless their individual rights were specifically articulated in our country's founding documents they would eventually be violated by those in power.

The Fourth Amendment, in particular, offers protections to individuals against the police powers of the government:

> *The right of the people to be secure in their persons, houses, papers, and effects, against unreasonable searches and seizures, shall not be violated, and no warrants shall issue, but upon probable cause, supported by oath or affirmation, and particularly describing the place to be searched, and the persons or things to be seized.*

Anyone who has watched one of the many police procedural dramas on television, like *Law & Order*, is very familiar with the two key elements of the amendment:

(1) "The right of the people to be secure in their persons, houses, papers, and effects, against unreasonable searches and seizures, shall not be violated."

(2) "No warrants shall issue, but upon probable cause, supported by oath or affirmation, and particularly describing the place to be searched, and the persons or things to be seized."

"The search-and-seizure provisions of the Fourth Amendment are all about privacy. To honor this freedom, the Fourth Amendment protects against 'unreasonable' searches and seizures by state or federal law enforcement authorities," according to Nolo.com:

> *The flip side is that the Fourth Amendment does permit searches and seizures that are reasonable. In practice, this means that the police may override your privacy concerns and conduct a search of you, your home, barn, car, boat, office, personal or business documents, bank account records, trash barrel, or whatever, if:*
>
> ** The police have probable cause to believe they can find evidence that you committed a crime, and a judge issues a warrant, or*
>
> ** The particular circumstances justify the search without a warrant first being issued.*

Over the past three decades, as part of "the war on drugs," agents of the government - at the federal, state, and local level - have revived a practice known as civil asset forfeiture, "in which officers and agents may lawfully seize the property or money of individuals they suspect of committing or helping to commit a crime. An individual targeted by civil asset forfeiture need not be arraigned in court, nor do they need to be convicted of a crime," as the Bill of Rights Institute notes. Many originalists believe this is a violation of the Fourth Amendment's prohibition "against unreasonable searches and seizures."

Until the Prohibition Era (1919-1933), civil asset forfeiture was rarely used. After the 18th Amendment prohibiting the sale of alcohol was passed in 1919, bootlegging - the illegal smuggling of alcohol into or within the United States exploded. When bootleggers who were transporting alcohol illegally were arrested with the goods in their possession, local and national law enforcement agencies seized the contraband alcohol.

"Forfeiture, the government seizure of property connected to illegal activity, has been a major weapon in the Federal government's 'war on drugs' since the mid-eighties," the Legal Information Institute notes:

> *In the words of former President George Bush, "Asset forfeiture laws allow the government to take the ill-gotten gains of drug kingpins and use them to put more cops on the streets." New York City Police Commissioner Howard Safir invoked deterrence when he said, "We believe that ... the threat of civil forfeiture and the possibility of losing one's car, have served to reduce the number of motorists who are willing to take the chance of being caught driving drunk." . . .*
>
> *Most forfeiture activity occurs under Federal law, and most of that is connected to the traffic in illegal drugs. The Department of Justice established the National Assets Seizure and Forfeiture Fund in 1985 and realized $27 million from drug-related forfeitures that year. By 1992 the total take had climbed to $875 million. Many states followed suit by establishing their own civil forfeiture programs. Cities and other municipal governments have cooperated in forfeiture actions under both Federal and state drug laws. They have used such laws on their own to deal with local concerns ranging from unsafe housing to prostitution, and now for the problem of drunk driving.*

The problem with civil asset forfeiture is that most citizens from whom property is seized by law enforcement have a very different idea than local law enforcement of what "unreasonable search and seizure" means. To them, and to most constitutional originalists, it is unreasonable to seize property from anyone who has not been convicted of a crime.

"The authority to seize property in this way is not inherent. Rather, it is established by statute. It is constrained by those authorizing laws and by the U.S. Constitution," the Legal Information Institute observes.

The seizure of private property without clear legal authority, critics argue, is simply the crime of theft committed by government authority, not a lawful taking.

"The expansion of forfeiture activity has not gone on without Constitutional challenge. The U.S. Supreme Court has heard at least half a dozen forfeiture cases during the nineties, but its rulings have not done much to rein in the practice," the Legal Information Institute notes.

Until the Prohibition Era (1919-1933), civil asset forfeiture was rarely used. After the 18th Amendment prohibiting the sale of alcohol was passed in 1919, bootlegging - the illegal smuggling of alcohol into or within the United States - exploded. When bootleggers who were transporting alcohol illegally were arrested with the goods in their possession, local and national law enforcement agencies seized the contraband alcohol.

Police in Detroit seize alcohol during the Prohibition Era

When Prohibition ended, the practice of civil asset forfeiture by law enforcement agencies lost favor.

For the next half a century, civil asset forfeiture was rarely used by law enforcement agencies. Everything changed, however, during the 1980s, when the illegal drug trade from South America and other foreign countries spiked, and the federal government declared the "War on Drugs."

Journalist Sarah Stillman argues that the passage of the Comprehensive Crime Control Act of 1984 led to the explosive growth in the use of civil asset forfeiture by law enforcement agencies.

Coast Guard seizes illegal drugs.

The law allowed law enforcement agencies to take for their own budgets the assets and cash they seized, as well as "extract swift penalties from white-collar criminals and offer restitution to victims of fraud."

"Despite the plain wording of the fourth amendment, the vast majority of courts view seizures of property pursuant to forfeiture laws as outside the purview of the warrant requirement, which mandates judicial authorization prior to government action," Ahok Aluja wrote more than 30 years ago in 1986 at the Yale Law and Policy Review when the practice of civil asset forfeiture was just beginning to take hold in law enforcement agencies at every level of government around the country:

> Moreover, civil forfeiture is on the rise as a preferred law enforcement tool. The Department of Justice encourages government attorneys "to use aggressively the forfeiture weapon in our continuing battle against crime." Forfeiture provisions are now incorporated into over 120 federal statutes. Furthermore, Congress recently extended the reach of the forfeiture statutes to include "[a]ll real property...intended to be used, in any manner... to facilitate the commission of... a violation" of the narcotics laws.

Examples of the abuses of civil asset forfeiture by law enforcement agencies abound.

The Daily Caller, for instance, offers these seven recent examples of civil asset forfeiture abuse:

1. Tan Nguyen hopped in his car excited about $50,000 in casino winnings. That excitement faded when he saw police lights in the rear view mirror. A Nevada police officer suspicious of the man's large sum of cash confiscated it, Forbes reports. Nguyen said the cop threatened to seize and tow his car if he spoke up about it.

After hiring a lawyer, Nguyen was able to get his $50,000 back with attorney's fees.

2. Matt Lee had his $2,400 cash confiscated from his car on a routine traffic stop. The worst part? It was taken by the same officer that targeted Nguyen: Deputy Lee Dove. In a shared settlement with Nguyen, Lee got his $2,400 back.

3. The Contemporary Art Institute of Detroit's monthly "Funk Night" party got weird in May of 2008. The all-night dance party was raging when police burst in around 2 a.m., the *Metro Times* reports. Officers alleged the establishment did not have a license. They passed out loitering tickets and impounded 40 vehicles just because they were driven to the party. They all got their cars back, except for one man who had his car stolen from the impound lot. Also, they each paid a $900 impound fee, totaling more than $35,000.

4. Mississippi police pulled over a man for a routine traffic stop in July of 2013. An officer's search of the vehicle found $360,000 in a secret compartment of the car. The police confiscated the money, though they had no proof the man committed a crime, ABC News reports. The report said cops "are not ruling out criminal activity."

5. A New Jersey man's stash of cash was taken by an officer when he traveled through Monterey, Tennessee. George Reby had $22,000 cash in his car when he was stopped by a police officer, News Channel 5 reported. The officer took the money because he suspected it was drug money. However, the man said he was going to use the money to buy a car, for which he had active bids on Ebay, something he was able to prove on his computer. When the officer wrote up the report, he failed to mention Reby's claim that he was going to buy a car.

"If somebody told me this happened to them, I absolutely would not believe this could happen in America," Reby told News Channel 5.

6. Even though they didn't charge her with a crime, Georgia police took $11,530 from Alda Gentile at a regular traffic stop, *The Associated Press* reports. They searched the car for drugs but found none. Gentile said she had the money for a house hunting trip to Florida.

Meridien, Mississippi police seized this cash, about $360,000, from a man stopped during a routine traffic stop. There is no record whether the man was ever charged with the crime. There is also no record as to whether local police kept 80 percent of the cash they seized, as state law allows.

7. A family in the Philadelphia suburbs had their home seized by police because their son sold drugs out of the house, CNN reports. The son was charged for selling $40 of heroin, but the parents say they didn't know about it.

"Civil forfeiture laws pose some of the greatest threats to property rights in the nation today, too often making it easy and lucrative for law enforcement to take and keep property - regardless of the owner's guilt or innocence," the Institute for Justice notes.

"Every year, police and prosecutors across the United States take hundreds of millions of dollars in cash, cars, homes and other property - regardless of the owners' guilt or innocence. Under civil forfeiture laws, the government can seize this property on the mere suspicion that it is connected to criminal activity. No charges or convictions are required. And once property is seized, owners must navigate a confusing, complex and often expensive legal process to try to win it back. Worst of all, most civil forfeiture laws give law enforcement agencies a powerful incentive to take property: a cut, or even all, of forfeiture proceeds," according to the Executive Summary of *Policing for Profits*:

Forfeiture activity has exploded, particularly in the new millennium.

Forfeited cash and proceeds from the sale of forfeited property generate revenue for the government - and provide an important measure of law enforcement's forfeiture activity.

In 1986, the Department of Justice's Assets Forfeiture Fund took in $93.7 million in revenue from federal forfeitures. By 2014, annual deposits had reached $4.5 billion - a 4,667 percent increase.

The forfeiture funds of the DOJ and Treasury Department together took in nearly $29 billion from 2001 to 2014, and combined annual revenue grew 1,000 percent over the period.

Total annual forfeiture revenue across 14 states more than doubled from 2002 to 2013. Those 14 states were the only states for which the Institute for Justice could obtain forfeiture revenues for an extended period.

"Nearly all expenditures of forfeiture proceeds are hidden from public view," *Policing for Profits* notes:

Forfeiture laws typically place few limits on law enforcement spending of forfeiture proceeds and impose even fewer checks to ensure that expenditures are proper or legal. Scant reporting requirements heighten the risk of abuse by shielding expenditures from public scrutiny.

Surprisingly, the Supreme Court has largely ruled in favor of the practice of civil asset forfeiture since the passage of the Comprehensive Crime Control Act of 1984. Several current lawsuits challenging civil asset forfeiture, however, may reach the Supreme Court in the coming years, and the outcome of those decisions may be different than those made over the past 30 years.

One recent lawsuit in particular suggests that judicial attitudes towards the constitutionality of civil asset forfeiture may be changing.

In June of 2017, "a federal appellate court ordered police to return $167,000 that was seized more than four years ago following two coordinated traffic stops along I-80 in Nevada," Matt Powers writes:

The opinion from the Ninth Circuit Court of Appeals casts a light on tactics that police use to seize money along the nation's highways. And, at least in some circumstances, the opinion finds those tactics unconstitutional.

"Civil forfeiture laws pose one of the greatest threats to property rights in the nation today. They encourage law enforcement to favor the pursuit of property over the pursuit of justice, and they typically give the innocent little recourse for recovering seized property. And without meaningful transparency, law enforcement faces little public accountability for its forfeiture activity or expenditures from forfeiture funds," the Institute for Justice notes.

"The best solution would be to simply abolish civil forfeiture. Short of that, lawmakers should eliminate financial incentives to take property, bolster property rights and due process protections, and demand transparency for forfeiture activity and spending. No one should lose property without being convicted of a crime, and law enforcement agencies should not profit from taking people's property," the Institute for Justice concludes.

Chapter Discussion Questions

(1) Would you suggest the right of personal privacy is stronger in the Fourth Amendment than the Third?

(2) To what extent, if any, is civil forfeiture similar to the writs of assistance in the colonial period of American history?

(3) In your opinion, is random drug testing a violation of the Fourth Amendment?

Chapter 14

The Fifth Amendment

Everyone who has watched a movie that includes a criminal trial or a Congressional hearing knows about one aspect of the Fifth Amendment: the right not to incriminate yourself.

"No person . . . shall be compelled in any criminal case to be a witness against himself," reads the relevant clause of the amendment.

Alleged crime boss Tony Accardo 'plead the 5th' nearly 200 times.

Alleged crime boss Tony Accardo took the Fifth Amendment more than 170 times during the 1951 Kefauver Hearings in the United States Senate, a dramatic event captured on live television.

But that important right is only one of five in the Fifth Amendment which guarantees individual liberties in civil and criminal trials and outlines "basic constitutional limits on police procedure," the Cornell Law Institute notes.

Here's how the full text of the Fifth Amendment reads:

No person shall be held to answer for a capital, or otherwise infamous crime, unless on a presentment or indictment of a grand jury, except in cases arising in the land or naval forces, or in the militia, when in actual service in time of war or public danger; nor shall any person be subject for the same offense to be twice put in jeopardy of life or limb; nor shall be compelled in any criminal case to be a witness against himself, nor be deprived of life, liberty, or property, without due process of law; nor shall private property be taken for public use, without just compensation.

Here's a more detailed breakdown so you can identify those five constitutional limits on police procedures more readily (emphasis added):

No person shall be held to answer for a capital, or otherwise infamous crime,

(1) unless on a presentment or indictment of a **grand jury**, except in cases arising in the land or naval forces, or in the militia, when in actual service in time of war or public danger

(2) nor shall any person be subject for the same offense to be **twice put in jeopardy** of life or limb (a concept known as **double jeopardy**)

(3) nor shall be **compelled in any criminal case to be a witness against himself**

(4) nor be deprived of life, liberty, or property, **without due process of law**

(5) nor shall private property be taken for public use, **without just compensation** (The government's ability to take private property for public use with just compensation is known as **eminent domain**)

Grand Jury

A grand jury is different from a trial jury, which is what most people think of when they hear the word "jury."

You are probably familiar with what a trial jury is: Twelve men or women who are "peers" of the accused who are empowered in a trial to determine whether or not the accused is guilty of the crime of which they are charged.

The accused is arrested by the police based on evidence that he or she has committed a crime. At the trial, which is presided over by a judge, the prosecuting attorney presents evidence for the jury that the accused - the defendant - is guilty of the crime, while the defense attorney argues that the evidence presented by the prosecuting attorney does not establish "beyond a reasonable doubt" that the defendant is guilty of the crime.

Once both the prosecuting attorney and defense attorney have presented their case, the judge provides the trial jury with instructions on the legal standards they should use in their deliberations. The jury then retires to complete their deliberations in private, and comes to a verdict: the defendant is either guilty or not guilty of the crime of which he or she is charged.

Unlike a trial jury, a grand jury plays a different role, but "not one that involves a finding of guilt or punishment of a party."

"Instead, a prosecutor will work with a grand jury to decide whether to bring criminal charges or an indictment against a potential defendant - usually reserved for serious felonies. Grand jury members may be called for jury duty for months at a time, but need only appear in court for a few days out of every month. Regular court trial juries are usually 6 or 12 people, but in the federal system, a grand jury can be 16 to 23 people," Findlaw.com notes:

> While all states have provisions in their laws that allow for grand juries, roughly half of the states don't use them. Courts often use preliminary hearings prior to criminal trials, instead of grand juries, which are adversarial in nature. As with grand juries, preliminary hearings are meant to determine whether there is enough evidence, or probable cause, to indict a criminal suspect.

In 1913, a grand jury convened in Boston went outside the courtroom to see first hand the site of the Arcadia Hotel fire.

Unlike a grand jury, a preliminary hearing is usually open to the public and involves lawyers and a judge (not so with grand juries, other than the prosecutor). Sometimes, a preliminary hearing preceeds a grand jury. One of the biggest differences between the two is the requirement that a defendant request a preliminary hearing, although the court may decline a request.

Grand jury proceedings are much more relaxed than normal court room proceedings. There is no judge present and frequently there are no lawyers except for the prosecutor. The prosecutor will explain the law to the jury and work with them to gather evidence and hear testimony. Under normal courtroom rules of evidence, exhibits and other testimony must adhere to strict rules before admission. However, a grand jury has broad power to see and hear almost anything they would like.

However, unlike the vast majority of trials, grand jury proceedings are kept in strict confidence.

Though independent entities, grand juries are heavily influenced by the prosecutors who convene them.

"In a bid to make prosecutors more accountable for their actions, Chief Judge [of the New York Court of Appeals] Sol Wachtler has proposed that the state scrap the grand jury system of bringing criminal indictments," the *New York Daily News* reported on January 31, 1985.

"Wachtler, who became the state's top judge earlier this month, said district attorneys now have so much influence on grand juries that 'by and large' they could get them to 'indict a ham sandwich,'" the News noted.

Not everyone agrees with Judge Wachtler, but it is rare for a grand jury to not return an indictment sought by the convening prosecutor.

Still, "[a] person being charged with a crime that warrants a grand jury has the right to challenge members of the grand juror for partiality or bias, but these challenges differ from peremptory challenges, which a defendant has when choosing a trial jury," the Cornell Law Institute notes:

When a defendant makes a peremptory challenge, the judge must remove the juror without making any proof, but in the case of a grand juror challenge, the challenger must establish the cause of the challenge by meeting the same burden of proof as the establishment of any other fact would require. Grand juries possess broad authority to investigate suspected crimes. They may not, however, conduct "fishing expeditions" or hire individuals not already employed by the government to locate testimony or documents. Ultimately, grand juries may make a presentment. During a presentment the grand jury informs the court that they have a reasonable suspicion that the suspect committed a crime.

Double Jeopardy

Under the double jeopardy clause of the Fifth Amendment, you can not be charged for the same crime a second time if you have been given a fair trial and found not guilty of those charges. It is designed to prevent prosecutorial abuses by the government.

"The government must place a defendant 'in jeopardy' for the Fifth Amendment clause to apply. The simple filing of criminal charges doesn't cause jeopardy to "attach" - the proceedings must get to a further stage," according to the Nolo.com legal encyclopedia.

"Generally, jeopardy attaches when the court swears in the jury. In a trial before a judge, jeopardy attaches after the first witness takes the oath and begins to testify," Nolo.com states.

"The Double Jeopardy Clause aims to protect against the harassment of an individual through successive prosecutions of the same alleged act, to ensure the significance of an acquittal, and to prevent the state from putting the defendant through the emotional, psychological, physical, and financial troubles that would accompany multiple trials for the same alleged offense," the Cornell Law Institute notes:

Two defendants thank their attorneys after being found not guilty by a jury in an Alaska state case of starting a forest fire. These two defendants can never again be charged with this specific crime, due to the double jeopardy clause of the Fifth Amendment.

Courts have interpreted the Double Jeopardy Clause as accomplishing these goals by providing the following three distinct rights: a guarantee that a defendant will not face a second prosecution after an acquittal, a guarantee that a defendant will not face a second prosecution after a conviction, and a guarantee that a defendant will not receive multiple punishments for the same offense. Courts, however, have not interpreted the Double Jeopardy Clause as either prohibiting the state from seeking review of a sentence or restricting a sentence's length on rehearing after a defendant's successful appeal.

Self-Incrimination

"The Fifth Amendment also protects criminal defendants from having to testify if they may incriminate themselves through the testimony. A witness may 'plead the Fifth' and not answer if the witness believes answering the question may be self-incriminatory," the Cornell Law Institute observes.

The Fifth Amendment's protection against self incrimination can also be invoked by witnesses called to testify before Congress. Such was the case in 2013 when IRS attorney Lois Lerner invoked her Fifth Amendment rights against self-incrimination when she appeared before a committee of the House of Representatives and refused to answer any questions. She subsequently resigned from the IRS after allegations were made that she unlawfully targeted conservative Tea Party groups for scrutiny not applied to other groups. After her resignation, she appeared before the same committee in 2014 and again invoked her Fifth Amendment rights and refused to testify before the committee.

Former IRS attorney Lois Lerner invoked her Fifth Amendment rights before a committee of the House of Representatives in 2014.

In recent history, the Supreme Court has extended the right of self-incrimination to the very beginning of the criminal proceedings process.

"In the landmark *Miranda v. Arizona* ruling, the United States Supreme Court extended the Fifth Amendment protections to encompass any situation outside of the courtroom that involves the curtailment of personal freedom. 384 U.S. 436 (1966)," the Cornell Law Institute reports:

Therefore, any time that law enforcement takes a suspect into custody, law enforcement must make the suspect aware of all rights. Known as Miranda rights, these rights include the right to remain silent, the right to have an attorney present during questioning, and the right to have a government-appointed attorney if the suspect cannot afford one.

If law enforcement fails to honor these safeguards, courts will often suppress any statements by the suspect as violative of the Fifth Amendment's protection against self-incrimination, provided that the suspect has not actually waived the rights. An actual waiver occurs when a suspect has made the waiver knowingly, intelligently, and voluntarily. To determine if a knowing, intelligent and voluntary waiver has occurred, a court will examine the totality of the circumstances, which considers all pertinent circumstances and events. If a suspect makes a spontaneous statement while in custody prior to being made aware of the Miranda rights, law enforcement can use the statement against the suspect, provided that police interrogation did not prompt the statement.

Due Process

Due process means that everyone in the United States is entitled to a fair trial.

In other countries where this right is not guaranteed, trials are sometimes not fair. These trials, known as "show trials" or "kangaroo courts" - where the guilty verdicts are determined before the trial even begins - are conducted for purposes of propaganda to advance the government's objectives, rather than justice for the accused.

"The guarantee of due process for all persons requires the government to respect all rights, guarantees, and protections afforded by the U.S. Constitution and all applicable statutes before the government can deprive any person of life, liberty, or property," the Cornell Law Institute notes:

Due process essentially guarantees that a party will receive a fundamentally fair, orderly, and just judicial proceeding. While the Fifth Amendment only applies to the federal government, the identical text in the Fourteenth Amendment explicitly applies this due process requirement to the states as well.

Courts have come to recognize that two aspects of due process exist: procedural due process and substantive due process. Procedural due process aims to ensure fundamental fairness by guaranteeing a party the right to be heard, ensuring that the parties receive proper notification throughout the litigation, and ensures that the adjudicating court has the appropriate jurisdiction to render a judgment. Meanwhile, substantive due process has developed during the 20th century as protecting those rights so fundamental as to be "implicit in the concept of ordered liberty."

Just Compensation

"While the federal government has a constitutional right to 'take' private property for public use, the Fifth Amendment's Just Compensation Clause requires the government to pay just compensation, interpreted as market value, to the owner of the property," the Cornell Law Institute notes.

"The U.S. Constitution does not explicitly grant condemnation powers to the federal government. Such power is generally inferred today from clauses of Article 1, Section 8, that give Congress authority to establish post offices and post roads as well as authority over property obtained for forts, arsenals, and other similar facilities, and from the takings clause of the Fifth Amendment," Professor Bruce Benson of Florida State wrote in 2004.

The clauses of Article I appear to limit federal takings by requiring the "consent of the legislature of the state" in which the property is located. This constraint raised the cost of federal seizures somewhat (the states faced no such constraint) and limited their use until the Supreme Court eliminated the constraint in **Kohl v. United States** *(91 U.S. 367 [1875]), in which the federal government was determined to have the power to take property directly in its own name. Before this case (which arose because Congress authorized the secretary of the Treasury to acquire land in Cincinnati for a public building, and federal officials condemned the land directly rather than obtaining it through state condemnation or voluntary exchange), the federal government had condemned land only through the intermediary of the state government.*

"James Madison, who wrote the Fifth Amendment, hoped to restrict the takings that had been made in the colonies under British rule and in the new states after the revolution because he wished to make individual property rights more secure, but he did not go as far as Jefferson would have liked, perhaps as a compromise to garner sufficient support for the Constitution. He chose instead to require compensation explicitly, and he used the term public use rather than public purpose, interest, benefit, or some other term in an effort to establish a narrower and more objective requirement than such alternative terms might require," Benson wrote.

"The U.S. Supreme Court has defined fair market value as the most probable price that a willing but unpressured buyer, fully knowledgeable of both the property's good and bad attributes, would pay. The government does not have to pay a property owner's attorney's fees, however, unless a statute so provides," the Cornell Law Institute notes.

> *In* **Kelo v. City of New London**, *the U.S. Supreme Court rendered a controversial opinion in which they held that a city could constitutionally seize private property for private commercial development. 545 U.S. 469 (2005).*

Susete Kelo, a nurse who owned "a little pink house" in New London, Connecticut was forced to sell it to the city of New London against her wishes based on that decision.

"The Supreme Court's 2005 ruling in *Kelo v. New London* was that year's blockbuster. Literally. The Court gave its blessing to the use of eminent domain to destroy blocks of housing so that city officials could pursue their dreams of a more wondrous community by seizing private property for a planned commercial development," George Leef wrote at *Forbes Magazine*:

The 2017 film "Little Pink House" stars Catherine Keener and is based on Susete Kelo's book.

> *That taking had been challenged on the grounds that the precise wording of the Fifth Amendment's provision allowing eminent domain – that the property had to be taken for "public use" – did not countenance takings where there was merely a purported "public purpose" in doing so. The Court's "liberal" wing didn't care either about the Constitution's precise words or the harm its ruling would inflict on lots of "little guy" owners whose modest properties stood in the way of grandiose political projects.*

> *Kelo is among the many cases demonstrating that ordinary Americans are served best by the strict rule of law rather than by "progressive" jurisprudence that empowers government officials.*

And that is the message strongly conveyed by the recently released movie about Susette Kelo's fight with the arrogant officials in New London, CT. Little Pink House premiered February 2 [2017] at the Santa Barbara film festival. In the film, Catherine Keener (who was nominated for an Oscar for her roles in Being John Malkovich and Capote) portrays Susette Kelo, the nurse who refused to meekly accept the city's decision to force her out of the small home she had fixed up and loved.

"In the end," Leef concluded, "the homes belonging to Susette Kelo and her neighbors were demolished for no purpose at all, since the hoped-for development collapsed. What was once a nice residential area is now acres of rubble. Perhaps some viewers will get the message that big government plans are prone to turning into boondoggles. Perhaps some others will get the point that it's morally wrong for government officials to treat property owners as pawns on a chessboard, easily exchanged for a positional advantage in the game."

Chapter Discussion Questions

(1) How do grand juries and trial juries function as checks within the judicial system?

(2) How would you balance the needs of the community and the rights of individuals when a government invokes the takings clause?

(3) How is the right against self incrimination related to the principle of limited government?

Chapter 15

The Sixth Amendment

The Sixth Amendment, like the Fourth Amendment and the Fifth Amendment, primarily focuses on the protection of individual liberties against the police powers of the state:

In all criminal prosecutions, the accused shall enjoy the right to a speedy trial, by an impartial jury of the State and district wherein the crime shall have been committed, which district shall have previously been ascertained by law, and to be informed of the nature and cause of the accusation; to be confronted with the witnesses against him; to have compulsory process for obtaining witnesses in his favor, and to have the Assistance of Counsel for his defence.

A good way to remember the Sixth Amendment is that it guarantees six very specific rights (emphasis added):

(1) If you ever are accused of a crime, and prosecuted criminally, you **have the right to a speedy and public trial.**

(2) You have a right to be **tried by an impartial jury of your peers**.

(3) You have the right to **know what crime you're being charged with and why.** In the parlance of the day used in the amendment, you had the right "to be informed of the nature and cause of the accusation."

(4) You have the right to **see, hear, and question - "to be confronted with" the witnesses against you.**

(5) You have the right to **bring your own witnesses to be heard on your behalf at trial.**

(6) You have the right to be **represented by a lawyer as "counsel for your defence."**

These rights seem obvious and commonplace to us today.

They were all well established in America at the time of the American Revolution, but had, at times, not been granted during the Colonial period.

Indeed, there was a period of time during the 17th Century when Colonial British America, as it was called at the time, suffered from the same lack of these rights, as did the mother country of England.

The abuses of these long-standing rights were perhaps most severe during the period of the reign of King Charles I from 1629 to 1640 when the king refused to call Parliament in to session.

It was during this decade that the infamous "Star Chamber" trials were conducted in secret and in French. The accused brought before these special tribunals, established for the purpose of prosecuting the political enemies of the king, did not have any of the rights now granted to every American as part of the Sixth Amendment.

John Lilburne, an early hero of popular resistance to the king's tyranny and a distant relative of our own Thomas Jefferson, was perhaps one of the most noteworthy Englishmen to be convicted and imprisoned by a Star Chamber trial.

"The tall and charismatic Lilburne entered the public eye in 1638, at the height of Charles I's era of personal rule. Only twenty-four at the time, Lilburne was arrested and tried for smuggling "unlicensed" Christian books from Holland to England," Michael Patrick Leahy wrote of Lilburne in his 2012 book, *Covenant of Liberty: The Ideological Origins of The Tea Party Movement*:

He was not tried in a common law court by a jury of twelve of his peers, where he would have been granted the right to his own legal counsel. Instead, his case was brought before the Star Chamber. Previously, this special court had been used for expedited hearings on matters involving important figures who might have influenced the outcome of common trials. Charles transformed the Star Chamber into his personal vehicle for eliminating enemies and forcing compliance with established regulations limiting dissent. By the time Lilburne was brought in chains before it, the Star Chamber had become the symbol of the abuse of power that characterized Charles's rule.

"Addressing Lilburne in the customary "Law French," of the Star Chamber, the judges demanded to hear his plea," Leahy wrote:

Lilburne refused to plead until he heard the charges in English. Angered by his defiance, the court ordered him to be stripped of his shirt and tied to an oxcart, behind which he walked for two miles. Crowds gathered to watch as he was lashed more than two hundred times with a three-tailed whip. When he arrived at his destination - the front yard of Westminster - he was untied from the cart and placed into a pillory.

"Defying his captors, Lilburne removed the banned religious books he had hidden in his pockets, threw them into the crowd, and loudly proclaimed that his punishment was a violation of his rights as an Englishman. His captors quickly gagged him, but he had won the hearts of his countrymen and became a symbol of resistance to the arbitrary power of the king," Leahy noted:

The price for this demonstration of courage was high. He remained in prison under severe conditions for more than two years, released only when Charles I was compelled to call Parliament into session to finance his "Bishops' Wars" against Scotland. He emerged severely malnourished. He no longer could use two of his fingers, casualties of two years of wrist chains.

More than three hundred years later, U.S. Supreme Court Justice Hugo Black paid tribute to Lilburne, "and cited his refusal to enter a plea to unknown charges as the basis for the Fifth Amendment - the protection against self-incrimination."

In 1959, Justice Black cited Lilburne's 17th century ordeal in England when he wrote his dissent in a case called *Barenblatt v. United States*. The Founding Fathers, he wrote, "believed that punishment was too serious a matter to be entrusted to any group other than an independent judiciary and a jury of twelve men acting on previously passed, unambiguous laws, with all the procedural safeguards they put in the Constitution as essential to a fair trial – safeguards which included the right to counsel, compulsory process for witnesses, specific indictments, confrontation of accusers, as well as protection against self-incrimination, double jeopardy and cruel and unusual punishment – in short, due process of law."

U.S. Supreme Court Justice Hugo Black

> *They believed this because not long before worthy men had been deprived of their liberties, and indeed their lives, through parliamentary trials without these safeguards. The memory of one John Lilburne – banished and disgraced by a parliamentary committee if he returned to his country – was particularly vivid when our Constitution was written. His attack on trials by such committees and his warning that "what is done unto any one, may be done unto every one," were part of the history of the times which moved those who wrote our Constitution to determine that no such occur over here.*

"It is the protection from arbitrary punishments through the right to a judicial trial with all these safeguards which over the years has distinguished America from lands where drumhead courts and other similar 'tribunals' deprive the weak and the unorthodox of life, liberty and property without due process of law," Black concluded.

Before serving as Cheif Justice of the U.S. Supreme Court, Earl Warren was the 30th Governor of California

In 1966, "Lilburne's Star Chamber trial was also cited as a significant historical precedent in the Supreme Court's majority opinion in the landmark case *Miranda v. Arizona*," Leahy noted in **Covenant of Liberty**.

Chief Justice Warren wrote specifically of that trial's influence on the Founding Fathers when they wrote the Fifth Amendment, but its due process protections apply to the Sixth Amendment as well.

"We sometimes forget how long it has taken to establish the privilege against self-incrimination, the sources from which it came, and the fervor with which it was defended. Its roots go back into ancient times," Chief Justice Earl Warren wrote in his majority opinion:

> *The critical historical event shedding light on its origins and evolution was the trial of one John Lilburn, a vocal anti-Stuart*

Leveller, who was made to take the Star Chamber Oath in 1637. The oath would have bound him to answer to all questions posed to him on any subject. He resisted the oath and declaimed the proceedings, stating:

"Another fundamental right I then contended for was that no man's conscience ought to be racked by oaths imposed to answer to questions concerning himself in matters criminal, or pretended to be so."

*On account of the Lilburn Trial, Parliament abolished the inquisitorial Court of Star Chamber and went further in giving him generous reparation. The lofty principles to which Lilburn had appealed during his trial gained popular acceptance in England. These sentiments worked their way over to the Colonies, and were implanted after great struggle into the Bill of Rights. Those who framed our Constitution and the Bill of Rights were ever aware of subtle encroachments on individual liberty. They knew that "illegitimate and unconstitutional practices get their first footing . . . by silent approaches and slight deviations from legal modes of procedure." **Boyd v. United States**, 116 U. S. 616, 635 (1886).*

"The privilege was elevated to constitutional status, and has always been 'as broad as the mischief against which it seeks to guard.' *Counselman v. Hitchcock*, 142 U. S. 547, 562 (1892). We cannot depart from this noble heritage," Warren concluded.

It is hard to overemphasize the English roots of American liberty, or the significance of Lilburne's part in that influence.

As it turns out, Lilburne was close friends with another young man from England who was undergoing his own trials after having arrived in America just a few years before Lilburne's Star Chamber trial. His name was Roger Williams, the founder of Rhode Island, who literally escaped from the Massachusetts Bay Colony with a death sentence hanging over his head because his ideas on religion differed with the founders of that colony.

As we mentioned in our earlier chapter on the First Amendment, it was Roger Williams' ideas about freedom of religion that ultimately prevailed a century and a half later when the American republic was founded, not those of the early leaders of the Massachusetts Bay Colony, who had restrictive ideas about how the Christian God should be worshiped and used the power of the state to enforce those ideas on others for some time.

Chapter Discussion Questions

(1) How might media coverage impact a defendant's right to a fair trial?

(2) Would you consider some of the procedural rights in the Sixth Amendment to be more important than others?

(3) If you were a judge and a defendant requested they not have a jury trial, would you honor that request?

(4) Are there circumstances where a defendant might not want a jury trial?

(5) Does the right to counsel mean a defendant has a right to competent counsel?

Chapter 16

The Seventh Amendment

The Seventh Amendment is one of those steady but unspectacular amendments that does not feature prominently in many Supreme Court cases, because it specifies two relatively straightforward rights: (1) trial by jury and (2) finding of facts made by a jury can not be appealed or "re-examined."

> *In suits at common law, where the value in controversy shall exceed twenty dollars, the right of trial by jury shall be preserved, and no fact tried by a jury shall be otherwise re-examined in any Court of the United States, than according to the rules of common law.*

You may note a phrase in that amendment with which you may not be familiar: "the rules of common law."

What, exactly, are "the rules of common law," and what, while we're at it, do we mean by "common law"?

The Oxford English Dictionary provides the simplest explanation of what is meant by common law: "The part of English law that is derived from custom and judicial precedent rather than statutes. Often contrasted with statutory law."

The Seventh Amendment continued English traditions in the establishment of what first year students at law school know as civil procedure. It does not apply at all to the other general area of law: criminal procedure.

Here is another important distinction to understand: the difference between civil law and criminal law.

"Criminal law deals with behavior that is or can be construed as an offense against the public, society, or the state - even if the immediate victim is an individual. Examples are murder, assault, theft, and drunken driving," the Encylopedia Britannica explains.

"Civil law deals with behavior that constitutes an injury to an individual or other private party, such as a corporation. Examples are defamation (including libel and slander), breach of contract, negligence resulting in injury or death, and property damage," the Encylopedia Britannica adds.

"Traditionally, the Supreme Court has treated the Seventh Amendment as preserving the right of trial by jury in civil cases as it 'existed under the English common law when the amendment was adopted'," the Legal Information Institute notes.

The Supreme Court added some details to what trial by jury "under the English common law" meant. The jury size could be the traditional "twelve men," but it could also be as small as six. Of equal importance, in civil trials, the jury verdict must be unanimous, again, as the Legal Information Institute notes:

Joseph Story served on the Supreme Court from 1811 to 1845.

The right was to "a trial by a jury of twelve men, in the presence and under the superintendence of a judge empowered to instruct them on the law and to advise them on the facts and (except in acquittal of a criminal charge) to set aside their verdict if in his opinion it is against the law or the evidence." Decision of the jury must be by unanimous verdict. In Colgrove v. Battin, however, the Court by a five-to-four vote held that rules adopted in a federal district court authorizing civil juries composed of six persons were permissible under the Seventh Amendment and congressional enactments.

The first judicial ruling on the Seventh Amendment came in 1812 in a case known as *United States v. Wonson*, where "the government challenged the accuracy of a jury verdict, and asked the appellate court to reverse the verdict or resubmit the case to a new jury," as Brandon Boxler wrote in the Richmond Journal of Law and the Public Interest:

Judge [Joseph] Story began his analysis by noting that, "when the constitution was submitted to the people for adoption, one of the most powerful objections urged against it was, that in civil causes it did not secure the trial of facts by a jury.

He reasoned that the Framers passed the Seventh Amendment "to remove the weight of this objection" and prevent judges from intruding either directly or indirectly - into the province of the jury.

Thus, because he was constitutionally prohibited from reexamining the jury's factual determinations, Judge Story denied the government's request for relief.

The *United States v. Wonson* case is a little bit unusual because it established a significant precedent not in a decision made by the Supreme Court, the highest court of the land, but in the Court of Appeals, which is the level of judiciary just below the Supreme Court.

As a reminder, the Constitution authorize Congress to establish the Supreme Court and "inferior" courts.

The Judiciary Act of 1789 did that by establishing a number of district courts around the county - where federal cases were initially heard. Litigants who lose

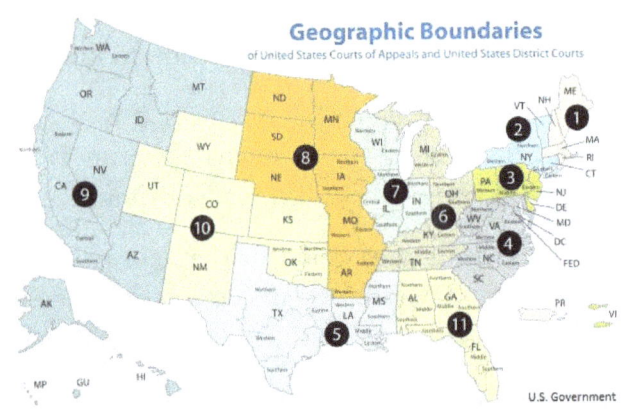

Today there are eleven Circuit Courts of appeal, each of which have about 16 judges.

at the district court level can appeal to the next level - the Circuit Court. There are eleven such Circuit Courts today, divided by geographical region of the country.

Litigants who lose in the Circuit Court have one final appeal - to the Supreme Court.

Since there is no higher court, the Supreme Court decision then becomes the precedent for all of the country to follow.

United States v. Wonson was never appealed to the Supreme Court, in part because the majority decision in the case was written by Associate Justice Joseph Story, while serving on the circuit court white at the time had one district judge and one Supreme Court Justice.

Story was one of the longest serving justices in the history of the Supreme Court, serving thirty-three years until his death in 1845.

He is perhaps best known for his majority decision in the famous *Amistad* case, which was made into a movie in 1997 by Stephen Spielberg.

Chapter Discussion Questions

(1) Should the 20-dollar stipulation of the Seventh Amendment be revised?

(2) What is the difference between the Seventh Amendment and the 'double jeopardy' clause in the Fifth Amendment?

Chapter 17

The Eighth Amendment

The Eighth Amendment contains one of the most famous phrases in American judicial history: "cruel and unusual punishment."

That phrase over the past half century has been the rallying cry around which opponents of capital punishment gather.

But the Eighth Amendment is an important protector of two other rights: the prohibition of excessive bail requirements and the prohibition of the imposition of excessive fines:

> *Excessive bail shall not be required, nor excessive fines imposed, nor cruel and unusual punishments inflicted.*

The amendment protects the rights of the individual by prohibiting three specific acts of the state:

(1) Excessive bail shall not be required.

(2) Excessive fines shall not be imposed.

(3) Cruel and unusual punishment shall not be inflicted.

We begin our discussion of the Eighth Amendment with the best known clause: the prohibition of "cruel and unusual punishment," which opponents of capital punishment have cited over the past half century as proof that the execution of prisoners for murder or any severe crime is not constitutional.

There are two elements here to consider.

First, the standard that applies is what the Framers considered to be "cruel and unusual punishment" at the time the amendment was ratified in 1791. The world two hundred years ago was much different than the world we live in today.

Some things people consider to be "cruel" today were, in many cases not given a second thought in 1791, nor were they considered out of the ordinary.

"Unusual punishment" in 1791 - even in the United States and England - has a different connotation than it does in modern America.

CRUEL AND UNUSUAL PUNISHMENT AND THE DEATH PENALTY (Capital Punishment)

"Capital punishment is currently authorized in 31 states, by the federal government and the U.S. military," according to the National Conference of State Legislatures:

> *In recent years, New Mexico (2009), Illinois (2011), Connecticut (2012) and Maryland (2013) have legislatively abolished the death penalty, replacing it with a sentence of life imprisonment with no possibility for parole. The Nebraska Legislature also abolished capital punishment in 2015, but it was reinstated by a statewide vote in 2016. Additionally, courts in Delaware recently ruled that the state's capital punishment law is unconstitutional. States across the country will continue to debate its fairness, reliability and cost of implementation.*

Since colonial days, capital punishment had been considered a legal and appropriate punishment for the crime of murder, and other similarly heinous offenses.

In the 1950s, political opposition and legal challenges to the death penalty began to increase. The number of executions for capital crimes began to decline.

In a 1972 case, *Furman v. Georgia*, the Supreme Court ruled in a 5 to 4 decision "that the imposition and carrying out of the death penalty in these cases constitute cruel and unusual punishment in violation of the Eighth and Fourteenth Amendments. The judgment in each case is therefore reversed insofar as it leaves undisturbed the death sentence imposed, and the cases are remanded for further proceedings."

31 states have the death penalty, 19 do not.

Four years later in 1976, the Supreme Court held in a 7 to 2 decision in the case of *Gregg v. Georgia* that capital punishment was constitutional:

> *The basic concern of Furman centered on those defendants who were being condemned to death capriciously and arbitrarily. Under the procedures before the Court in that case, sentencing authorities were not directed to give attention to the nature or circumstances of the crime committed or to the character or record of the defendant. Left unguided, juries imposed the death sentence in a way that could only be called freakish. The new Georgia sentencing procedures, by contrast, focus the jury's attention on the particularized nature of the crime and the particularized characteristics of the individual defendant. While the jury is permitted to consider any aggravating or mitigating circumstances, it must find and identify at least one statutory aggravating factor before it may impose a penalty of death. In this way, the jury's discretion is channeled. No longer [p207] can a jury wantonly and freakishly impose the death sentence; it is always circumscribed by the legislative guidelines. In addition, the review function of the Supreme Court of Georgia affords additional assurance that the concerns that prompted our decision in Furman are not present to any significant degree in the Georgia procedure applied here.*

> *For the reasons expressed in this opinion, we hold that the statutory system under which Gregg was sentenced to death does not violate the Constitution.*

The political and legal arguments for and against capital punishment continue.

"There are two reasons for arguing that the death penalty is a 'cruel and unusual punishment', and thus unconstitutional," The Economist Magazine, a long-established British publication that covers American political and legal issues, argued in 2014:

> One was on grim display in Arizona on July 23rd, when Joseph Wood, a double-murderer, took nearly two gasping, choking hours to die by lethal injection. The other came under legal attack on July 16th, when a federal judge, Cormac Carney, struck down capital punishment in California for being too slow and capricious.
>
> Of the more than 900 people California has sentenced to death since 1978, only 13 have been executed. The last one died in 2006. The same year, a federal court ruled that California's mode of lethal injection carried a risk that "an inmate will suffer pain so extreme" that it should be considered cruel and unusual.

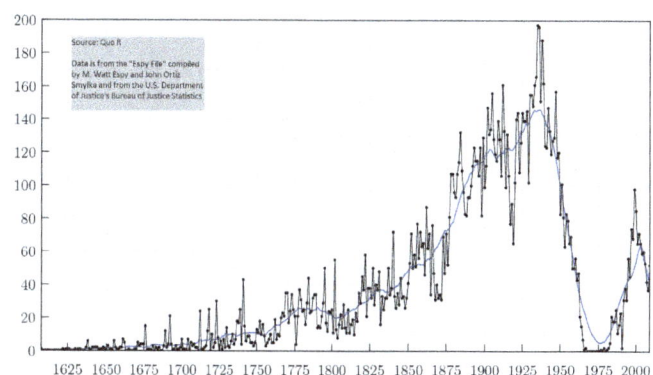

On a per capita basis, there were more executions for those convicted of capital crimes in the United States in the decades following the ratification of the Eighth Amendment than there are today.

> With Mr. Carney's ruling, the state's system of capital punishment has been judged doubly unfit. The average prisoner who is executed in California has spent 25 years on death row - much longer than the national average of nearly 16 years. Such long delays make it unlikely that capital punishment deters other potential murderers, ruled Mr. Carney.

"Nonsense," say supporters of maintaining capital punishment for those who commit heinous crimes.

"No serious constitutional argument can be made against the death penalty. The endless campaigns to ban it cost taxpayers millions to defend," attorneys David Rivkin Jr. and Andrew Grossman wrote in an op-ed at the *Los Angeles Times* in 2011:

> Every legal argument against the death penalty begins with the 8th or 5th Amendment. The 8th bars "cruel and unusual punishments," and the 5th guarantees "due process of law" before a person can be "deprived of life, liberty or property." But there is no serious constitutional argument against the death penalty. The 5th Amendment itself recognizes the existence of "capital" crimes, and executions were common before and after the Constitution's framing. No framer ever suggested that the Constitution divested states of this part of their historical punishment power, nor has there been a constitutional amendment that does so.
>
> Matters not addressed by the Constitution are left to the democratic process and, in the main, to the states. As in Europe and Canada, a solid majority of American citizens supports the death penalty, believing it to serve both as a deterrent and an appropriate societal response to particularly heinous crimes. Unlike in Europe and Canada, however, U.S. courts and political leaders have not overridden public opinion to end the practice.
>
> But they have tried. At the tail end of the criminal rights revolution of the 1960s and 1970s, the Supreme Court put a halt to all executions. While the public acquiesced or supported other innovations in

criminal law, such as Miranda warnings, the death penalty moratorium was less well received. Pushed by their citizens, states passed new laws requiring juries to find specific "aggravating factors" justifying the death penalty, and in 1976, the court allowed executions to resume on that basis.

A Gallup Poll conducted in 2004 found "that three-fourths (75%) of Americans agree that 'states should be allowed to execute prisoners sentenced to the death penalty by means of lethal injection.' Twenty-one percent said it should not be permitted because it is a form of cruel and unusual punishment."

OTHER APPLICATIONS OF CRUEL AND UNUSUAL PUNISHMENT

The "cruel and unusual punishment" clause has been applied to punishments other than capital punishment as well. One such punishment is loss of citizenship.

"Divestiture of the citizenship of a natural born citizen was held in *Trop v. Dulles*, again by a divided Court, to be constitutionally forbidden as a penalty more cruel and 'more primitive than torture,' inasmuch as it entailed statelessness or 'the total destruction of the individual's status in organized society,'" the Legal Information Institute noted.

EXCESSIVE BAIL

Chief Justice Fred Vinson's majority opinion in the 1951 case *Stack v. Boyle* expressed the Court's view on excessive bail.

"This traditional right to freedom before conviction permits the unhampered preparation of a defense, and serves to prevent the infliction of punishment prior to conviction . . . Unless this right to bail before trial is preserved, the presumption of innocence, secured only after centuries of struggle, would lose its meaning," Vinson wrote.

"The bail clause was lifted with slight changes from the English Bill of Rights Act. In England that clause has never been thought to accord a right to bail in all cases, but merely to provide that bail shall not be excessive in those cases where it is proper to grant bail. When this clause was carried over into our Bill of Rights, nothing was said that indicated any different concept," Justice Stanley Reed wrote a year later, in the Court's majority opinion in *Carlson v. Landon*.

Chief Justice Frederick Moore Vinson served on the U.S. Supreme Court from 1946 to 1953.

EXCESSIVE FINES

The excessive fines clause of the Eighth Amendment was largely a footnote for some time, but that has changed in the past several decades.

"The 'excessive fines' clause surfaces (among other places) in cases of civil and criminal forfeiture, for example when property is seized during a drug raid," the Legal Information Institute reports.

"For years the Supreme Court had little to say with reference to excessive fines," the Legal Information Institute reported:

In an early case, it held that it had no appellate jurisdiction to revise the sentence of an inferior court, even though the excessiveness of the fines was apparent on the face of the record. In a dissent, Justice

Brandeis once contended that the denial of second-class mailing privileges to a newspaper on the basis of its past conduct imposed additional mailing cost, a fine in effect, which, since the costs grew indefinitely each day, was an unusual punishment proscribed by this Amendment. The Court has elected to deal with the issue of fines levied upon indigents, resulting in imprisonment upon inability to pay, in terms of the equal protection clause, thus obviating any necessity to develop the meaning of "excessive fines" as applied to the person sentenced. So too, the Court has held the Clause inapplicable to civil jury awards of punitive damages in cases between private parties, "when the government neither has prosecuted the action nor has any right to receive a share of the damages awarded."

As political controversies over the death penalty and civil asset forfeitures continue to expand, the Eighth Amendment is likely to be an increasingly relevant part of the Constitution in future Supreme Court decisions.

Chapter Discussion Questions

(1) In your view, has the meaning of "cruel and unusual punishment" changed over time?

(2) In your opinion, should there be a death penalty because a majority of people support it?

Chapter 18

The Ninth Amendment
By: Claudia Henneberry

The Constitution was written for one particular purpose - to limit the powers of the general, or, national, government, therein *securing the blessings of liberty* by protecting the individual's natural rights. It is simply outlined in the Preamble, drafted brilliantly by Gouverneur Morris, a native New Yorker who represented Pennsylvania at the Constitutional Convention, and made clear the primary purposes for the Constitution - that the people are the ones for whom and by whom it was created beginning with the revolutionary words, *We the People.*

During the consideration of the Bill of Rights, the concern by the Federalists was that if they specified certain rights of the people to be guarded by the national government, what if they neglected others? How could they be sure that all the people's God-given rights would be protected?

Among others, this was a major concern for James Wilson, a Pennsylvania lawyer who would later be appointed to serve on the first Supreme Court. Supporters of the Constitution, or Federalists, such as James Wilson and Alexander Hamilton, argued that a bill of rights would be dangerous. Enumerating any rights, Wilson argued, might imply that all those not listed were surrendered. And, because it was impossible to enumerate all the rights of the people, a bill of rights might actually be construed to justify the government's power to limit any liberties of the people that were not enumerated, or, listed.

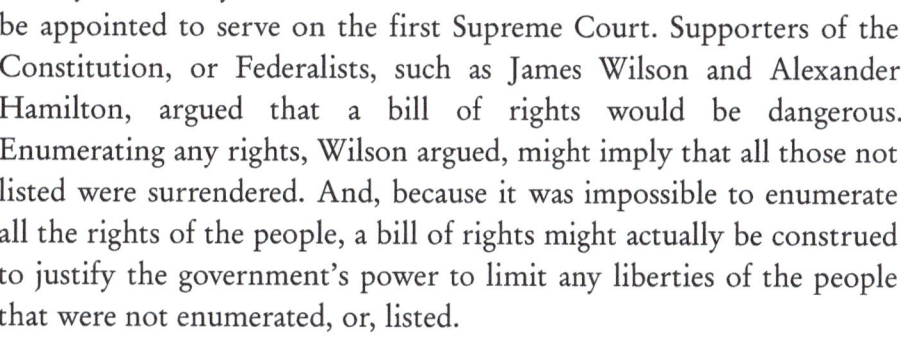
Gouverneur Morris

Justice James Wilson

Actually, what the Federalists really believed about the Bill of Rights in general, not just about the Ninth Amendment, was that this list of rights would diminish the power of the national government.

James Madison basically agreed with Wilson's idea that rights not included in the Bill of Rights may be abused by the national government, but he may have had a solution. In a speech given on June 8, 1789 in the first federal Congress under the newly adopted Constitution, Madison now supported the "bill of rights." He suggested that "It has been objected also against a bill of rights, that, by enumerating particular exceptions to the grant of power, it would disparage those rights which were not placed in that enumeration, and it might follow by implication, that those rights which were not singled out, were intended to be assigned into the hands of the general government, and were consequently insecure. This is one of the most plausible arguments I have ever heard urged against the admission of a bill of rights into this system; but, I conceive, that may be guarded against."

Madison's speech included his proposed solution that would become the Ninth Amendment: "The exceptions here or elsewhere in the constitution, made in favor of particular rights, shall not be so construed as to diminish the just importance of other rights retained by the people; or as to enlarge the powers delegated by the constitution; but either as actual limitations of such powers, or as inserted merely for greater caution."

Congress re-worded Madison's proposal and it became the Ninth Amendment to the Constitution:

The enumeration in the Constitution of certain rights shall not be construed to deny or disparage others retained by the people.

The Ninth Amendment is probably the least understood of the Bill of Rights. The words literally mean: The enumeration (listing) in the Constitution of certain rights shall not be construed (understood or interpreted) to deny (keep from) or disparage (put down or belittle) others retained (always held) by the people.

It means that each individual person, not groups of people, is born with certain natural rights and those rights always belonged to that person before the establishment of any government and that those rights, whether listed or not, must be protected by the government.

Roger Sherman, a representative from Connecticut, explained it as, "The people have certain natural rights which are retained by them when they enter into Society." Sherman, who served on the House Select Committee to draft the Bill of Rights in 1791, went on to give examples of natural rights, "Such are the rights of conscience in matters of religion; of acquiring property, and of pursuing happiness & Safety; of Speaking, writing and publishing their Sentiments with decency and freedom; of peaceably assembling to consult their common good, and of applying to Government by petition or remonstrance for redress of grievances."

Of course, most of those rights are enumerated in the First Amendment and others, such as acquiring property, pursuing happiness and safety are not, yet these rights were commonly understood by our framers like Sherman and George Mason to be natural. Many state constitutions named these as rights of their citizens.

Representative Roger Sherman from Connecticut, helped to draft the Bill of Rights

The Ninth Amendment makes clear that the people are separate from the national (and the state) governments, that only they have rights. The people give powers to the governments, but the people also have rights that are not delegated to either the national nor state governments.

Because the Ninth Amendment does not specifically identify certain rights, it has been up to the courts to decide what is and what is not covered. The amendment is regarded as a preventative measure to keep the government from expanding its power. There has never been a judicial decision based solely on the Ninth Amendment. It has simply been cited along with other amendments in court decisions.

In 1833, the Supreme Court ruled in *Barron v. Baltimore* that the Ninth Amendment pertained to the national courts only and not to state governments. Basically, that meant that, originally, the amendment protected the rights of the people from expanding power of the national government which is a government of enumerated powers.

By July of 1868, the Fourteenth Amendment was ratified that contains the "privileges or immunities clause" which limits the powers of the state governments. The Ninth and the Fourteenth work together to ensure all rights are protected at every level of government.

The right to privacy, for example, is not specifically mentioned in our Constitution, however, the Supreme Court has regarded it as one of those unenumerated rights guaranteed by the Ninth and Fourteenth Amendments. In the case of *Griswold v. Connecticut* (1965), the Director of Planned Parenthood, Estelle Griswold, and a medical doctor had opened a birth control clinic. They were arrested for violating Connecticut's 1879 law prohibiting the use of "any drug, medicinal article, or instrument for the purpose of preventing conception."

In a seven to two decision, the court ruled that the Connecticut law was unconstitutional, that it violated the "right to marital privacy," and that even though the Bill of Rights does not mention "privacy," it is inherent and implied in other protections provided by the Constitution, and that the "right to privacy" is seen as a right of individuals to be protected against governmental intrusion into their lives. This is an example of the court's use of the Ninth and Fourteenth Amendments.

The Ninth Amendment is sometimes referred to as "the silent amendment" due to its controversial and misunderstood meaning. In 1987, Robert Bork, a U. S. District judge, legal scholar and an advocate of originalism (interpreting the Constitution according to the founders' intentions), referred to the Ninth as an "inkblot" which hid its true meaning. He said just as judges should not guess what was under an inkblot, they should not guess the amendment's meaning.

The Ninth Amendment is a testament to the framers of this nation in their keen understanding that we are born with certain unalienable rights that must be protected. They ensured with this amendment that the national government could not exploit those rights not listed in the Constitution that are sacred and also retained by We the People.

Chapter Discussion Questions

(1) What are the advantages and disadvantages of having the judiciary determine the meaning of the Ninth Amendment?

(2) Do you agree with the justice in the Griswold decision that privacy was a right contained in the Ninth Amendment?

Chapter 19

Revisiting the Tenth Amendment

As we wrote about extensively in Chapter Five, the foundational concept of Federalism in the United States Constitution is most specifically outlined in the Tenth Amendment:

The powers not delegated to the United States by the Constitution, nor prohibited by it to the States, are reserved to the States respectively, or to the people.

One aspect of the Tenth Amendment very relevant to contemporary issues is that it makes absolutely no mention of reserving any powers not delegated to the federal government to cities or counties that are subdivisions of state governments.

Indeed, the Constitution grants powers to only three entities - (1) the federal government, which it grants limited and enumerated powers, (2) the state governments, which along with (3) the people - and by that the Founders meant each of us as individuals - have all the powers not specifically delegated to the federal government reserved to them.

The text of the Constitution clearly enumerates 33 specific powers granted to the national government, as we explained in Chapter Six on the Separation of Powers:

Article 1, Section 8 of the Constitution enumerates 19 specific powers granted to the legislative branch of the national government.

Article II, Sections 2 and 3 of the Constitution enumerates 13 specific powers granted to the executive branch of the national government.

Article III, Sections 1 and 2 of the Constitution enumerates 1 specific power granted to the judicial branch of the national government.

The important point to remember about the Tenth Amendment is this: If a power is not one of these 33 specific powers granted to the national government, it is reserved to the States, or to the people.

As a reminder, and a recap from Chapter Five, Article I, Section 8 enumerates these 19 specific powers granted to the Congress:

Section 8

(1) The Congress shall have Power To lay and collect Taxes, Duties, Imposts and Excises,

(2) to pay the Debts and provide for the common Defence and general Welfare of the United States; but all Duties, Imposts and Excises shall be uniform throughout the United States;

(3) To borrow Money on the credit of the United States;

(4) To regulate Commerce with foreign Nations, and among the several States, and with the Indian Tribes;

(5) To establish an uniform Rule of Naturalization, and uniform Laws on the subject of Bankruptcies throughout the United States;

(6) To coin Money, regulate the Value thereof, and of foreign Coin, and fix the Standard of Weights and Measures;

(7) To provide for the Punishment of counterfeiting the Securities and current Coin of the United States;

(8) To establish Post Offices and post Roads;

(9) To promote the Progress of Science and useful Arts, by securing for limited Times to Authors and Inventors the exclusive Right to their respective Writings and Discoveries;

(10) To constitute Tribunals inferior to the supreme Court;

(11) To define and punish Piracies and Felonies committed on the high Seas, and Offences against the Law of Nations;

(12) To declare War, grant Letters of Marque and Reprisal, and make Rules concerning Captures on Land and Water;

(13) To raise and support Armies, but no Appropriation of Money to that Use shall be for a longer Term than two Years;

(14) To provide and maintain a Navy;

(15) To make Rules for the Government and Regulation of the land and naval Forces;

(16) To provide for calling forth the Militia to execute the Laws of the Union, suppress Insurrections and repel Invasions;

(17) To provide for organizing, arming, and disciplining, the Militia, and for governing such Part of them as may be employed in the Service of the United States, reserving to the States respectively, the Appointment of the Officers, and the Authority of training the Militia according to the discipline prescribed by Congress;

(18) To exercise exclusive Legislation in all Cases whatsoever, over such District (not exceeding ten Miles square) as may, by Cession of particular States, and the Acceptance of Congress, become the Seat of the Government of the United States, and to exercise like Authority over all Places purchased by the Consent of the Legislature of the State in which the Same shall be, for the Erection of Forts, Magazines, Arsenals, dock-Yards, and other needful Buildings; - And

(19) To make all Laws which shall be necessary and proper for carrying into Execution the foregoing

Powers, and all other Powers vested by this Constitution in the Government of the United States, or in any Department or Officer thereof.

Article II, Sections 2 and 3 enumerate these 13 specific powers granted to the president:

Section 2

The President shall be

(1) Commander in Chief of the Army and Navy of the United States, and

(2) of the Militia of the several States, when called into the actual Service of the United States;

(3) he may require the Opinion, in writing, of the principal Officer in each of the executive Departments, upon any Subject relating to the Duties of their respective Offices, and

(4) he shall have Power to grant Reprieves and Pardons for Offences against the United States, except in Cases of Impeachment.

(5) He shall have Power, by and with the Advice and Consent of the Senate, to make Treaties, provided two thirds of the Senators present concur; and

(6) he shall nominate, and by and with the Advice and Consent of the Senate, shall appoint Ambassadors, other public Ministers and Consuls, Judges of the supreme Court, and all other Officers of the United States, whose Appointments are not herein otherwise provided for, and which shall be established by Law: but the Congress may by Law vest the Appointment of such inferior Officers, as they think proper, in the President alone, in the Courts of Law, or in the Heads of Departments.

(7) The President shall have Power to fill up all Vacancies that may happen during the Recess of the Senate, by granting Commissions which shall expire at the End of their next Session.

Section 3

(8) He shall from time to time give to the Congress Information of the State of the Union, and recommend to their Consideration such Measures as he shall judge necessary and expedient; he may, on extraordinary Occasions,

(9) convene both Houses, or either of them, and in Case of Disagreement between them,

(10) with Respect to the Time of Adjournment, he may adjourn them to such Time as he shall think proper;

(11) he shall receive Ambassadors and other public Ministers;

(12) he shall take Care that the Laws be faithfully executed, and

(13) shall Commission all the Officers of the United States.

Article III, Sections 1 and 2 of the Constitution enumerates 1 specific power granted to the judicial branch of the national government. Section 1 vests the judicial power in the judicial branch, and Section 2 defines that power:

Section 1

(1) The judicial Power of the United States shall be vested in one supreme Court, and in such inferior

Courts as the Congress may from time to time ordain and establish. The Judges, both of the supreme and inferior Courts, shall hold their Offices during good Behaviour, and shall, at stated Times, receive for their Services a Compensation, which shall not be diminished during their Continuance in Office.

Section 2

The judicial Power shall extend to all Cases, in Law and Equity, arising under this Constitution, the Laws of the United States, and Treaties made, or which shall be made, under their Authority; - to all Cases affecting Ambassadors, other public Ministers and Consuls; - to all Cases of admiralty and maritime Jurisdiction; - to Controversies to which the United States shall be a Party; - to Controversies between two or more States; - between a State and Citizens of another State; - between Citizens of different States; - between Citizens of the same State claiming Lands under Grants of different States, and between a State, or the Citizens thereof, and foreign States, Citizens or Subjects.

Over the past several decades, a number of local governments have challenged the supremacy of the federal government in the enumerated powers granted to it by the Constitution, and the state governments, in those powers reserved to them by the Constitution.

These local governments - all of which are chartered and authorized by their respective state governments - are essentially claiming their own sovereignty over both the federal and state governments in areas that are clearly defined as authorities granted only to the federal and state governments.

The most blatant area in which this claim of unconstitutional sovereignty is advanced by state and local governments is in the area of immigration law, and specifically in their adoption of what are referred to as "sanctuary city laws" that protect illegal aliens residing in their jurisdiction from the enforcement of federal laws.

This argument is primarily political, but the tactics used by the local governments to claim sovereignty are in the legal system as well.

"According to tracking by the Center for Immigration Studies," CNN notes, "roughly 300 sanctuary jurisdictions rejected more than 17,000 detention requests [from the federal government], between January 1, 2014 and September 30, 2015."

One of the coming battles that center around the Tenth Amendment will deal with the claim by local jurisdictions that they have sovereignty over the federal government as well as their respective state governments.

Chapter Discussion Questions

(1) What criteria would you use to determine if a power was reserved to the states or to the people?

(2) Why were the Anti-Federalists in favor of the Tenth Amendment?

(3) Why were the Federalists opposed to the Tenth Amendment?

Chapter 20

Judicial Review

The **Separation of Powers** and **Federalism** are two foundational concepts of the Constitution, based on the idea that checks and balances between competing interests will prevent any one individual or group from obtaining and exercising abusive powers within our republic.

In the national government, the checks and balances of the Separation of Powers were designed within the Constitution, which gave specific powers to the three equal branches of government - executive, legislative, and judicial - but also placed limits on the powers of each branch.

The legislative branch, which passes laws, approves Presidential nominations for Cabinet positions, the Supreme Court, other federal courts, and other appointments, appropriates money, and can impeach the president and federal judges.

The executive branch can veto legislation, nominate judges, and administers the day-to-day operations of the government.

The Separation of Powers

The judicial branch has asserted, without much resistance, the power to declare laws passed by Congress and Presidential actions unconstitutional - a principle commonly known as "judicial review."

Unlike the powers granted the two other branches - the executive and the legislative - "judicial review" is not explicitly spelled out in the text of the Constitution, though it has become "one of the distinctive features of United States constitutional law," according to FindLaw.com.

"It is no small wonder, then, to find that the power of the federal courts to test federal and state legislative enactments and other actions by the standards of what the Constitution grants and withholds is nowhere expressly conveyed," FindLaw.com noted:

But it is hardly noteworthy that its legitimacy has been challenged from the first, and, while now accepted generally, it still has detractors and its supporters disagree about its doctrinal basis and its application. Although it was first asserted in Marbury v. Madison to strike down an act of Congress as inconsistent with the Constitution, judicial review did not spring full-blown from the brain of Chief Justice Marshall.

"Although judicial review is consistent with several provisions of the Constitution and the argument for its existence may be derived from these provisions, they do not compel the conclusion that the Framers intended judicial review nor that it must exist," FindLaw.com concluded.

As University of San Diego Professor of Law Michael Rappaport, director of the Center for the Study of Constitutional Originalism, wrote in 2010, "judicial review is not just made up."

"In recent years, scholars have argued persuasively that the Framers expected judicial review of the Constitution," he pointed out.

John Marshall served as Chief Justice of the Supreme Court from 1801 to 1835 and wrote the landmark Marbury v. Madison decision.

Still, since there is no specific text to explicitly support the concept of judicial review in the Constitution, our current acceptance of the principle derives from the precedent established in one peculiar case that did not seem particularly earth-shaking at the time the Marshall Court announced its decision on it in 1803: *Marbury v. Madison*.

"William Marbury, a self-made man and Adams loyalist, was one of the 'midnight' justices whom John Adams appointed during his last days in office. The Federalist Senate confirmed his appointment on Adams's last day as president, but after Jefferson assumed office and found that Marbury's commission had still not been delivered, he ordered that it be withheld. Marbury subsequently sought from the Supreme Court a writ of mandamus that would compel Secretary of State Madison to deliver his commission," Lynne Cheney wrote in her biography of the fourth president, ***James Madison: A Life Reconsidered***.

William Marbury, plaintiff in Marbury v. Madison

John Marshall, a Virginia Federalist, former Secretary of State for President Adams, and staunch opponent of President Thomas Jefferson (despite the fact they were third-cousins), had become the nation's fourth Chief Justice of the Supreme Court just two months before Adams gave Marbury his last minute position. Ironically, it was Marshall who had failed to deliver Marbury his commission when it was first issued by President Adams because he was still Secretary of State at the time - he held both offices concurrently for the last two months of the Adams administration.

Marbury did not sue Marshall, however, he sued James Madison, his successor as Secretary of State under President Jefferson, who also failed to deliver the commission.

"In 1803, the [Supreme Court] issued its opinion, saying that Marbury was entitled to the commission, but that the Supreme Court could not issue the writ [requiring Madison to deliver the commission] because the section of the Judiciary Act of 1789 that would have permitted the court to do so was unconstitutional," Cheney wrote:

> *On the surface, the outcome seemed positive for the Jefferson administration. But Marshall's decision also allowed the chief justice to avoid direct confrontation with the administration, which was riding high, even while the president, whom he despised as only one Virginia cousin could another, had broken the law.*

As Oyez.org framed the questions in the case:

> *(1) Do the plaintiffs have a right to receive their commissions?*
>
> *(2) Can they sue for their commissions in court?*
>
> *(3) Does the Supreme Court have the authority to order the delivery of their commissions?*

In 1803, at the time of the Marbury v. Madison decision, two branches of government had their own buildings. The executive branch was housed in The White House and the legislative branch had the Capitol Building. The Supreme Court was relegated to a modest room at the Capitol. By 1810, it moved into these more gracious chambers in the Capitol, where it met until 1860. It moved into the Old Senate Chamber in 1860, where it met until it finally moved into its own building in 1935.

The four members of the six member court who were present for the oral arguments in the case (Chief Justice Marshall, William Paterson, Samuel Chase, and Bushrod Washington were present. Alfred Moore and William Cushing were absent due to illness) unanimously decided in Marbury's favor. There was, however, a twist to the case.

"Though Marbury was entitled to it, the Court was unable to grant it because Section 13 of the Judiciary Act of 1789 conflicted with Article III Section 2 of the U.S. Constitution and was therefore null and void," Oyez.org noted.

"Of all the disappointed office seekers in American history, only William Marbury obtained the honor of having his portrait hang in the chambers of the United States Supreme Court. In the Justices' small dining room designated by Chief Justice Warren Burger as "the John Marshall room," Chief Justice Burger placed the portraits of Marbury and James Madison, Marbury's legal adversary, as if the two men, in partnership, had given the Chief Justice his commission to practice judicial review," Professor David Forte wrote in his 1996 article, *"Marbury's Travail: Federalist Politics and William Marbury's Appointment as Justice of the Peace."*

"Particularly in contrast with the annexation of Louisiana [in 1803], the decision handed down by the Supreme Court in *Marbury v. Madison* seemed at the time of little significance," Cheney wrote.

But, as it turns out, it was of very great significance.

"The decision in *Marbury v. Madison* has never been disturbed, although it has been criticized and has had opponents throughout our history. It not only carried the day in the federal courts, but from its announcement judicial review by state courts of local legislation under local constitutions made rapid progress and was securely established in all States by 1850," FindLaw.com noted.

The Justia US Law website identifies a total of 165 "acts of Congress held unconstitutional in whole or in part by the Supreme Court of the United States," between 1803 and 2008.

"[T]he concept of judicial review has made the courts - and in particular the U.S. Supreme Court - the ultimate arbiter of whether a state or federal law violates the Constitution. Just as baseball umpires are sometimes criticized for their calls on the playing field, the exercise of judicial review has periodically exposed the Court to complaints that it has erred either by being too aggressive in striking down laws (in conventional parlance, 'judicial activism'), or by not being aggressive enough in overturning laws (sometimes called 'judicial passivity')," Mark Pulliam wrote at National Review in 2015.

In the end, however, the standard for judicial review is left to the discretion of the majority of the nine justices who serve on the Supreme Court.

And sometimes when exercising this standard, they get it wrong, as they did the second time they struck down a law passed by Congress as unconstitutional fifty-four years after *Marbury v. Madison*. The Supreme Court used the power of judicial review in the 1857 Dred Scott decision, perhaps the worst decision ever made by the Supreme Court.

Chief Justice Roger Taney, along with four other members of the Supreme Court in 1857, was a slave owner.

That decision declared the Missouri Compromise of 1820 unconstitutional and returned Dred Scott, a slave whose owner brought him into free territory and consequently claimed his freedom, to slavery:

Not until 1857 - fifty-four years after Marbury - was a second act of Congress declared unconstitutional by the Supreme Court. In the infamous Dred Scott case (Scott v. Sandford), the Court held that the Missouri Compromise of 1820 was unconstitutional. This compromise - in addition to admitting Missouri to the Union as a slave state and Maine as a free state - had divided the remaining U.S. territory along the 36°30° north latitude line. Slavery was "forever prohibited" above the line, except for Missouri. The Court ruled in 1857 that Congress lacked the power to exclude slavery from any territory. The decision intensified the debate over slavery, which eventually exploded into the Civil War. The Dred Scott ruling was undone by the Thirteenth and Fourteenth Amendments, which outlawed slavery and extended equal protection under the law to all U.S. citizens.

In March 1861, during his first inaugural address, President Abraham Lincoln indirectly criticized the exercise of judicial review by the Supreme Court in the Dred Scot decision, an error that helped plunge the country into the Civil War:

I do not forget the position assumed by some that constitutional questions are to be decided by the Supreme Court, nor do I deny that such decisions must be binding in any case upon the parties to a suit as to the object of that suit, while they are also entitled to very high respect and consideration in all parallel cases by all other departments of the Government.

And while it is obviously possible that such decision may be erroneous in any given case, still the evil effect following it, being limited to that particular case, with the chance that it may be overruled and never become a precedent for other cases, can better be borne than could the evils of a different practice.

"At the same time, the candid citizen must confess that if the policy of the Government upon vital questions affecting the whole people is to be irrevocably fixed by decisions of the Supreme Court, the instant they are made in ordinary litigation between parties in personal actions the people will have ceased to be their own rulers, having to that extent practically resigned their Government into the hands of that eminent tribunal," Lincoln concluded.

One hundred and fifty years and more than 150 Supreme Court rulings in which judicial review has been exercised later, the principle remains controversial.

"Our supreme law - ratified by the states and binding on succeeding generations - is the Constitution (not the Declaration of Independence). The Constitution embodies legitimate rights, which the courts are not just permitted, but obligated, to enforce. At the same time, the Supreme Court has invented many 'rights' that appear nowhere in the Constitution and are, in fact, entirely the product of the justices' own personal predilections," Pulliam wrote in his 2015 National Review article:

"After the 1857 Supreme Court decision that ruled against his freedom, Dred Scott was returned to slavery, but was manumitted and given his freedom two months later in May 1857. He died of tuberculosis in 1858.

> *If a legitimate constitutional right is implicated, a court does not engage in "activism" by striking down a law that violates it. That is the court's duty. Indeed, the court would be guilty of passivity (or outright abdication) if it upheld the law. Courts are supposed to uphold laws that do not violate a legitimate constitutional right, no matter how foolish the judges may think they are. That is exercising "judicial restraint" (a good thing). Conversely, if a court fails to strike down a law that does violate the Constitution (as the Supreme Court arguably did with Obamacare in NFIB v. Sebelius [2012]), it is not engaged in "judicial restraint," but is guilty of passivity/abdication (a bad thing). However, giving the Court carte blanche to overturn laws for reasons not grounded in the Constitution invites judicial usurpation, which is both unprincipled and undemocratic.*

With the Supreme Court in 2016 divided between four "conservative" originalists, four "liberal" living Constitution proponents, and one swing vote, the death of the leading originalist on the Court that year,, Antonin Scalia, set off a political firestorm that displayed the kind of checks and balances envisioned by the Framers.

Then-President Obama, a Democrat, nominated Merrick Garland to the Supreme Court, a well-respected jurist whose ideology clearly aligned with the "liberal" living Constitution proponents. Replacing an originalist with a liberal would have dramatically changed the court's balance, in which a number of 5-4 cases were decided by the "swing" vote, Justice Anthony Kennedy.

The Republican controlled Senate, led by Majority Leader Mitch McConnell (R-Kentucky), refused to confirm or even hold hearings on Garland's nomination.

With the Presidential election of 2016 looming, the Republicans argued, let the next President elected by the American people pick this ninth critical Supreme Court justice.

When Republican Donald Trump won that election, he quickly nominated an originalist, Neil Gorsuch, to succeed Justice Scalia on the Supreme Court.

The Senate, still controlled by the Republicans, confirmed Gorsuch in 2017, but only after they took advantage of a new reading of the Senate rules introduced only a few years earlier by the Democrats, which allowed them to break a filibuster by the Democrats.

The entire process was dramatic and contentious, an example of just the sort of checks and balances the Framers had in mind at the Constitutional Convention in 1787.

When Justice Anthony Kennedy announced his retirement from the Supreme Court in June 2018, another round of checks and balances drama began.

Cooper Moran, then a rising senior at Lincoln County High School and winner of the *2018 Tennessee Star Constitution Bee*, was there to witness the drama first hand. He was in the Capitol Rotunda on July 10, 2018 just as Vice President Mike Pence escorted President Trump's Supreme Court nominee, Brett Kavanaugh, to meet several US Senators for the first time.

After a lengthy series of controversial hearings, Kavanaugh was confirmed to the Supreme Court by the U.S. Senate in a 50-48 vote on October 6, 2018.

Chapter Discussion Questions

(1) In your opinion, if the courts have the power of judicial review, does that mean the courts are unchecked by the other branches?

(2) Does it surprise you that judicial review has largely been uncontroversial?

(3) Why do you think the first use of judicial review was not controversial but the second use was?

Chapter 21

December 15, 1791:
The Date Our American Republic Was Fully Formed

On December 15, 1791, the legislature of the state of Virginia ratified ten of the 12 amendments to the Constitution proposed by Congress two years earlier, making the Bill of Rights the law of the land, and completing our country's founding document.

It had been over 15 years since the Declaration of Independence had been approved on July 4, 1776 by the Second Continental Congress. Now, after a bloody war, many fits-and-starts, and the admission of Vermont nine months earlier on March 4 as the 14th state, the complete covenant that bound the new republic had been sealed.

It had also been more than four years since Benjamin Franklin, stepping out of the final day of the Constitutional Convention, told Mrs. Powel the delegates had given the citizens of the fledgling United States, "a Republic, if you can keep it." All four years had been necessary to fulfill the agreement made to the Anti-Federalists in Massachusetts, New Hampshire, South Carolina, Virginia, and New York, during the ratification conventions in those states that in return for ratifying the Constitution, amendments would be supported in the first federal Congress.

Thanks largely to James Madison, and the integrity of all those leaders who sided with the Federalists, that commitment was fulfilled. While it is interesting to speculate on whether the new republic would have lasted had a Bill of Rights not been proposed and adopted, such speculation, thankfully, remains just that.

In the subsequent two centuries plus, we've added seventeen additional amendments to the Constitution.

Independence Hall, Philadelphia, Pennsylvania

The good news that we could tell Mr. Franklin and Ms. Powel, should they by some mysterious act return to our day and time to check up on America is this: we have kept the republic - so far.

But as Franklin said, and President Ronald Reagan reminded us, "we are but one generation away from losing freedom forever."

Though some may argue that the current generation of leadership in America has set a rather low bar on keeping the republic and preserving freedom in America, as of 2019, the printing of this first edition of *The Star News Digital Media Guide to the Constitution and the Bill of Rights for Secondary School Students*, we still have our republic.

The challenge of keeping our republic for the balance of the 21st century, and even into the 22nd, will soon be in the hands of the generation of secondary school students reading this book, not the generation of this book's authors.

Chapter Discussion Questions

(1) Do you agree that the secular covenant that established the United States of America was not fully formed until the Bill of Rights was ratified on December 15, 1791 and became part of the Constitution?

(2) Do you - as a secondary school student in the 2019-2020 academic year - have a civic duty throughout your lifetime as a citizen of the United States to ensure that we "keep the republic"?

(3) If so, what are the elements of that civic duty?

(4) If not, why not?

Acknowledgements

This 2019 first edition of *The Star News Digital Media Guide to the Constitution and Bill of Rights for Secondary School Students* began as a series of articles first published in 2017 by *The Tennessee Star*, which is now owned by Star News Digital Media, Inc., a company formed in 2018 for the purpose of operating news sites, including *The Tennessee Star, The Ohio Star, The Virginia Star*, and more; and publishing books about the Constitution, American history, civics, and other elements of the American experience for secondary school students.

In the fall of 2017, the series led to the idea of organizing the first *Tennessee Star Constitution Bee*, a competition for secondary school students in Tennessee that tested knowledge of the Constitution based upon a pilot edition of this book, which was published in July 2017 and contained the most important articles from *The Tennessee Star Constitution Series*.

We thank The Polk Foundation, whose financial support helped us conduct the 2017 *Tennessee Star Constitution Bee*, and two subsequent bees for secondary school students in Tennessee in 2018 and 2019, as well as the Andrew Woodfin Miller Foundation, whose financial support provided scholarships to the winners of the 2018 and 2019 *Tennessee Star Constitution Bees*.

We also thank the volunteers who have helped make *The Tennessee Star Constitution Bee* possible: Mike Sheppard, Claudia Henneberry, John Harris, David Garcia, Laura and Kevin Baigert, and Norman Bobo, among others.

The 2017 pilot edition of *The Tennessee Star Guide to the Constitution and the Bill of Rights for Secondary School Students* was followed by the 2018 first edition of *The Tennessee Star Guide to the Constitution and Bill of Rights for Secondary School Students*, which in turn has been followed by this 2019 first edition of *The Star News Digital Media Guide to the Constitution and Bill of Rights for Secondary School Students*.

In 2021, we published a second printing of this first edition followed by a third printing in 2025.

Finally, we express our gratitude and thanks to Professor John Kaminski, Director of the Center for the Study of the American Constitution at the University of Wisconsin-Madison, for fact checking this 2019 first edition of *The Star News Digital Media Guide to the Constitution and Bill of Rights for Secondary School Students*.

Appendix

The United States Constitution and The Bill of Rights
Amendments 1 - 10

The United States Constitution

We the People of the United States, in Order to form a more perfect Union, establish Justice, insure domestic Tranquility, provide for the common defence, promote the general Welfare, and secure the Blessings of Liberty to ourselves and our Posterity, do ordain and establish this Constitution for the United States of America.

Article I (Article 1 - Legislative)

Section 1

All legislative Powers herein granted shall be vested in a Congress of the United States, which shall consist of a Senate and House of Representatives.

Section 2

1: The House of Representatives shall be composed of Members chosen every second Year by the People of the several States, and the Electors in each State shall have the Qualifications requisite for Electors of the most numerous Branch of the State Legislature.

2: No Person shall be a Representative who shall not have attained to the Age of twenty five Years, and been seven Years a Citizen of the United States, and who shall not, when elected, be an Inhabitant of that State in which he shall be chosen.

3: Representatives and direct Taxes shall be apportioned among the several States which may be included within this Union, according to their respective Numbers, which shall be determined by adding to the whole Number of free Persons, including those bound to Service for a Term of Years, and excluding Indians not taxed, three fifths of all other Persons. The actual Enumeration shall be made within three Years after the first Meeting of the Congress of the United States, and within every subsequent Term of ten Years, in such Manner as they shall by Law direct. The Number of Representatives shall not exceed one for every thirty Thousand, but each State shall have at Least one Representative; and until such enumeration shall be made, the State of New Hampshire shall be entitled to chuse three, Massachusetts eight, Rhode-Island and Providence Plantations one, Connecticut five, New-York six, New Jersey four, Pennsylvania eight, Delaware one, Maryland six, Virginia ten, North Carolina five, South Carolina five, and Georgia three.

4: When vacancies happen in the Representation from any State, the Executive Authority thereof shall issue Writs of Election to fill such Vacancies.

5: The House of Representatives shall chuse their Speaker and other Officers; and shall have the sole Power of Impeachment.

Section 3

1: The Senate of the United States shall be composed of two Senators from each State, chosen by the Legislature thereof, for six Years; and each Senator shall have one Vote.

2: Immediately after they shall be assembled in Consequence of the first Election, they shall be divided as equally as may be into three Classes. The Seats of the Senators of the first Class shall be vacated at the Expiration of the second Year, of the second Class at the Expiration of the fourth Year, and of the third Class at the Expiration of the sixth Year, so that one third may be chosen every second Year; and if Vacancies happen by Resignation, or otherwise, during the Recess of the Legislature of any State, the Executive thereof may make temporary Appointments until the next Meeting of the Legislature, which shall then fill such Vacancies.

3: No Person shall be a Senator who shall not have attained to the Age of thirty Years, and been nine Years a Citizen of the United States, and who shall not, when elected, be an Inhabitant of that State for which he shall be chosen.

4: The Vice President of the United States shall be President of the Senate, but shall have no Vote, unless they be equally divided.

5: The Senate shall chuse their other Officers, and also a President pro tempore, in the Absence of the Vice President, or when he shall exercise the Office of President of the United States.

6: The Senate shall have the sole Power to try all Impeachments. When sitting for that Purpose, they shall be on Oath or Affirmation. When the President of the United States is tried, the Chief Justice shall preside: And no Person shall be convicted without the Concurrence of two thirds of the Members present.

7: Judgment in Cases of impeachment shall not extend further than to removal from Office, and disqualification to hold and enjoy any Office of honor, Trust or Profit under the United States: but the Party convicted shall nevertheless be liable and subject to Indictment, Trial, Judgment and Punishment, according to Law.

Section 4

1: The Times, Places and Manner of holding Elections for Senators and Representatives, shall be prescribed in each State by the Legislature thereof; but the Congress may at any time by Law make or alter such Regulations, except as to the Places of chusing Senators.

2: The Congress shall assemble at least once in every Year, and such Meeting shall be on the first Monday in December, unless they shall by Law appoint a different Day.

Section 5

1: Each House shall be the Judge of the Elections, Returns and Qualifications of its own Members, and a Majority of each shall constitute a Quorum to do Business; but a smaller Number may adjourn from day to day, and may be authorized to compel the Attendance of absent Members, in such Manner, and under such Penalties as each House may provide.

2: Each House may determine the Rules of its Proceedings, punish its Members for disorderly Behaviour, and, with the Concurrence of two thirds, expel a Member.

3: Each House shall keep a Journal of its Proceedings, and from time to time publish the same, excepting such Parts as may in their Judgment require Secrecy; and the Yeas and Nays of the Members of either House on any question shall, at the Desire of one fifth of those Present, be entered on the Journal.

4: Neither House, during the Session of Congress, shall, without the Consent of the other, adjourn for more than three days, nor to any other Place than that in which the two Houses shall be sitting.

Section 6

1: The Senators and Representatives shall receive a Compensation for their Services, to be ascertained by Law, and paid out of the Treasury of the United States. They shall in all Cases, except Treason, Felony and Breach of the Peace, be privileged from Arrest during their Attendance at the Session of their respective Houses, and in going to and returning from the same; and for any Speech or Debate in either House, they shall not be questioned in any other Place.

2: No Senator or Representative shall, during the Time for which he was elected, be appointed to any civil Office under the Authority of the United States, which shall have been created, or the Emoluments whereof shall have been encreased during such time; and no Person holding any Office under the United States, shall be a Member of either House during his Continuance in Office.

Section 7

1: All Bills for raising Revenue shall originate in the House of Representatives; but the Senate may propose or concur with Amendments as on other Bills.

2: Every Bill which shall have passed the House of Representatives and the Senate, shall, before it become a Law, be presented to the President of the United States; If he approve he shall sign it, but if not he shall return it, with his Objections to that House in which it shall have originated, who shall enter the Objections at large on their Journal, and proceed to reconsider it. If after such Reconsideration two thirds of that House shall agree to pass the Bill, it shall be sent, together with the Objections, to the other House, by which it shall likewise be reconsidered, and if approved by two thirds of that House, it shall become a

Law. But in all such Cases the Votes of both Houses shall be determined by yeas and Nays, and the Names of the Persons voting for and against the Bill shall be entered on the Journal of each House respectively. If any Bill shall not be returned by the President within ten Days (Sundays excepted) after it shall have been presented to him, the Same shall be a Law, in like Manner as if he had signed it, unless the Congress by their Adjournment prevent its Return, in which Case it shall not be a Law.

3: Every Order, Resolution, or Vote to which the Concurrence of the Senate and House of Representatives may be necessary (except on a question of Adjournment) shall be presented to the President of the United States; and before the Same shall take Effect, shall be approved by him, or being disapproved by him, shall be repassed by two thirds of the Senate and House of Representatives, according to the Rules and Limitations prescribed in the Case of a Bill.

Section 8

1: The Congress shall have Power To lay and collect Taxes, Duties, Imposts and Excises, to pay the Debts and provide for the common Defence and general Welfare of the United States; but all Duties, Imposts and Excises shall be uniform throughout the United States;

2: To borrow Money on the credit of the United States;

3: To regulate Commerce with foreign Nations, and among the several States, and with the Indian Tribes;

4: To establish an uniform Rule of Naturalization, and uniform Laws on the subject of Bankruptcies throughout the United States;

5: To coin Money, regulate the Value thereof, and of foreign Coin, and fix the Standard of Weights and Measures;

6: To provide for the Punishment of counterfeiting the Securities and current Coin of the United States;

7: To establish Post Offices and post Roads;

8: To promote the Progress of Science and useful Arts, by securing for limited Times to Authors and Inventors the exclusive Right to their respective Writings and Discoveries;

9: To constitute Tribunals inferior to the supreme Court;

10: To define and punish Piracies and Felonies committed on the high Seas, and Offences against the Law of Nations;

11: To declare War, grant Letters of Marque and Reprisal, and make Rules concerning Captures on Land and Water;

12: To raise and support Armies, but no Appropriation of Money to that Use shall be for a longer Term than two Years;

13: To provide and maintain a Navy;

14: To make Rules for the Government and Regulation of the land and naval Forces;

15: To provide for calling forth the Militia to execute the Laws of the Union, suppress Insurrections and repel Invasions;

16: To provide for organizing, arming, and disciplining, the Militia, and for governing such Part of them as may be employed in the Service of the United States, reserving to the States respectively, the Appointment of the Officers, and the Authority of training the Militia according to the discipline prescribed by Congress;

17: To exercise exclusive Legislation in all Cases whatsoever, over such District (not exceeding ten Miles square) as may, by Cession of particular States, and the Acceptance of Congress, become the Seat of the Government of the United States, and to exercise like Authority over all Places purchased by the Consent of the Legislature of the State in which the Same shall be, for the Erection of Forts, Magazines, Arsenals, dock-Yards, and other needful Buildings;—And

18: To make all Laws which shall be necessary and proper for carrying into Execution the foregoing Powers, and all other Powers vested by this Constitution in the Government of the United States, or in any Department or Officer thereof.

Section 9

1: The Migration or Importation of such Persons as any of the States now existing shall think proper to admit, shall not be prohibited by the Congress prior to the Year one thousand eight hundred and eight, but a Tax or duty may be imposed on such Importation, not exceeding ten dollars for each Person.

2: The Privilege of the Writ of Habeas Corpus shall not be suspended, unless when in Cases of Rebellion or Invasion the public Safety may require it.

3: No Bill of Attainder or ex post facto Law shall be passed.

4: No Capitation, or other direct, Tax shall be laid, unless in Proportion to the Census or Enumeration herein before directed to be taken.

5: No Tax or Duty shall be laid on Articles exported from any State.

6: No Preference shall be given by any Regulation of Commerce or Revenue to the Ports of one State over those of another: nor shall Vessels bound to, or from, one State, be obliged to enter, clear, or pay Duties in another.

7: No Money shall be drawn from the Treasury, but in Consequence of Appropriations made by Law; and a regular Statement and Account of the Receipts and Expenditures of all public Money shall be published from time to time.

8: No Title of Nobility shall be granted by the United States: And no Person holding any Office of Profit or Trust under them, shall, without the Consent of the Congress, accept of any present, Emolument, Office, or Title, of any kind whatever, from any King, Prince, or foreign State.

Section 10

1: No State shall enter into any Treaty, Alliance, or Confederation; grant Letters of Marque and Reprisal; coin Money; emit Bills of Credit; make any Thing but gold and silver Coin a Tender in Payment of Debts; pass any Bill of Attainder, ex post facto Law, or Law impairing the Obligation of Contracts, or grant any Title of Nobility.

2: No State shall, without the Consent of the Congress, lay any Imposts or Duties on Imports or Exports, except what may be absolutely necessary for executing it's inspection Laws: and the net Produce of all Duties and Imposts, laid by any State on Imports or Exports, shall be for the Use of the Treasury of the United States; and all such Laws shall be subject to the Revision and Controul of the Congress.

3: No State shall, without the Consent of Congress, lay any Duty of Tonnage, keep Troops, or Ships of War in time of Peace, enter into any Agreement or Compact with another State, or with a foreign Power, or engage in War, unless actually invaded, or in such imminent Danger as will not admit of delay.

Article II (Article 2 - Executive)

Section 1

1: The executive Power shall be vested in a President of the United States of America. He shall hold his Office during the Term of four Years, and, together with the Vice President, chosen for the same Term, be elected, as follows

2: Each State shall appoint, in such Manner as the Legislature thereof may direct, a Number of Electors, equal to the whole Number of Senators and Representatives to which the State may be entitled in the Congress: but no Senator or Representative, or Person holding an Office of Trust or Profit under the United States, shall be appointed an Elector.

3: The Electors shall meet in their respective States, and vote by Ballot for two Persons, of whom one at least shall not be an Inhabitant of the same State with themselves. And they shall make a List of all the Persons voted for, and of the Number of Votes for each; which List they shall sign and certify, and transmit sealed to the Seat of the Government of the United States, directed to the President of the Senate. The President of the Senate shall, in the Presence of the Senate and House of Representatives, open all the Certificates, and the Votes shall then be counted. The Person having the greatest Number of Votes shall be the President, if such Number be a Majority of the whole Number of Electors appointed; and if there be more than one who have such Majority, and have an equal Number of Votes, then the House of Representatives shall immediately chuse by Ballot one of them for President; and if no Person have a Majority, then from the five highest on the List the said House shall in like Manner chuse the President. But in chusing the President, the Votes shall be taken by States, the Representation from each State having one Vote; A quorum for this Purpose shall consist of a Member or Members from two thirds of the States, and a Majority of all the States shall be necessary to a Choice. In every Case, after the Choice of the President, the Person having the greatest Number of Votes of the Electors shall be the Vice President. But if there should remain two or more who have equal Votes, the Senate shall chuse from them by Ballot the Vice President.

4: The Congress may determine the Time of chusing the Electors, and the Day on which they shall give their Votes; which Day shall be the same throughout the United States.

5: No Person except a natural born Citizen, or a Citizen of the United States, at the time of the Adoption of this Constitution, shall be eligible to the Office of President; neither shall any Person be eligible to that Office who shall not have attained to the Age of thirty five Years, and been fourteen Years a Resident within the United States.

6: In Case of the Removal of the President from Office, or of his Death, Resignation, or Inability to discharge the Powers and Duties of the said Office, the Same shall devolve on the VicePresident, and the Congress may by Law provide for the Case of Removal, Death, Resignation or Inability, both of the President and Vice President, declaring what Officer shall then act as President, and such Officer shall act accordingly, until the Disability be removed, or a President shall be elected.

7: The President shall, at stated Times, receive for his Services, a Compensation, which shall neither be encreased nor diminished during the Period for which he shall have been elected, and he shall not receive within that Period any other Emolument from the United States, or any of them.

8: Before he enter on the Execution of his Office, he shall take the following Oath or Affirmation:—"I do solemnly swear (or affirm) that I will faithfully execute the Office of President of the United States, and will to the best of my Ability, preserve, protect and defend the Constitution of the United States."

Section 2

1: The President shall be Commander in Chief of the Army and Navy of the United States, and of the Militia of the several States, when called into the actual Service of the United States; he may require the Opinion, in writing, of the principal Officer in each of the executive Departments, upon any Subject relating to the Duties of their respective Offices, and he shall have Power to grant Reprieves and Pardons for Offences against the United States, except in Cases of Impeachment.

2: He shall have Power, by and with the Advice and Consent of the Senate, to make Treaties, provided two thirds of the Senators present concur; and he shall nominate, and by and with the Advice and Consent of the Senate, shall appoint Ambassadors, other public Ministers and Consuls, Judges of the supreme Court, and all other Officers of the United States, whose Appointments are not herein otherwise provided for, and which shall be established by Law: but the Congress may by Law vest the Appointment of such inferior Officers, as they think proper, in the President alone, in the Courts of Law, or in the Heads of Departments.

3: The President shall have Power to fill up all Vacancies that may happen during the Recess of the Senate, by granting Commissions which shall expire at the End of their next Session.

Section 3

He shall from time to time give to the Congress Information of the State of the Union, and recommend to their Consideration such Measures as he shall judge necessary and expedient; he may, on extraordinary Occasions, convene both Houses, or either of them, and in Case of Disagreement between them, with Respect to the Time of Adjournment, he may adjourn them to such Time as he shall think proper; he shall receive Ambassadors and other public Ministers; he shall take Care that the Laws be faithfully executed, and shall Commission all the Officers of the United States.

Section 4

The President, Vice President and all civil Officers of the United States, shall be removed from Office on Impeachment for, and Conviction of, Treason, Bribery, or other high Crimes and Misdemeanors.

Article III (Article 3 - Judicial)

Section 1

The judicial Power of the United States, shall be vested in one supreme Court, and in such inferior Courts as the Congress may from time to time ordain and establish. The Judges, both of the supreme and inferior Courts, shall hold their Offices during good Behaviour, and shall, at stated Times, receive for their Services, a Compensation, which shall not be diminished during their Continuance in Office.

Section 2

1: The judicial Power shall extend to all Cases, in Law and Equity, arising under this Constitution, the Laws of the United States, and Treaties made, or which shall be made, under their Authority;—to all Cases affecting Ambassadors, other public Ministers and Consuls;—to all Cases of admiralty and maritime Jurisdiction;—to Controversies to which the United States shall be a Party;—to Controversies between two or more States;—between a State and Citizens of another State;—between Citizens of different States,—between Citizens of the same State claiming Lands under Grants of different States, and between a State, or the Citizens thereof, and foreign States, Citizens or Subjects.

2: In all Cases affecting Ambassadors, other public Ministers and Consuls, and those in which a State shall be Party, the supreme Court shall have original Jurisdiction. In all the other Cases before mentioned, the supreme Court shall have appellateJurisdiction, both as to Law and Fact, with such Exceptions, and under such Regulations as the Congress shall make.

3: The Trial of all Crimes, except in Cases of Impeachment, shall be by Jury; and such Trial shall be held in the State where the said Crimes shall have been committed; but when not committed within any State, the Trial shall be at such Place or Places as the Congress may by Law have directed.

Section 3

1: Treason against the United States, shall consist only in levying War against them, or in adhering to their Enemies, giving them Aid and Comfort. No Person shall be convicted of Treason unless on the Testimony of two Witnesses to the same overt Act, or on Confession in open Court.

2: The Congress shall have Power to declare the Punishment of Treason, but no Attainder of Treason shall work Corruption of Blood, or Forfeiture except during the Life of the Person attainted.

Article IV (Article 4 - States' Relations)

Section 1

Full Faith and Credit shall be given in each State to the public Acts, Records, and judicial Proceedings of every other State. And the Congress may by general Laws prescribe the Manner in which such Acts, Records and Proceedings shall be proved, and the Effect thereof.

Section 2

1: The Citizens of each State shall be entitled to all Privileges and Immunities of Citizens in the several States.

2: A Person charged in any State with Treason, Felony, or other Crime, who shall flee from Justice, and be found in another State, shall on Demand of the executive Authority of the State from which he fled, be delivered up, to be removed to the State having Jurisdiction of the Crime.

3: No Person held to Service or Labour in one State, under the Laws thereof, escaping into another, shall, in Consequence of any Law or Regulation therein, be discharged from such Service or Labour, but shall be delivered up on Claim of the Party to whom such Service or Labour may be due.

Section 3

1: New States may be admitted by the Congress into this Union; but no new State shall be formed or erected within the Jurisdiction of any other State; nor any State be formed by the Junction of two or more States, or Parts of States, without the Consent of the Legislatures of the States concerned as well as of the Congress.

2: The Congress shall have Power to dispose of and make all needful Rules and Regulations respecting the Territory or other Property belonging to the United States; and nothing in this Constitution shall be so construed as to Prejudice any Claims of the United States, or of any particular State.

Section 4

The United States shall guarantee to every State in this Union a Republican Form of Government, and shall protect each of them against Invasion; and on Application of the Legislature, or of the Executive (when the Legislature cannot be convened) against domestic Violence.

Article V (Article 5 - Mode of Amendment)

The Congress, whenever two thirds of both Houses shall deem it necessary, shall propose Amendments to this Constitution, or, on the Application of the Legislatures of two thirds of the several States, shall call a Convention for proposing Amendments, which, in either Case, shall be valid to all Intents and Purposes, as Part of this Constitution, when ratified by the Legislatures of three fourths of the several States, or by Conventions in three fourths thereof, as the one or the other Mode of Ratification may be proposed by the Congress; Provided that no Amendment which may be made prior to the Year One thousand eight hundred and eight shall in any Manner affect the first and fourth Clauses in the Ninth Section of the first Article; and that no State, without its Consent, shall be deprived of its equal Suffrage in the Senate.

Article VI (Article 6 - Prior Debts, National Supremacy, Oaths of Office)

1: All Debts contracted and Engagements entered into, before the Adoption of this Constitution, shall be as valid against the United States under this Constitution, as under the Confederation.

2: This Constitution, and the Laws of the United States which shall be made in Pursuance thereof; and all Treaties made, or which shall be made, under the Authority of the United States, shall be the supreme Law of the Land; and the Judges in every State shall be bound thereby, any Thing in the Constitution or Laws of any State to the Contrary notwithstanding.

3: The Senators and Representatives before mentioned, and the Members of the several State Legislatures, and all executive and judicial Officers, both of the United States and of the several States, shall be bound by Oath or Affirmation, to support this Constitution; but no religious Test shall ever be required as a Qualification to any Office or public Trust under the United States.

Article VII (Article 7 - Ratification)

The Ratification of the Conventions of nine States, shall be sufficient for the Establishment of this Constitution between the States so ratifying the Same.

done in Convention by the Unanimous Consent of the States present the Seventeenth Day of September in the Year of our Lord one thousand seven hundred and Eighty seven and of the Independence of the United States of America the Twelfth In witness whereof **We have hereunto subscribed our Names,**

Attest William Jackson Secretary

Go: Washington -Presidt. and deputy from Virginia Showing George Washington's signature.

Delaware

Geo: Read

Gunning Bedford jun

John Dickinson

Richard Bassett

Jaco: Broom

Maryland

James McHenry

Dan of St Thos. Jenifer

Danl Carroll.

Virginia

John Blair—

James Madison Jr.

North Carolina

Wm Blount

Richd. Dobbs Spaight.

Hu Williamson

South Carolina

J. Rutledge

Charles Cotesworth Pinckney

Charles Pinckney

Pierce Butler.

Georgia

William Few

Abr Baldwin

New Hampshire

John Langdon

Nicholas Gilman

Massachusetts

Nathaniel Gorham

Rufus King

Connecticut

Wm. Saml. Johnson

Roger Sherman

New York

Alexander Hamilton

New Jersey

Wil. Livingston

David Brearley.

Wm. Paterson.

Jona: Dayton

Pennsylvania

B Franklin

Thomas Mifflin

Robt Morris

Geo. Clymer

Thos. FitzSimons

Jared Ingersoll

James Wilson.

Gouv Morris

The Bill of Rights

Amendments 1 - 10

The Preamble to The Bill of Rights

Congress of the United States

begun and held at the City of New-York, on

Wednesday the fourth of March, one thousand seven hundred and eighty nine.

THE Conventions of a number of the States, having at the time of their adopting the Constitution, expressed a desire, in order to prevent misconstruction or abuse of its powers, that further declaratory and restrictive clauses should be added: And as extending the ground of public confidence in the Government, will best ensure the beneficent ends of its institution.

RESOLVED by the Senate and House of Representatives of the United States of America, in Congress assembled, two thirds of both Houses concurring, that the following Articles be proposed to the Legislatures of the several States, as amendments to the Constitution of the United States, all, or any of which Articles, when ratified by three fourths of the said Legislatures, to be valid to all intents and purposes, as part of the said Constitution; viz.

ARTICLES in addition to, and Amendment of the Constitution of the United States of America, proposed by Congress, and ratified by the Legislatures of the several States, pursuant to the fifth Article of the original Constitution.

Amendment I

Congress shall make no law respecting an establishment of religion, or prohibiting the free exercise thereof; or abridging the freedom of speech, or of the press; or the right of the people peaceably to assemble, and to petition the Government for a redress of grievances.

Amendment II

A well regulated Militia, being necessary to the security of a free State, the right of the people to keep and bear Arms, shall not be infringed.

Amendment III

No Soldier shall, in time of peace be quartered in any house, without the consent of the Owner, nor in time of war, but in a manner to be prescribed by law.

Amendment IV

The right of the people to be secure in their persons, houses, papers, and effects, against unreasonable searches and seizures, shall not be violated, and no Warrants shall issue, but upon probable cause, supported by Oath or affirmation, and particularly describing the place to be searched, and the persons or things to be seized.

Amendment V

No person shall be held to answer for a capital, or otherwise infamous crime, unless on a presentment or indictment of a Grand Jury, except in cases arising in the land or naval forces, or in the Militia, when in actual service in time of War or public danger; nor shall any person be subject for the same offence to be twice put in jeopardy of life or limb; nor shall be compelled in any criminal case to be a witness against himself, nor be deprived of life, liberty, or property, without due process of law; nor shall private property be taken for public use, without just compensation.

Amendment VI

In all criminal prosecutions, the accused shall enjoy the right to a speedy and public trial, by an impartial jury of the State and district wherein the crime shall have been committed, which district shall have been previously ascertained by law, and to be informed of the nature and cause of the accusation; to be confronted with the witnesses against him; to have compulsory process for obtaining witnesses in his favor, and to have the Assistance of Counsel for his defence.

Amendment VII

In Suits at common law, where the value in controversy shall exceed twenty dollars, the right of trial by jury shall be preserved, and no fact tried by a jury, shall be otherwise re-examined in any Court of the United States, than according to the rules of the common law.

Amendment VIII

Excessive bail shall not be required, nor excessive fines imposed, nor cruel and unusual punishments inflicted.

Amendment IX

The enumeration in the Constitution, of certain rights, shall not be construed to deny or disparage others retained by the people.

Amendment X

The powers not delegated to the United States by the Constitution, nor prohibited by it to the States, are reserved to the States respectively, or to the people.

Amendments 11 - 27

AMENDMENT XI

Passed by Congress March 4, 1794. Ratified February 7, 1795.

Note: Article III, section 2, of the Constitution was modified by amendment 11.

The Judicial power of the United States shall not be construed to extend to any suit in law or equity, commenced or prosecuted against one of the United States by Citizens of another State, or by Citizens or Subjects of any Foreign State.

AMENDMENT XII

Passed by Congress December 9, 1803. Ratified June 15, 1804.

Note: A portion of Article II, section 1 of the Constitution was superseded by the 12th amendment.

The Electors shall meet in their respective states and vote by ballot for President and Vice-President, one of whom, at least, shall not be an inhabitant of the same state with themselves; they shall name in their ballots the person voted for as President, and in distinct ballots the person voted for as Vice-President, and they shall make distinct lists of all persons voted for as President, and of all persons voted for as Vice-President, and of the number of votes for each, which lists they shall sign and certify, and transmit sealed to the seat of the government of the United States, directed to the President of the Senate; -- the President of the Senate shall, in the presence of the Senate and House of Representatives, open all the certificates and the votes shall then be counted; -- The person having the greatest number of votes for President, shall be the President, if such number be a majority of the whole number of Electors appointed; and if no person have such majority, then from the persons having the highest numbers not exceeding three on the list of those voted for as President, the House of Representatives shall choose immediately, by ballot, the President. But in choosing the President, the votes shall be taken by states, the representation from each state having one vote; a quorum for this purpose shall consist of a member or members from two-thirds of the states, and a majority of all the states shall be necessary to a choice. [And if the House of Representatives shall not choose a President whenever the right of choice shall devolve upon them, before the fourth day of March next following, then the Vice-President shall act as President, as in case of the death or other constitutional disability of the President. --]* The person having the greatest number of votes as Vice-President, shall be the Vice-President, if such number be a majority of the whole number of Electors appointed, and if no person have a majority, then from the two highest numbers on the list, the Senate shall choose the Vice-President; a quorum for the purpose shall consist of two-thirds of the whole number of Senators, and a majority of the whole number shall be necessary to a choice. But no person constitutionally ineligible to the office of President shall be eligible to that of Vice-President of the United States.

*Superseded by section 3 of the 20th amendment.

AMENDMENT XIII

Passed by Congress January 31, 1865. Ratified December 6, 1865.

Note: A portion of Article IV, section 2, of the Constitution was superseded by the 13th amendment.

Section 1.

Neither slavery nor involuntary servitude, except as a punishment for crime whereof the party shall have been duly convicted, shall exist within the United States, or any place subject to their jurisdiction.

Section 2.

Congress shall have power to enforce this article by appropriate legislation.

AMENDMENT XIV

Passed by Congress June 13, 1866. Ratified July 9, 1868.

Note: Article I, section 2, of the Constitution was modified by section 2 of the 14th amendment.

Section 1.

All persons born or naturalized in the United States, and subject to the jurisdiction thereof, are citizens of the United States and of the State wherein they reside. No State shall make or enforce any law which shall abridge the privileges or immunities of citizens of the United States; nor shall any State deprive any person of life, liberty, or property, without due process of law; nor deny to any person within its jurisdiction the equal protection of the laws.

Section 2.

Representatives shall be apportioned among the several States according to their respective numbers, counting the whole number of persons in each State, excluding Indians not taxed. But when the right to vote at any election for the choice of electors for President and Vice-President of the United States, Representatives in Congress, the Executive and Judicial officers of a State, or the members of the Legislature thereof, is denied to any of the male inhabitants of such State, being twenty-one years of age,* and citizens of the United States, or in any way abridged, except for participation in rebellion, or other crime, the basis of representation therein shall be reduced in the proportion which the number of such male citizens shall bear to the whole number of male citizens twenty-one years of age in such State.

Section 3.

No person shall be a Senator or Representative in Congress, or elector of President and Vice-President, or hold any office, civil or military, under the United States, or under any State, who, having previously taken an oath, as a member of Congress, or as an officer of the United States, or as a member of any State legislature, or as an executive or judicial officer of any State, to support the Constitution of the United States, shall have engaged in insurrection or rebellion against the same, or given aid or comfort to the enemies thereof. But Congress may by a vote of two-thirds of each House, remove such disability.

Section 4.

The validity of the public debt of the United States, authorized by law, including debts incurred for payment of pensions and bounties for services in suppressing insurrection or rebellion, shall not be questioned. But neither the United States nor any State shall assume or pay any debt or obligation incurred in aid of insurrection or rebellion against the United States, or any claim for the loss or emancipation of any slave; but all such debts, obligations and claims shall be held illegal and void.

Section 5.

The Congress shall have the power to enforce, by appropriate legislation, the provisions of this article.

Changed by section 1 of the 26th amendment.

AMENDMENT XV

Passed by Congress February 26, 1869. Ratified February 3, 1870.

Section 1.

The right of citizens of the United States to vote shall not be denied or abridged by the United States or by any State on account of race, color, or previous condition of servitude--

Section 2.

The Congress shall have the power to enforce this article by appropriate legislation.

AMENDMENT XVI

Passed by Congress July 2, 1909. Ratified February 3, 1913.

Note: Article I, section 9, of the Constitution was modified by amendment 16.

The Congress shall have power to lay and collect taxes on incomes, from whatever source derived, without apportionment among the several States, and without regard to any census or enumeration.

AMENDMENT XVII

Passed by Congress May 13, 1912. Ratified April 8, 1913.

Note: Article I, section 3, of the Constitution was modified by the 17th amendment.

The Senate of the United States shall be composed of two Senators from each State, elected by the people thereof, for six years; and each Senator shall have one vote. The electors in each State shall have the qualifications requisite for electors of the most numerous branch of the State legislatures.

When vacancies happen in the representation of any State in the Senate, the executive authority of such State shall issue writs of election to fill such vacancies: Provided, That the legislature of any State may empower the executive thereof to make temporary appointments until the people fill the vacancies by election as the legislature may direct.

This amendment shall not be so construed as to affect the election or term of any Senator chosen before it becomes valid as part of the Constitution.

AMENDMENT XVIII

Passed by Congress December 18, 1917. Ratified January 16, 1919. Repealed by amendment 21.

Section 1.

After one year from the ratification of this article the manufacture, sale, or transportation of intoxicating liquors within, the importation thereof into, or the exportation thereof from the United States and all territory subject to the jurisdiction thereof for beverage purposes is hereby prohibited.

Section 2.

The Congress and the several States shall have concurrent power to enforce this article by appropriate legislation.

Section 3.

This article shall be inoperative unless it shall have been ratified as an amendment to the Constitution by the legislatures of the several States, as provided in the Constitution, within seven years from the date of the submission hereof to the States by the Congress.

AMENDMENT XIX

Passed by Congress June 4, 1919. Ratified August 18, 1920.

The right of citizens of the United States to vote shall not be denied or abridged by the United States or by any State on account of sex.

Congress shall have power to enforce this article by appropriate legislation.

AMENDMENT XX

Passed by Congress March 2, 1932. Ratified January 23, 1933.

Note: Article I, section 4, of the Constitution was modified by section 2 of this amendment. In addition, a portion of the 12th amendment was superseded by section 3.

Section 1.

The terms of the President and the Vice President shall end at noon on the 20th day of January, and the terms of Senators and Representatives at noon on the 3d day of January, of the years in which such terms would have ended if this article had not been ratified; and the terms of their successors shall then begin.

Section 2.

The Congress shall assemble at least once in every year, and such meeting shall begin at noon on the 3d day of January, unless they shall by law appoint a different day.

Section 3.

If, at the time fixed for the beginning of the term of the President, the President elect shall have died, the Vice President elect shall become President. If a President shall not have been chosen before the time fixed for the beginning of his term, or if the President elect shall have failed to qualify, then the Vice President elect shall act as President until a President shall have qualified; and the Congress may by law provide for the case wherein neither a President elect nor a Vice President elect shall have qualified, declaring who shall then act as President, or the manner in which one who is to act shall be selected, and such person shall act accordingly until a President or Vice President shall have qualified.

Section 4.

The Congress may by law provide for the case of the death of any of the persons from whom the House of Representatives may choose a President whenever the right of choice shall have devolved upon them, and for the case of the death of any of the persons from whom the Senate may choose a Vice President whenever the right of choice shall have devolved upon them.

Section 5.

Sections 1 and 2 shall take effect on the 15th day of October following the ratification of this article.

Section 6.

This article shall be inoperative unless it shall have been ratified as an amendment to the Constitution by the legislatures of three-fourths of the several States within seven years from the date of its submission.

AMENDMENT XXI

Passed by Congress February 20, 1933. Ratified December 5, 1933.

Section 1.

The eighteenth article of amendment to the Constitution of the United States is hereby repealed.

Section 2.

The transportation or importation into any State, Territory, or possession of the United States for delivery or use therein of intoxicating liquors, in violation of the laws thereof, is hereby prohibited.

Section 3.

This article shall be inoperative unless it shall have been ratified as an amendment to the Constitution by conventions in the several States, as provided in the Constitution, within seven years from the date of the submission hereof to the States by the Congress.

AMENDMENT XXII

Passed by Congress March 21, 1947. Ratified February 27, 1951.

Section 1.

No person shall be elected to the office of the President more than twice, and no person who has held the office of President, or acted as President, for more than two years of a term to which some other person was elected President shall be elected to the office of the President more than once. But this Article shall not apply to any person holding the office of President when this Article was proposed by the Congress, and shall not prevent any person who may be holding the office of President, or acting as President, during the term within which this Article becomes operative from holding the office of President or acting as President during the remainder of such term.

Section 2.

This article shall be inoperative unless it shall have been ratified as an amendment to the Constitution by the legislatures of three-fourths of the several States within seven years from the date of its submission to the States by the Congress.

AMENDMENT XXIII

Passed by Congress June 16, 1960. Ratified March 29, 1961.

Section 1.

The District constituting the seat of Government of the United States shall appoint in such manner as the Congress may direct:

A number of electors of President and Vice President equal to the whole number of Senators and Representatives in Congress to which the District would be entitled if it were a State, but in no event more than the least populous State; they shall be in addition to those appointed by the States, but they shall be considered, for the purposes of the election of President and Vice President, to be electors appointed by a State; and they shall meet in the District and perform such duties as provided by the twelfth article of amendment.

Section 2.

The Congress shall have power to enforce this article by appropriate legislation.

AMENDMENT XXIV

Passed by Congress August 27, 1962. Ratified January 23, 1964.

Section 1.

The right of citizens of the United States to vote in any primary or other election for President or Vice President, for electors for President or Vice President, or for Senator or Representative in Congress, shall not be denied or abridged by the United States or any State by reason of failure to pay any poll tax or other tax.

Section 2.

The Congress shall have power to enforce this article by appropriate legislation.

AMENDMENT XXV

Passed by Congress July 6, 1965. Ratified February 10, 1967.

Note: Article II, section 1, of the Constitution was affected by the 25th amendment.

Section 1.

In case of the removal of the President from office or of his death or resignation, the Vice President shall become President.

Section 2.

Whenever there is a vacancy in the office of the Vice President, the President shall nominate a Vice President who shall take office upon confirmation by a majority vote of both Houses of Congress.

Section 3.

Whenever the President transmits to the President pro tempore of the Senate and the Speaker of the House of Representatives his written declaration that he is unable to discharge the powers and duties of his office, and until he transmits to them a written declaration to the contrary, such powers and duties shall be discharged by the Vice President as Acting President.

Section 4.

Whenever the Vice President and a majority of either the principal officers of the executive departments or of such other body as Congress may by law provide, transmit to the President pro tempore of the Senate and the Speaker of the House of Representatives their written declaration that the President is unable to discharge the powers and duties of his office, the Vice President shall immediately assume the powers and duties of the office as Acting President.

Thereafter, when the President transmits to the President pro tempore of the Senate and the Speaker of the House of Representatives his written declaration that no inability exists, he shall resume the powers and duties of his office unless the Vice President and a majority of either the principal officers of the executive department or of such other body as Congress may by law provide, transmit within four days to the President pro tempore of the Senate and the Speaker of the House of Representatives their written declaration that the President is unable to discharge the powers and duties of his office. Thereupon Congress shall decide the issue, assembling within forty-eight hours for that purpose if not in session. If the Congress, within twenty-one days after receipt of the latter written declaration, or, if Congress is not in session, within twenty-one days after Congress is required to assemble, determines by two-thirds vote of both Houses that the President is unable to discharge the powers and duties of his office, the Vice President shall continue to discharge the same as Acting President; otherwise, the President shall resume the powers and duties of his office.

AMENDMENT XXVI

Passed by Congress March 23, 1971. Ratified July 1, 1971.

Note: Amendment 14, section 2, of the Constitution was modified by section 1 of the 26th amendment.

Section 1.

The right of citizens of the United States, who are eighteen years of age or older, to vote shall not be denied or abridged by the United States or by any State on account of age.

Section 2.

The Congress shall have power to enforce this article by appropriate legislation.

AMENDMENT XXVII

Originally proposed Sept. 25, 1789. Ratified May 7, 1992.

No law, varying the compensation for the services of the Senators and Representatives, shall take effect, until an election of Representatives shall have intervened.

Glossary
A helpful guide to terms used

Abolition – The act of putting an end to a system, practice, or institution, as in slavery.

Abrogate – To abolish by formal or official means; annul by an authoritative act; repeal.

Act – The formal product of a legislative body. Statute.

Amendment – A change, addition, or an alteration to a document such as the U. S. Constitution.

American Revolution – The war that took place from 1775-1783 when the 13 British colonies in North America rebelled against their Mother country, Great Britain.

Anti-Federalist – An opponent of the proposed U. S. Constitution, some of whom refused to adopt the Constitution before it was amended.

Apportionment – The distribution of representatives among and within the states based on population.

Articles of Confederation – The contract between the 13 states proposed by the Continental Congress in November 1777 and adopted in March 1781. The first constitution for the United States.

Assembly – Meeting together to converse freely.

Baptists of Danbury – Baptists of Danbury, CT, wrote a letter to President Thomas Jefferson in 1801 expressing their concern that their state may infringe on their religious liberty. Jefferson responded by citing the first Amendment, that Congress could make no law establishing a religion nor prohibiting the free exercise thereof, "thus building a wall of separation between Church and State."

Bicameral – A legislature consisting of two houses, as in the House, representing the people and the Senate, representing the states.

Bill – A draft of a proposed law submitted for consideration by a legislative body.

Bill of Rights – The first ten amendments to the U. S. Constitution intended to protect certain unalienable natural and civil rights.

Bipartisan – Relating to or involving cooperation, agreement, or compromise between two or more political parties.

Bureaucracy – A body of unelected government officials.

Cabinet – A body of advisors to a head of state or to a President.

Central Government – A government that governs satellite or surrounding principalities such as states. The federal or national government.

Checks and Balances – A system that allows each branch of a government to limit acts of another branch so as to prevent one branch from exceeding or abusing its prescribed powers listed in the U.S. Constitution.

Chief Justice – The presiding judge of the U. S. Supreme Court.

Citizen – A native or naturalized person of a sovereign state who owes allegiance to and is entitled to protection from that state.

Civil Law – Deals with behavior that causes injury to an individual or other private party, such as a corporation. Examples: libel, slander, breach of contract, negligence resulting in injury or death, and property damage.

Clause – A distinct article in a formal document.

Concurrent Powers – Powers held by both state and federal governments.

Congress – The chief lawmaking body of the U. S. which consists of the House of Representatives and the Senate.

Connecticut Compromise – Also known as Roger Sherman's Great Compromise which satisfied the debate between the large states and the small states at the Constitutional Convention of 1787, whereby representation in the House of Representatives would be based on population, to satisfy the larger states, and representation in the Senate would be equal for each state, appeasing the smaller states.

Conservative – The ideology based on traditional values, smaller government, a strict interpretation of the U. S. Constitution, the rule of law, and freedom; One who ascribes to the conservative ideology.

Constitution – A written instrument embodying the rules of a political organization or nation.

Continental Congress – A meeting of delegates from the original colonies. The governing body of the United States during the American Revolution from 774 to 1781.

Convention of States – Described in Article V of the U. S. Constitution as the right of three-fourths of the state legislatures or conventions to ratify amendments to the Constitution.

Covenant – A solemn agreement between two or more parties.

Criminal Law – Deals with behavior that is or can be construed as an offense against the public, society, or the state, even if the victim is an individual. Examples: murder, assault, theft, driving while impaired.

Declaration of Independence – Document drafted by Thomas Jefferson and adopted by the Second Continental Congress on July 4, 1776 which declared that the thirteen original colonies were no longer under the control of Great Britain. It listed the grievances against King George III, his ministers, and parliament and stated key concepts of American liberty.

Delegate – An elected or appointed representative of a political body.

Democracy – Type of government in which decisions are made by a vote of the majority.

Direct Election – An election in which the people vote directly.

District - A territorial division of a region, state, or municipality for electoral purposes.

Double Jeopardy – A clause of the Fifth Amendment that guarantees that no one may be tried twice for the same crime if once found not guilty of that crime.

Due Process – A guarantee provided in the Fifth and Fourteenth Amendments which provides that people must receive a fair trial respecting all rights and protections from both the federal government (Fifth Amendment) and state governments (Fourteenth Amendment).

Eighth Amendment – Prohibits excessive bail, fines, and cruel and unusual punishment.

Elastic Clause – Also known as the "necessary and proper" clause in Article I, Section 8 of the U. S. Constitution, states that Congress has the power "To make all Laws. . . necessary and proper for carrying into Execution the foregoing Powers, and all other Powers vested by this Constitution in the Government of the United States, or in any Department or Officer thereof."

Elector – One who is appointed to participate in the official election of the U. S. President in his/her state by casting and signing a ballot for President and Vice President.

Electoral College – The method of electing the U. S. President and Vice President. Each state legislature appoints a number of electors equal to the number of U. S. Representatives plus the number of U. S. Senators for the respective state, who will cast ballots following the general election for President. The signed Certificates of Vote by each elector are transmitted to the U. S. Senate where the President of the Senate opens all the Certificates in the presence of members of both houses.

Eminent Domain – The right of a government to take private property for public use with payment of just compensation to the owner.

Enumerated Powers – The list of specific powers granted to Congress in Article I, Section 8 of the U. S. Constitution.

Establishment Clause – The Clause in the First Amendment that prohibits Congress from making a law respecting an official religion.

Executive Branch – The branch of government that enforces laws.

Faith – "Strong belief in God or the doctrines of a religion." (from Lexico.com)

Faithless Elector – An elector who goes against his/her state's popular vote winner in the Presidential election when casting his/her vote in the Electoral College.

Federal government – The national or central government under the Constitution.

Federalism – One of the foundational concepts of the U. S. Constitution that protects the freedoms and liberties guaranteed to individuals by balancing the governance and responsibilities between a national government and each sovereign state government.

Federalist – An individual who favored a stronger federal government and the adoption of the U. S. Constitution. Most Federalists did not think a Bill of Rights was necessary.

Federalist Papers – 85 essays written by Alexander Hamilton (51), James Madison (29), and John Jay (5), printed in New York City newspapers in 1788 under the pseudonym Publius, trying to persuade New Yorkers to ratify the proposed U. S. Constitution.

Fifth Amendment – Guarantees that no one may be denied a fair trial with access to a grand jury; may not be tried for the same offense twice; shall not be compelled to testify against himself; may not be denied life, liberty, or property without due process of law; nor may property be taken without just compensation.

Filibuster – A prolonged speech preventing progress of a piece of legislation. In recent times, a rule in the Senate by which measures must be passed by a vote of at least sixty senators.

First Amendment – Guarantees freedom of religion, freedom of speech, freedom of the press, peaceably assembly, and the right to petition.

Founders – The Founding Fathers

Founding Fathers – Those men who wrote our founding documents and designed the form of government for the United States. Usually refers to seven specific early Americans: George Washington, Benjamin Franklin, Thomas Jefferson, Alexander Hamilton, James Madison, John Adams, and John Jay.

Fourth Amendment – Guarantees protections from unreasonable searches and seizures and from warrants issued without probable cause.

Framers – The 55 delegates to the Constitutional Convention who convened in Philadelphia in 1787.

Freedom – "The power or right to act, speak, or think as one wants without hindrance." (from Lexico.com)

General Welfare – Concern of the government for the health, peace, morality, and safety of the people.

Gerrymander – The partisan drawing of electoral district boundaries with the intent of benefitting one political party over the other.

Glorious Revolution – The political uprising that placed William and Mary on the English throne. This promoted the "rule of law" through the passage of the English Bill of Rights in 1689 that protected individual liberties of British subjects wherever they lived in the world.

Golden Triangle of Freedom – The concept introduced by Os Guinness. Freedom requires Virtue, Virtue requires Faith of some sort, and Faith of any sort requires Freedom.

Great Compromise – The agreement between the small states and the large states during the Constitutional Convention in 1787 that apportioned representation in the House of Representatives based on population and equal state representation in the Senate. Also known as the Connecticut Compromise.

House of Representatives – One of the two houses of the legislative branch of government of the United States whose representation is based on population of the respective states.

Impeach – The formal indictment of a public official for serious offenses.

Inalienable – Incapable of being taken away or sold. Used interchangeably with Unalienable. Examples: Life, Liberty, and the Pursuit of Happiness.

Inherent Powers – Those powers held by the U. S. President not specified in the Constitution, but may be necessary to perform the duties of the office.

Judicial Branch – The branch of government that interprets laws and tries cases in violation of laws or settles controversies between contending parties.

Judicial Review – The power of a court to declare laws or executive actions unconstitutional.

Jurisdiction – The extent of power of a legal authority over political territories, geographic regions, or in types of legal matters.

Justice – The quality of being fair and reasonable.

King George III– The monarch of Great Britain and Ireland from 1760-1801, then King of the United Kingdom of Great Britain and Ireland until his death in 1820. He was King during the American Revolution.

Legislative Branch – The branch of government that makes laws.

Liberalism – A political ideology founded by John Locke in the 17th century advocating natural rights, freedom, and a republican form of government. Modern liberalism, however, favors a broader interpretation of the U. S. Constitution and a larger and more powerful federal government which tends to go against its original meaning of less government and more freedom.

Liberty – "The state of being free within society from oppressive restrictions imposed by authority on one's way of life, behavior, or political views." (from Lexico.com)

Lobbyist – An individual or group that conducts activities to influence members of a legislative body or public officials.

Magna Carta – An English document signed by King John in 1215 guaranteeing fundamental rights and privileges.

Mandate – To officially require someone to do something or for something to take place.

Massachusetts Compromise – Proposed by John Hancock in the Massachusetts ratifying convention of 1788, an agreement between Federalist and Antifederalist delegates which secured ratification of the Constitution while instructing future members of Congress to support nine specific amendments to the Constitution..

Naturalization – The legal act or process by which a non-citizen may acquire citizenship.

Natural Rights – Those rights individuals are born with given to them by their Creator. An example of a natural right is the right to defend oneself and one's property.

Ninth Amendment – The rights listed in the Constitution shall not be understood to deny or disparage other rights not listed.

Original Intent – The theory of interpreting a state or federal constitution by determining the authors' intentions at the time of its drafting.

Parliament – The law-making body of England, consisting of the House of Commons, House of Lords, and the monarch.

Petition – A formal written request signed by people appealing to authority with respect to a specific cause.

Preamble – The opening statement to the U. S. Constitution explaining the reasons why the Framers designed our government as a republic.

Probable Cause – Reasonable suspicion that a person has committed a crime or there is the presence of evidence of criminality.

Quartering Act – Passed in 1767, this act provided that soldiers could reside in private homes, primarily in Boston, without the owners' consent or could be housed in barracks at the expense of the colonies. This led to the addition of the Third Amendment to the Constitution. Ironically, quartering of troops was declared illegal in England by the English Bill of Rights many years prior to the American Revolution.

Quorum – The number of members of a group or body that must be present for any business to be done by the body.

Ratify – The act of giving formal consent to.

Repeal – To abolish by formal or official means; to put an end to.

Republic- The form of government in which leaders or representatives are elected by those who have the right to vote. A republic is based on the Rule of Law applying to all.

Rule of Law – The concept of being governed by laws passed by a legislative body of representatives of the people. The laws apply to everyone equally.

Second Amendment – Guarantees the right to keep and bear arms.

Secular Covenant – A solemn agreement, as in the agreement by the citizens of the United States to be governed by the Constitution and the Bill of Rights through their ratification.

Sedition – The act of defaming a government or government official.

Self-Incrimination – Testifying against oneself in a court of law or before a magistrate of the court.

Separation of Powers – One of the foundational concepts of the U.S. Constitution that protects freedoms and liberties by dividing governmental powers among three equal branches of government: Legislative, Executive, and Judicial.

Seventh Amendment – Guarantees the right to a trial-by-jury in civil cases.

Sixth Amendment – Guarantees the right to a fair and speedy criminal trial.

Sovereignty – A nation's or state's supreme power or authority within its borders.

Tenth Amendment – Guarantees the states (or the people) the powers not delegated to the national government by the Constitution.

Third Amendment – Guarantees that no soldier will be quartered in any house without consent by the owner; it may apply in non-originalist cases having to do with "zones of privacy."

Treaty – A binding agreement or contract between two or more nations or communities.

Tyrannical Government – A government run by a dictator who controls its citizens through fear.

Unalienable – Incapable of being taken away or denied such as Life, Liberty, and the Pursuit of Happiness.

Unconstitutional – Unauthorized by or inconsistent with a constitution.

Unicameral – A one-chamber legislative body.

Usurp – To abuse one's power or go beyond one's prescribed or enumerated powers.

Veto – The act of refusing to accept or to reject a proposal submitted by a law-making body.

Virtue – "Behavior showing high moral standards." (from Lexico.com)

Warrant – Legal document authorizing search and/or seizure of property, arrest of individuals, or the execution of a legal judgment.

Endnotes
Sources and Links for Interactive Learning

pg 01 - But, as Ronald Reagan famously said, "freedom is never more than one generation away from extinction."

https://www.youtube.com/watch?v=SDouNtnR_IA

pg 02 - Guinness introduced the simple term "The Golden Triangle of Freedom," which captures this fundamental concept, in his 2012 book *A Free Peoples's Suicide: Sustainable Freedom and the American Future*.

https://www.amazon.com/Free-Peoples-Suicide-Sustainable-American/dp/0830834656

pg 15 - The first 52 words of the Constitution – the Preamble – lay out The Who, the Why, the What, and the How of the 4,000 plus words that followed in the document it introduced...

https://constitutioncenter.org/interactive-constitution/preamble

pg 16 - See 'Madison's Notes on the Debates in the Federal Convention' for September 8, 1787

http://avalon.law.yale.edu/18th_century/debates_908.asp

pg 16 - ... according to Constitutionland.com

https://constitutionland.com/preamble-street

pg 16 - "Born into a New York family distinguished for its wealth, lineage, and political influence, [Gouverneur] Morris . . . graduated from King's College (now Columbia University) and in 1771 was admitted to the bar"

https://web.archive.org/web/20200428153102/https://www.history.com/topics/american-revolution/gouverneur-morris

pg 17 - "... Gouverneur was never a governor, but he served in the Continental Congress, Constitutional Convention and U.S. Senate"

https://www.history.com/news/10-things-you-may-not-know-about-the-oddest-founding-father

pg 18 - In August 1787, before Morris was given the editorial responsibilities, the preamble, as circulated in a draft of the entire Constitution as it existed one month before the final signing given to the delegates, read as follows

https://www.gilderlehrman.org/sites/default/files/content-images/00819.01.jpg

pg 18 - "When he was still a young one, age thirty-five, Mr. Morris drafted the Constitution of the United States," biographer Richard Brookhiser wrote

https://www.amazon.com/gp/product/0743256026/

pg 19 - In fact, as Constitution Law notes, only one time in the history of all Supreme Court decisions – *Jacobson v. Mass, 197 U.S. 11* (1904) – did the Supreme Court cite the Preamble:

https://www.conlaw.org/cites2.htm

pg 19 - The numerous state conventions that were called, in Marshall's mind, are the original source of the federal government's power under the US Constitution," Constitutionland.com notes

https://constitutionland.com/preamble-street

pg 20 - "[T]he Preamble has important implications for who has the ultimate power of constitutional interpretation"

https://constitutioncenter.org/interactive-constitution/preamble/the-preambles-significance-for-constitutional-interpretation-by-michael-sto/interp/37

pg 20 - "The Preamble to the Constitution has been largely ignored by lawyers and courts through American history"
https://constitutioncenter.org/interactive-constitution/preamble/giving-meaning-to-the-preamble-by-erwin-chemerinsky/interp/37

pg 20 - "When challenged on the federal government's constitutional authority to create welfare programs, meddle in education or run a national healthcare system, progressives will almost always appeal to the 'general welfare clause' [of the Preamble and Article I Section 8]"

http://tenthamendmentcenter.com/

pg 21- "Clearly, the words general welfare must mean something other than a grant of power for Congress to do whatever it pleased. What exactly did the framers mean?" Maharrey asks rhetorically:

http://www.michaelmaharrey.com/constitution101-the-general-welfare-clause-820/

pg 33 - Federalism is a foundational concept framed in the Constitution of the United States which defines the relationship between the national government and each of the state governments that comprise our republic (thirteen such state governments in 1789, fifty now in 2017).

https://www.archives.gov/founding-docs/constitution-transcript

pg 33 - "In the compound republic of America, the power surrendered by the people is first divided between two distinct governments, and then the portion allotted to each subdivided among distinct and separate departments"

http://avalon.law.yale.edu/18th_century/fed51.asp

pg 34 - Article I, Section 8 of the Constitution enumerates 19 specific powers granted to the legislative branch of the national government, one of the most important of which is the "Power to lay and collect Taxes, Duties, Imposts, and Excises."

https://www.archives.gov/founding-docs/constitution-transcript

pg 34 - Article II, Sections 2 and 3 of the Constitution enumerates 13 specific powers granted to the executive branch of the national government, the most significant of which states that "The President shall be Commander in Chief of the Army and Navy of the United States, and of the Militia of the several States."

https://www.archives.gov/founding-docs/constitution-transcript

pg 33 - Article III, Section 2 of the Constitution enumerates one specific power granted to the judicial branch of the national government: "The judicial Power shall extend to all Cases, in Law and Equity, arising under this Constitution, the Laws of the United States, and Treaties made, or which shall be made, under their Authority."

https://www.archives.gov/founding-docs/constitution-transcript

pg 35 - It also defines 8 specific types of cases to which the judicial power of the judicial branch of the national government shall apply.

https://www.archives.gov/founding-docs/constitution-transcript

pg 39 - "It is safe to say that a respect for the principle of separation of powers is deeply ingrained in every American," the National Archives website says

https://www.archives.gov/education/lessons/separation-powers

pg 40 - "... Because men are not angels - because they are so often actuated by private interest and ambition - these very motives themselves must be employed to keep the departments of government within their limited, constitutional boundaries"

http://www.heritage.org/political-process/report/james-madison-father-the-constitution

pg 40 - "The accumulation of all powers, legislative, executive, and judiciary, in the same hands, whether of one, a few, or many, and whether hereditary, self appointed, or elective, may justly be pronounced the very definition of tyranny"

https://www.congress.gov/resources/display/content/The+Federalist+Papers#TheFederalistPapers-47

pg 44 - Dictionary.com defines "abrogate" as "to abolish by formal or official means; annul by an authoritative act; repeal," or "to put aside; put an end to."

http://www.dictionary.com/browse/abrogate

pg 47 - "The executive Power shall be vested in a President of the United States of America. He shall hold his Office during the Term of four Years, and, together with the Vice President, chosen for the same Term, be elected, as follows"

https://www.archives.gov/founding-docs/constitution-transcript

pg 47 - "This language in fact paralleled the provisions for state legislative appointment of congressional delegates in the Articles of Confederation, and of U.S. Senators under Article I of the Constitution"

http://www.heritage.org/constitution/#!/articles/2/essays/79/presidential-electors

pg 49 - Alexander Hamilton commented extensively on this in Federalist No. 68, published in the New York Packet on March 14, 1788

http://avalon.law.yale.edu/18th_century/fed68.asp

pg 51 - Because the Constitution did not distinguish between President and Vice-President in the votes cast by each state's electors in the Electoral College, both Jefferson and his running mate Aaron Burr received 73 votes"

https://www.archives.gov/legislative/features/1800-election/1800-election.html

pg 51 - "Passed by Congress December 9, 1803, and ratified June 15, 1804, the 12th Amendment provided for separate Electoral College votes for President and Vice President, correcting weaknesses in the earlier electoral system which were responsible for the controversial Presidential Election of 1800"

https://www.archives.gov/historical-docs/todays-doc/index.html?dod-date=1209

pg 52 - In one of the bitter ironies of history, Aaron Burr killed Alexander Hamilton in a duel on July 11, 1804 (Hamilton died the following day), less than a month after the 12th Amendment was ratified.

http://www.alexanderhamiltonexhibition.org/about/Ron%20Chernow%20Interview.pdf

pg 53 - Our democratic ethos increasingly embraced popular elections, leading all state legislatures by 1880 to provide for popular election of presidential electors, and the Sixteenth Amendment in 1913 mandated the same for Senators"

http://www.heritage.org/constitution/#!/articles/2/essays/79/presidential-electors

pg 58 - "When the Constitution was signed on the 17th of September, the question was, "Shall we take it to Congress?""

http://teachingamericanhistory.org/ratification/stageone/

pg 58 - In the end, the Pennsylvania Assembly "decided to go to Congress" for approval before deciding to hold a ratifying convention in the state.

http://teachingamericanhistory.org/ratification/stageone/

pg 59 - William Jackson, who had taken the actual Constitution document on parchment with him to the Confederation Congress in New York "made his way back to Pennsylvania with the Constitution on the very day [September 29] that the Pennsylvania Assembly was supposed to adjourn"

http://teachingamericanhistory.org/ratification/stageone/

pg 61 - "I propose, in a series of papers, to discuss the following interesting particulars," Hamilton wrote in this first "general introduction" article, capitalizing each of the six "particulars" for emphasis

https://www.congress.gov/resources/display/content/The+Federalist+Papers#TheFederalistPapers-1

pg 61 - "...Quite to the contrary they were concerned about the loss of liberties"

http://econfaculty.gmu.edu/wew/articles/00/billofrights.html

pg 61 - "The Pennsylvania State Legislature was in session when the new Constitution was proposed, so the ratification campaign proceeded immediately, and a large public meeting held October 6, 1787, in the State House (Independence Hall) yard to nominate delegates to the next Pennsylvania Legislature became a forum for debate on ratification"

http://www.constitution.org/afp/jwilson0.htm

pg 61 - "Wilson ... was asked to speak to the gathering to explain the proposed Constitution and answer some of the criticisms that had been made of it. His speech was printed in the Pennsylvania Packet on October 10, 1787, and it was soon reprinted throughout the states, receiving more coverage than the more detailed arguments made [later] in The Federalist"

http://www.constitution.org/afp/jwilson0.htm

pg 61 - "In delegating federal powers," Wilson began, "the congressional power is to be collected, not from tacit implication, but from the positive grant expressed in the instrument of the union.

http://www.constitution.org/afp/jwilson0.htm

pg 61 - "This distinction being recognized, will furnish an answer to those who think the omission of a bill of rights a defect in the proposed constitution; for it would have been superfluous and absurd to have stipulated with a federal body of our own creation, that we should enjoy those privileges of which we are not divested, either by the intention or the act that has brought the body into existence"

http://www.constitution.org/afp/jwilson0.htm

pg 62 - Bills of Rights have "no application to constitutions professedly founded upon the power of the people, and executed by their immediate representatives and servants. Here, in strictness, the people surrender nothing; and as they retain every thing they have no need of particular reservations"

https://www.congress.gov/resources/display/content/The+Federalist+Papers#TheFederalistPapers-84 pg 62 - They would contain various exceptions to powers not granted; and, on this very account, would afford a colorable pretext to claim more than were granted ... [it] would furnish, to men disposed to usurp, a plausible pretense for claiming that power

https://www.congress.gov/resources/display/content/The+Federalist+Papers#TheFederalistPapers-84

pg 64 - The delegates complained that the State House facilities were overcrowded. On January 17, the convention moved to the Long Lane Congregational Church.

http://teachingamericanhistory.org/ratification/massachusettstimeline/

pg 65 - What is clear is that the Massachusetts Compromise secured the victory for the proponents of the Constitution because roughly ten delegates changed their mind to secure ratification by a 187-168 vote

http://teachingamericanhistory.org/ratification/massachusetts/

pg 65 - The Massachusetts Centinel, a Federalist newspaper "published in Boston on Wednesdays and Saturdays by Benjamin Russell (1761–1845) ... specialized in the brief article that, in vigorous and colorful language, extolled the Constitution or scored its critic

http://csac.history.wisc.edu/ma_centinel_boston.pdf

pg 65 - Up next was New Hampshire, where, as Professor Lloyd noted, "many a campaign has fallen on hard times . . . in February.

http://teachingamericanhistory.org/ratification/stagefour/

pg 66 - Given the concerns expressed by the delegates from Maryland and South Carolina at the Philadelphia Convention, one might anticipate that there would be quite a confrontation in Maryland and South Carolina

http://teachingamericanhistory.org/ratification/stagefour/

pg 66 - New Hampshire was 52-52, Virginia was 84-84, and New York was 19 in favor and 46 against by what today we might call 'entrance polls.' It was going to be an extremely close call

http://teachingamericanhistory.org/ratification/stagefive/

pg 67 - Governor Edmund Randolph presented the proposed Constitution to the Virginia Assembly in mid-October 1787 and the legislative branch provided for the election of delegates to a state ratifying convention

http://teachingamericanhistory.org/ratification/stagefive/

pg 67 - Now the Mid-Atlantic states were connected to the South, but New England remained separated by New York, which, "in many ways, was at the center of the ratification controversy

http://teachingamericanhistory.org/ratification/stagefive/

pg 67 - On June 16, 1788 the New York ratification convention convened in Poughkeepsie, 90 miles north of New York City. Alexander Hamilton was the most prominent Federalist delegate in attendance

http://teachingamericanhistory.org/ratification/stagefive/

pg 69 - Learning that Congress endorsed a version of Madison's Bill of Rights proposal, North Carolina held a second ratifying convention. This time, on November 21, 1789, the delegates ratified the Constitution

http://teachingamericanhistory.org/ratification/stagesix/

pg 69 - They also had the nerve to propose that the First Congress recommend the adoption of a bill of rights as well as amendments to the Philadelphia Constitution

http://teachingamericanhistory.org/ratification/stagesix/

pg 69 - Residents of the former British colony rejected the first effort to approve the Constitution by a margin of 10-to-1

http://www.politico.com/story/2014/05/this-day-in-politics-107177

pg 69 - Rhode Island convention finally ratified the Constitution "on May 29, 1790 (over a year after President George Washington's inauguration) by a vote of 34-32

https://www.constitutionfacts.com/us-constitution-amendments/fascinating-facts/

pg 73 - The Congress, whenever two thirds of both Houses shall deem it necessary, shall propose Amendments to this Constitution, or, on the Application of the Legislatures of two thirds of the several States, shall call a Convention for proposing Amendments

https://constitutioncenter.org/interactive-constitution/articles/article-v

pg 73 - The Ratification of the Conventions of nine States, shall be sufficient for the Establishment of this Constitution between the States so ratifying the Same

https://constitutioncenter.org/interactive-constitution/articles/article-vii

pg 76 - Article V of the Constitution stated that amendments proposed by either the Congress or an Article V convention "shall be valid to all Intents and Purposes, as Part of this Constitution, when ratified by the Legislatures of three fourths of the several States, or by Conventions in three fourths thereof, as the one or the other Mode of Ratification may be proposed by the Congress"

https://constitutioncenter.org/interactive-constitution/articles/article-v

pg 76 - "His influence over the legislature was so evident that George Washington observed that 'He has only to say let this be Law–and it is Law,'" Professor Richard Labunski wrote in his 2006 book, James Madison and the Struggle for the Bill of Rights.

https://books.google.com/books/about/James_Madison_and_the_Struggle_for_the_B.html?id=JvmZbFMxCHsC

pg 77 - On February 5, 1789, the state legislature of New York passed its own Article V petition to Congress, and Federalists worried that more states might join them

http://foavc.org/01page/Amendments/001_Annals_of_Congress%20%20%20Pg%2000029%20%20Yr%201789-NY-General%20Call%20for%20an%20Article%20V%20Convention_HL.JPG

pg 78 - This he believed was not the case until two-thirds of the State Legislatures concurred in such application, and then it is out of the power of Congress to decline complying

http://foa5c.org/01page/Amendments/001_Annals_of_Congress_00259_1789_HL.JPG

pg 81 - In 1982, a college undergraduate student, Gregory Watson, discovered that the proposed amendment could still be ratified and started a grassroots campaign. Watson was also an aide to Texas state senator Ric Williamson

https://constitutioncenter.org/blog/how-a-c-grade-college-term-paper-led-to-a-constitutional-amendment/

pg 85 - The first amendment is the most important in the American Constitution because it protects the things that make us what we are, including talking, and writing, and worshiping

https://www.facebook.com/HillsdaleCollegeOnlineCourses/posts/1048517321846817

pg 86 - "The only foundation for a useful education in a republic is to be laid in religion. Without this, there can be no virtue, and without virtue there can be no liberty, and liberty is the object and life of all republican governments,"

http://www.westillholdthesetruths.org/quotes/110/the-only-foundation-for-a-useful

pg 86 - To which "religion" does the First Amendment refer?

https://www.goodreads.com/author/quotes/138426.W_Cleon_Skousen

pg 88 - Madison said that the Sedition Act attacked the "right of freely examining public characters and measures and of free communication among the people."

https://billofrightsinstitute.org/founding-documents/primary-source-documents/virginia-and-kentucky-resolutions/

pg 89 - The Sedition Act passed the Senate on a 22-9 party line vote, and in the House on a 60-46 party line vote. Adams quickly signed it into law.

https://www.amazon.com/gp/product/0062066331/

pg 89 - A cannon blast saluted the president

https://www.amazon.com/gp/product/0062066331/

pg 90 - President Adams, Bache wrote in *The Aurora*, "has appointed Alexander Hamilton inspector general of the Army, the same Hamilton who published a book to prove he is an adulterer . . . Mr. Adams ought hereafter to be silent about French principles."

https://www.amazon.com/gp/product/0062066331/

pg 93 - Abraham Lincoln once called 'the right of peaceable assembly' part of 'the Constitutional substitute for revolution'

http://law.wustl.edu/faculty_profiles/documents/inazu/ForgottenFreedomAssembly.pdf

pg 93 - Groups invoking the right of assembly have inherently been those that dissent from the majority and consensus standards endorsed by government

http://law.wustl.edu/faculty_profiles/documents/inazu/ForgottenFreedomAssembly.pdf

pg 93 - These three themes - the dissenting assembly, the public assembly, and the expressive assembly - emerge from the groups that have gathered throughout our nation's history

http://law.wustl.edu/faculty_profiles/documents/inazu/ForgottenFreedomAssembly.pdf

pg 94 - In 1836, the U. S. House of Representatives decided that it would not entertain petitions concerning slavery nor concerning the abolition of slavery. Those would simply be "tabled."

http://history.house.gov/Historical-Highlights/1800-1850/The-House-of-Representatives-instituted-the-%E2%80%9Cgag-rule%E2%80%9D/

pg 98 - "The very text of the Second Amendment implicitly recognizes the pre-existence of the right and declares only that 'it shall not be infringed'," Supreme Court Justice Antonin Scalia wrote in the majority opinion in the landmark case *District of Columbia v. Heller, 554 U.S. 570, 128 S. Ct. 2783* (2008)

https://www.supremecourt.gov/opinions/boundvolumes/554bv.pdf

pg 98 - Scalia went on to note that this pre-existing right was recognized in 17th century England, the country of origin for the majority of colonists in British North America.

https://www.supremecourt.gov/opinions/boundvolumes/554bv.pdf

pg 99 - In the article titled "The Right to Keep and Bear Arms in the Light of Its Historical Development," Emery wrote

https://www.jstor.org/stable/1326865?seq=1

pg 100 - By the 1930s, when President Franklin Roosevelt had appointed four of the nine members of the Supreme Court, this "collective rights approach" to the Second Amendment was embraced by the highest court in the land, as Cornell Law School's Legal Information Institution notes

https://www.law.cornell.edu/wex/second_amendment

pg 100 - Writing in 2004, Professor Randy Barnett previewed what this more originalist court meant for the Second Amendment, in his article "Was the Right to Keep and Bear Arms Conditioned on Service in An Organized Militia?" Barnett concluded that it was not.

https://scholarship.law.georgetown.edu/cgi/viewcontent.cgi?article=1858&context=facpub

pg 100 - Four years later, in 2008, the Supreme Court re-established the "individual rights approach" to the Second Amendment, as Cornell Law School's Legal Information Institution notes

https://www.law.cornell.edu/wex/second_amendment

pg 101 - Respondent argues that it protects an individual right to possess a firearm unconnected with service in a militia, and to use that arm for traditionally lawful purposes, such as self-defense within the home," Justice Scalia wrote in the 5-4 majority decision in District of Columbia v. Heller

https://www.supremecourt.gov/opinions/boundvolumes/554bv.pdf

pg 101 - "… His description of it cannot possibly be thought to tie it to militia or military service," Scalia noted

https://www.supremecourt.gov/opinions/boundvolumes/554bv.pdf

pg 102 - "Three important founding-era legal scholars interpreted the Second Amendment in published writings. All three understood it to protect an individual right unconnected with militia service. All three understood it to protect an individual right unconnected with military service," Scalia continued

https://www.supremecourt.gov/opinions/boundvolumes/554bv.pdf

pg 102 - [N]othing in our opinion should be taken to cast doubt on longstanding prohibitions on the possession of firearms by felons or the mentally ill, or laws forbidding the carrying of firearms in sensitive places such as schools and government buildings, or laws imposing conditions and qualifications on the commercial sale of arms," Scalia concluded

https://www.supremecourt.gov/opinions/boundvolumes/554bv.pdf

pg 103 - Justice Clarence Thomas described how the New York statute was applied to Koch and Nash at the start of his majority opinion in the case

https://www.supremecourt.gov/opinions/21pdf/597us1r54_7648.pdfhttps://www.supremecourt.gov/opinions/21pdf/597us1r54_7648.pdf

pg 103 - Thomas then explained how state courts in New York interpreted "proper cause."

https://www.supremecourt.gov/opinions/21pdf/597us1r54_7648.pdf

pg 104 - We know of no other constitutional right that an individual may exercise only after demonstrating to government officers some special need," Justice Alito wrote in his concurring opinion

https://www.supremecourt.gov/opinions/21pdf/597us1r54_7648.pdf

pg 104 - Political controversy over the Second Amendment continues, as is evidenced by the dissenting opinion in Bruen by Justice Breyer, who wrote

https://www.supremecourt.gov/opinions/21pdf/597us1r54_7648.pdf

pg 107 - To modern eyes, the Third Amendment seems anachronistic. To the Founders, however, it was a critical protection of individual liberty

http://www.pbs.org/wnet/supremecourt/democracy/sources_document3.html

pg 107 - The Third Amendment seems to have no direct constitutional relevance at present; indeed, not only is it the least litigated amendment in the Bill of Rights, but the Supreme Court has never decided a case on the basis of it

https://constitutioncenter.org/interactive-constitution/amendments/amendment-iii

pg 108 - The idea of quartering soldiers in private homes without the owners' consent, even in wartime, had been illegal in England for many years before the American Revolution. The English Bill of Rights of 1689 listed the right of the king's subjects 'not to be burdened with the sojourning of soldiers against their will.'

http://www.crf-usa.org/images/pdf/quarteringofsoldiersincolonialaamerica.pdf

pg 109 - "The brief congressional debates on the text [in 1789] make clear that the amendment reflects an effort to balance private property rights and the potential wartime need for military quarters"

http://www.heritage.org/constitution/#!/amendments/3/essays/143/quartering-of-troops

pg 109 - For example, the Court cited it in the name of marital privacy as support for constitutional restrictions on state governments' abilities to regulate the sale of contraceptives in *Griswold v. Connecticut* (1965)

http://www.heritage.org/constitution/#!/amendments/3/essays/143/quartering-of-troops

pg 113 - The Fourth Amendment, in particular, offers protections to individuals against the police powers of the state

https://www.law.cornell.edu/constitution/fourth_amendment

pg 113 - The search-and-seizure provisions of the Fourth Amendment are all about privacy. To honor this freedom, the Fourth Amendment protects against "unreasonable" searches and seizures by state or federal law enforcement authorities

http://www.nolo.com/legal-encyclopedia/search-seizure-criminal-law-30183.html

pg 114 - Forfeiture, the government seizure of property connected to illegal activity, has been a major weapon in the Federal government's 'war on drugs' since the mid-eighties

https://www.law.cornell.edu/wex/forfeiture

pg 114 - The authority to seize property in this way is not inherent. Rather, it is established by statute. It is constrained by those authorizing laws and by the U.S. Constitution

https://www.law.cornell.edu/wex/forfeiture

pg 114 - The expansion of forfeiture activity has not gone on without Constitutional challenge. The U.S. Supreme Court has heard at least half a dozen forfeiture cases during the nineties, but its rulings have not done much to rein in the practice

https://www.law.cornell.edu/wex/forfeiture

pg 115 - *The Daily Caller*, for instance, offers these seven recent examples of civil asset forfeiture abuse

http://dailycaller.com/2015/01/30/the-7-most-egregious-examples-of-civil-asset-forfeiture/

pg 116 - Civil forfeiture laws pose some of the greatest threats to property rights in the nation today, too often making it easy and lucrative for law enforcement to take and keep property - regardless of the owner's guilt or innocence

http://ij.org/report/policing-for-profit/

pg 117 - Worst of all, most civil forfeiture laws give law enforcement agencies a powerful incentive to take property: a cut, or even all, of forfeiture proceeds

http://ij.org/report/policing-for-profit/executive-summary/

pg 117 - In June of 2017, "a federal appellate court ordered police to return $167,000 that was seized more than four years ago following two coordinated traffic stops along I-80 in Nevada

http://ij.org/appeals-court-roadside-stop-seize-violated-constitution/

pg 121 - Alleged crime boss Tony Accardo took the Fifth Amendment more than 170 times during the 1951 Kefauver Hearings in the United States Senate

https://www.youtube.com/watch?v=HfjaLLdOaJQ

pg 121 - But that important right is only one of five in the Fifth Amendment which guarantees individual liberties in civil and criminal trials and outlines "basic constitutional limits on police procedure

https://www.law.cornell.edu/wex/fifth_amendment

pg 122 - Regular court trial juries are usually 6 or 12 people, but in the federal system, a grand jury can be 16 to 23 people

http://criminal.findlaw.com/criminal-procedure/how-does-a-grand-jury-work.html

pg 123 - In a bid to make prosecutors more accountable for their actions, Chief Judge [of the New York Court of Appeals] Sol Wachtler has proposed that the state scrap the grand jury system of bringing criminal indictments,

http://www.barrypopik.com/index.php/new_york_city/entry/indict_a_ham_sandwich/

pg 123 - Wachtler, who became the state's top judge earlier this month, said district attorneys now have so much influence on grand juries that 'by and large' they could get them to 'indict a ham sandwich'

http://www.barrypopik.com/index.php/new_york_city/entry/indict_a_ham_sandwich/

pg 123 - [a] person being charged with a crime that warrants a grand jury has the right to challenge members of the grand juror for partiality or bias, but these challenges differ from peremptory challenges, which a defendant has when choosing a trial jury

https://www.law.cornell.edu/wex/fifth_amendment

pg 123 - The simple filing of criminal charges doesn't cause jeopardy to "attach" - the proceedings must get to a further stage

http://www.nolo.com/legal-encyclopedia/the-prohibition-against-double-jeopardy.html

pg 123 - Generally, jeopardy attaches when the court swears in the jury. In a trial before a judge, jeopardy attaches after the first witness takes the oath and begins to testify

http://www.nolo.com/legal-encyclopedia/the-prohibition-against-double-jeopardy.html

pg 124 - The Double Jeopardy Clause aims to protect against the harassment of an individual through successive prosecutions of the same alleged act, to ensure the significance of an acquittal, and to prevent the state from putting the defendant through the emotional, psychological, physical, and financial troubles that would accompany multiple trials for the same alleged offense

https://www.law.cornell.edu/wex/fifth_amendment

pg 124 - The Fifth Amendment protects criminal defendants from having to testify if they may incriminate themselves through the testimony. A witness may 'plead the Fifth' and not answer if the witness believes answering the question may be self-incriminatory

https://www.law.cornell.edu/wex/fifth_amendment

pg 124 - Such was the case in 2013 when IRS attorney Lois Lerner invoked her Fifth Amendment rights against self-incrimination when she appeared before a committee of the House of Representatives and refused to answer any questions.

https://www.washingtonpost.com/politics/lois-lerner-invokes-fifth-amendment-in-house-hearing-on-irs-targeting/2013/05/22/03539900-c2e6-11e2-8c3b-0b5e9247e8ca_story.html

pg 124 - After her resignation, she appeared before the same committee in 2014 and again invoked her Fifth Amendment rights and refused to testify before the committee.

https://www.c-span.org/video/?318121-1/lois-lerner-contempt-hearing-thursday-9am-et

pg 124 - "In the landmark *Miranda v. Arizona* ruling, the United States Supreme Court extended the Fifth Amendment protections to encompass any situation outside of the courtroom that involves the curtailment of personal freedom. 384 U.S. 436 (1966)

https://www.law.cornell.edu/wex/fifth_amendment

pg 125 - The guarantee of due process for all persons requires the government to respect all rights, guarantees, and protections afforded by the U.S. Constitution and all applicable statutes before the government can deprive any person of life, liberty, or property

https://www.law.cornell.edu/wex/fifth_amendment

pg 125 - While the federal government has a constitutional right to 'take' private property for public use, the Fifth Amendment's Just Compensation Clause requires the government to pay just compensation, interpreted as market value, to the owner of the property

https://www.law.cornell.edu/wex/fifth_amendment

pg 125 - The U.S. Constitution does not explicitly grant condemnation powers to the federal government. Such power is generally inferred today from clauses of Article 1, Section 8, that give Congress authority to establish post offices and post roads as well as authority over property obtained for forts, arsenals, and other similar facilities, and from the takings clause of the Fifth Amendment

http://www.independent.org/pdf/tir/tir_12_03_04_benson.pdf

pg 126 - James Madison, who wrote the Fifth Amendment, hoped to restrict the takings that had been made in the colonies under British rule and in the new states after the revolution because he wished to make individual property rights more secure...

http://www.independent.org/pdf/tir/tir_12_03_04_benson.pdf

pg 126 - The government does not have to pay a property owner's attorney's fees, however, unless a statute so provides

https://www.law.cornell.edu/wex/fifth_amendment

pg 126 - She wrote a book about her case, which was recently made into a movie.

https://www.youtube.com/watch?v=cVJQgQuFqSM

pg 126 - The Supreme Court's 2005 ruling in *Kelo v. New London* was that year's blockbuster.

https://www.forbes.com/sites/georgeleef/2017/03/19/little-pink-house-movie-exposes-the-tyranny-of-eminent-domain/#38cc6a9542b8

pg 134 - The privilege was elevated to constitutional status, and has always been "as broad as the mischief against which it seeks to guard.

https://supreme.justia.com/cases/federal/us/142/547/case.html

pg 137 - The Oxford English Dictionary provides the simplest explanation of what is meant by common law: "The part of English law that is derived from custom and judicial precedent rather than statutes. Often contrasted with statutory law.

https://en.oxforddictionaries.com/definition/us/common_law

pg 137 - Criminal law deals with behavior that is or can be construed as an offense against the public, society, or the state - even if the immediate victim is an individual. Examples are murder, assault, theft, and drunken driving

https://www.britannica.com/demystified/what-is-the-difference-between-criminal-law-and-civil-law

pg 137 - Civil law deals with behavior that constitutes an injury to an individual or other private party, such as a corporation. Examples are defamation (including libel and slander), breach of contract, negligence resulting in injury or death, and property damage

https://www.law.cornell.edu/anncon/html/amdt7frag1_user.html#amdt7_hd4

pg 137 - Traditionally, the Supreme Court has treated the Seventh Amendment as preserving the right of trial by jury in civil cases as it 'existed under the English common law when the amendment was adopted'

https://www.law.cornell.edu/anncon/html/amdt7frag1_user.html#amdt7_hd4

pg 138 - The first judicial ruling on the Seventh Amendment came in 1812 in a case known as United States v. Wonson, where "the government challenged the accuracy of a jury verdict, and asked the appellate court to reverse the verdict or resubmit the case to a new jury

http://scholarship.law.wm.edu/cgi/viewcontent.cgi?article=1009&context=studentpubs

pg 144 - Capital punishment is currently authorized in 31 states, by the federal government and the U.S. military

http://www.ncsl.org/research/civil-and-criminal-justice/death-penalty.aspx

pg 144 - In a 1972 case, *Furman v. Georgia*, the Supreme Court ruled in a 5 to 4 decision "that the imposition and carrying out of the death penalty in these cases constitute cruel and unusual punishment in violation of the Eighth and Fourteenth Amendments.

https://www.law.cornell.edu/supremecourt/text/408/238#writing-USSC_CR_0408_0238_ZO

pg 144 - Four years later in 1976, the Supreme Court held in a 7 to 2 decision in the case of *Gregg v. Georgia* that capital punishment was constitutional

https://www.law.cornell.edu/supremecourt/text/428/153#writing-USSC_CR_0428_0153_ZO

pg 145 - There are two reasons for arguing that the death penalty is a "cruel and unusual punishment", and thus unconstitutional

https://www.economist.com/news/united-states/21608773-judge-strikes-blow-against-capital-punishment-cruel-and-unusual

pg 145 - No serious constitutional argument can be made against the death penalty. The endless campaigns to ban it cost taxpayers millions to defend

http://articles.latimes.com/2011/oct/26/opinion/la-oe-rivkin-death-penalty-20111026

pg 146 - A Gallup Poll conducted in 2004 found "that three-fourths (75%) of Americans agree that 'states should be allowed to execute prisoners sentenced to the death penalty by means of lethal injection.'

http://www.gallup.com/poll/11716/lethal-injections-cruel-unusual-punishment.aspx

pg 146 - Chief Justice Fred Vinson's majority opinion in the 1951 case *Stack v. Boyle* expressed the Court's view on excessive bail.

https://supreme.justia.com/cases/federal/us/342/1/case.html

pg 146 - This traditional right to freedom before conviction permits the unhampered preparation of a defense, and serves to prevent the infliction of punishment prior to conviction. ... Unless this right to bail before trial is preserved, the presumption of innocence, secured only after centuries of struggle, would lose its meaning

https://supreme.justia.com/cases/federal/us/342/1/case.html

pg 146 - The "excessive fines" clause surfaces (among other places) in cases of civil and criminal forfeiture, for example when property is seized during a drug raid

https://www.law.cornell.edu/constitution/eighth_amendment

pg 146 - For years the Supreme Court had little to say with reference to excessive fines

https://www.law.cornell.edu/constitution-conan/amendment-8/excessive-fines

pg 160 - "roughly 300 sanctuary jurisdictions rejected more than 17,000 detention requests [from the federal government], between January 1, 2014 and September 30, 2015."

http://edition.cnn.com/2017/01/25/politics/sanctuary-cities-explained

pg 163 - Unlike the powers granted the two other branches–the executive and the legislative–"judicial review" is not explicitly spelled out in the text of the Constitution, though it has become "one of the distinctive features of United States constitutional law

http://constitution.findlaw.com/article3/annotation13.html

pg 164 - "judicial review is not just made up."

http://www.libertylawsite.org/2013/01/24/the-constitutional-basis-for-judicial-review/

pg 164 - William Marbury, a self-made man and Adams loyalist, was one of the "midnight" justices whom John Adams appointed during his last days in office.

https://www.amazon.com/gp/product/0143127039

pg 165 - (1) Do the plaintiffs have a right to receive their commissions? (2) Can they sue for their commissions in court? (3) Does the Supreme Court have the authority to order the delivery of their commissions?

https://www.oyez.org/cases/1789-1850/5us137

pg 165 - Particularly in contrast with the annexation of Louisiana [in 1803], the decision handed down by the Supreme Court in *Marbury v. Madison* seemed at the time of little significance

https://www.amazon.com/gp/product/0143127039

pg 165 - The decision in *Marbury v. Madison* has never been disturbed, although it has been criticized and has had opponents throughout our history

http://constitution.findlaw.com/article3/annotation13.html

pg 166 - The Justia US Law website identifies a total of 165 "acts of Congress held unconstitutional in whole or in part by the Supreme Court of the United States," between 1803 and 2008.

http://law.justia.com/constitution/us/046-acts-of-congress-held-unconstitutional.html

pg 166 - That decision declared the Missouri Compromise of 1820 unconstitutional and returned Dred Scott, a slave whose owner brought him into free territory and consequently claimed his freedom, to slavery

https://web.archive.org/web/20151109052405/http://www.cqpress.com/context/constitution/docs/legislation.html

pg 166 - In March 1861, during his first inaugural address, President Abraham Lincoln indirectly criticized the exercise of judicial review by the Supreme Court in the Dred Scot decision, an error that helped plunge the country into the Civil War

https://www.loc.gov/teachers/newsevents/events/lincoln/pdf/avalonFirst.pdf

pg 167 - At the same time, the candid citizen must confess that if the policy of the Government upon vital questions affecting the whole people is to be irrevocably fixed by decisions of the Supreme Court, the instant they are made in ordinary litigation between parties in personal actions the people will have ceased to be their own rulers, having to that extent practically resigned their Government into the hands of that eminent tribunal

https://www.loc.gov/teachers/newsevents/events/lincoln/pdf/avalonFirst.pdf

pg 167 - At the same time, the Supreme Court has invented many "rights" that appear nowhere in the Constitution and are, in fact, entirely the product of the justices' own personal predilections

http://www.nationalreview.com/article/416590/quandary-judicial-review-mark-pulliam

About the Authors

Michael Patrick Leahy is the CEO of *Star News Digital Media* and the host of *The Michael Patrick Leahy Show* on WENO AM760 The Flame. Leahy was one of the early leaders of the Tea Party Movement, and is the author of *Covenant of Liberty: The Ideological Origins of The Tea Party Movement*. He is a graduate of Harvard University, and earned his MBA from Stanford University. He lives in the Nashville area with his wife and has two adult daughters.

Claudia Daniel Henneberry graduated from Meredith College in Raleigh, North Carolina, in 1979, with degrees in History and Secondary Education. She taught Social Studies and English in North Carolina and is now retired. Since her retirement, Claudia has substitute taught, tutored, and has been involved in reviewing textbooks. She testified before the Tennessee Textbook Commission and the Tennessee Senate Education Committee in 2013 on inaccuracies, biases, and omissions in the social studies texts. Claudia started a "Ladies for Liberty" group with a neighbor to encourage women to learn about the Constitution and get involved in the political arena. She also helped organize several summers of Camp Constitution held in Brentwood, Tennessee.

First Edition
November 2025
Third Printing